*International directory
of programmed instruction*

*Répertoire international
d'enseignement programmé*

International directory of programmed instruction

Compiled under the direction of the Centre de Documentation sur l'Enseignement Programmé of the Institut National pour la Formation des Adultes, Paris, and revised with the assistance of the International Centre for Advanced Technical and Vocational Training, Turin

Répertoire international d'enseignement programmé

Etabli sous la direction du Centre de documentation sur l'enseignement programmé de l'Institut national pour la formation des adultes (Paris) et revisé avec l'aide du Centre international de perfectionnement professionnel et technique de Turin

Unesco   Paris 1973

This work is a sequel to / Cet ouvrage fait suite à
Programmed instruction: an international directory /
L'enseignement programmé: un répertoire international
(S. Spaulding, ed.). Pittsburgh, International Education
Clearinghouse, University of Pittsburgh; Paris, Unesco,
1967. 189 p.

Published by the
United Nations Educational,
Scientific and Cultural Organization
7, Place de Fontenoy, 75700 Paris

Publié par
l'Organisation des Nations Unies
pour l'éducation, la science et la culture
7, place de Fontenoy, 75700 Paris
Imprimerie Joseph Floch, Mayenne

© Unesco, 1973
Printed in France

ISBN.92-3-001102-9
LC No. 73-79981

PREFACE

The generic term "programmed instruction" covers a whole range of methods and techniques developed over roughly ten years past in order to apply recent technological advances to educational purposes. The introduction of these methods and techniques, the outcome of advanced study of theories of learning and teaching, has been the subject of much experiment and research over the past decade. This is shown by the number of conferences devoted to this new view of education, and by the experimental projects launched by Unesco in Central Africa, in South East Asia and in the Ivory Coast.

However, the findings of this research and the lessons drawn from these experiments are often difficult of access, despite growing interest in programmed instruction. Unesco, therefore, feels it should make available the information at its disposal to all those research workers and educators, whether theorists or practitioners who are interested in such new methods and techniques.

In 1967, Unesco, jointly with the University of Pittsburgh, published an international directory of organizations and specialists in the field of programmed instruction. To produce the directory, Unesco called on Dr. Seth Spaulding, at that time Chairman of the "Graduate Program in International and Development Education" of the university's School of Education. The directory quickly became out of print, and it was found necessary to prepare a new one in which greater emphasis would be placed on information received from countries farthest advanced in programmed instruction. To this end, Unesco sent a questionnaire to the National Commissions of countries having institutes or bodies partially or entirely devoted to the theory or practice of such teaching. For its part, the Centre de Documentation sur l'Enseignement Programmé of the Institut National pour la Formation des Adultes in Paris (CDEP), sent the same questionnaire to all bodies which it believed might supply useful information. CDEP assumed responsibility for sorting and analysing the replies, and the joint unit of the Unesco-ILO International Centre for Advanced Technical and Vocational Training in Turin was entrusted with checking the material collected.

All entries in this directory are in English alphabetical order of countries. Naturally, the designations employed and the presentation of the material imply no expression of opinion on the part of the Unesco Secretariat concerning the legal status or the system of government of any country, or concerning the delimitation of its frontiers.

The Unesco Secretariat wishes to thank the National Commissions which undertook the indispensable task of distributing the questionnaires, and also all those national bodies and specialists whose answers made it possible to compile the information contained in this directory.

The directory in its present form does not claim to be exhaustive but it may be considered the first version of a publication which can be brought up to date periodically as programmed instruction develops.

In this connexion, the Unesco Secretariat will welcome any information that readers and users of the directory may be willing to provide.

PREFACE

Le terme générique d' "enseignement programmé" désigne un ensemble de méthodes et de techniques élaborées depuis une dizaine d'années en vue de mettre les progrès récents de la technologie au service de l'éducation. La mise en oeuvre de ces méthodes et techniques, issues d'une étude poussée des théories de l'apprentissage et de l'enseignement proprement dit, a fait l'objet de nombreuses expériences, et aussi de nombreuses recherches, au cours de la dernière décennie. Les colloques consacrés à cette nouvelle conception de l'enseignement, de même que les projets expérimentaux lancés par l'Unesco en Afrique centrale, en Asie du Sud-Est et en Côte-d'Ivoire, en sont la preuve.

Cependant, les résultats de ces recherches et les leçons tirées de ces expériences sont souvent difficilement accessibles, en dépit de l'intérêt croissant que suscite l'enseignement programmé. C'est pourquoi l'Unesco a estimé qu'il lui appartenait de faire bénéficier des informations dont elle disposait tous ceux - chercheurs, éducateurs, théoriciens ou praticiens - qui s'intéressent à ces méthodes et techniques nouvelles.

Dès 1967, elle publiait, conjointement avec l'Université de Pittsburgh, un répertoire international des organismes et spécialistes s'occupant d'enseignement programmé. Pour élaborer cet ouvrage, elle avait fait appel à la compétence du Dr Seth Spaulding, alors président du Graduate Programme in International and Development Education de l'Institut de pédagogie de cette université. Ce répertoire ayant été rapidement épuisé, il a paru nécessaire d'en préparer un nouveau, dans lequel l'accent serait mis davantage sur les informations reçues des pays les plus avancés en matière d'enseignement programmé. A cet effet, l'Unesco a adressé un questionnaire aux commissions nationales des pays où existaient des institutions ou organismes consacrant tout ou partie de leurs activités à la théorie ou à la pratique de cet enseignement. De son côté, le Centre de documentation sur l'enseignement programmé (CDEP) de l'Institut national pour la formation des adultes, de Paris, a adressé ce même questionnaire à toutes les organisations qui lui paraissaient être en mesure de fournir des informations utiles. Le dépouillement et l'analyse des réponses ont été confiés au CDEP et la vérification des éléments ainsi recueillis à l'Unité conjointe Unesco-BIT du Centre international de perfectionnement professionnel et technique de Turin.

Toutes les notices du présent répertoire sont présentées dans l'ordre alphabétique anglais des noms de pays. Il va de soi que les désignations employées et la présentation adoptée ne sauraient être interprétées comme exprimant une prise de position du Secrétariat de l'Unesco sur le statut légal ou le régime d'un pays non plus que sur le tracé de ses frontières.

Le Secrétariat de l'Unesco tient à exprimer sa gratitude aux commissions nationales qui ont bien voulu se charger de la diffusion des questionnaires et sans lesquelles ce travail n'aurait pu être mené à bien, ainsi qu'à tous les organismes nationaux et aux spécialistes qui, en répondant à ces questionnaires, ont permis de rassembler les informations contenues dans le présent répertoire.

Tel qu'il se présente, cet ouvrage n'a pas la prétention d'être complet; on peut le considérer néanmoins comme le premier état d'une publication susceptible de recevoir une mise à jour périodique en fonction du développement de l'enseignement programmé.

A cet égard, le Secrétariat de l'Unesco accueillera avec gratitude toutes les informations que les lecteurs et utilisateurs du présent répertoire voudront bien lui adresser.

TABLE OF CONTENTS/TABLE DES MATIERES

Introduction 13
Introduction 15
Argentina/Argentine 17
Austria/Autriche 19
Belgium/Belgique 22
Bulgaria/Bulgarie 30
Czechoslovakia/Tchécoslovaquie 35
Finland/Finlande 47
France 49
Germany, Federal Republic of/
Allemagne, République fédérale d' 67
Hungary/Hongrie 76
India/Inde 82
Israel/Israël 86
Italy/Italie 90
Japan/Japon 103
Korea, Republic of/Corée,
République de 112
Mexico/Mexique 114
Netherlands/Pays-Bas 118
Norway/Norvège 121
Peru/Pérou 122
Poland/Pologne 124
Romania/Roumanie 132
Singapore/Singapour 134
Spain/Espagne 135
Sweden/Suède 140
Switzerland/Suisse 145
Syrian Arab Republic/République
arabe syrienne 153
Thailand/Thaïlande 154
Tunisia/Tunisie 155
Union of Soviet Socialist Republics/
Union des républiques socialistes
soviétiques 157
United Kingdom/Royaume-Uni 161
United States of America/Etats-Unis
d'Amérique 177
Venezuela 189

INTRODUCTION

The present directory replaces the book "Programmed Instruction: an International Directory", published jointly by Unesco and the University of Pittsburgh in 1967, which gave sometimes rather fragmentary information about 67 countries. In this new version, the reader will find what is on the whole fuller information about 31 countries' activities in the field of programmed instruction. If some of the countries which appeared in the first directory are not included, this is because they did not answer the questionnaire and because CDEP, for its part, was unable to obtain any facts concerning them.

The information compiled has been grouped for each country, under three headings, subdivided into a number of sub-headings:

ORGANIZATIONS AND ACTIVITIES

This heading includes information on:
(i) Centres concerned with programmed instruction (including, in each case, the name, address and type of centre: private body, university, etc.);
(ii) Activities (conferences, symposia, seminars, etc.). The information provided under this sub-heading generally includes the title of each activity, the name of the organizing body, dates and place of the gathering, status of participants and mention of the bodies responsible for publishing the proceedings;
(iii) Specialized publishers with name, address and nature of business;
(iv) Periodicals (title, publisher, address, frequency of publication and subject matter);
(v) Professional organizations using programmed instruction (name, address, public catered for);
(vi) Manufacturers of teaching machines (name, address, type of machines, characteristics);
(vii) Training organizations (name and type, address, public for which training is designed);
(viii) Documentation centres (address and nature of services).

PUBLICATIONS

This heading, which is of particular interest to readers in search of fuller information on recent development in programmed instruction, lists:
(i) Books (author, title, place of publication, name and address of publisher, year of publication, number of pages);
(ii) Articles (author and title of each article, periodical in which published, number of issue, year and month of publication, number of pages, subject of article);
(iii) Bibliographies.

RESEARCH AND APPLICATIONS

Among the achievements of the last few years, the most important concern:
(i)   <u>Research</u> (topic, sponsoring body, public concerned);
(ii) <u>Published programmed courses</u> (similar presentation to that used for books, under heading <u>publications</u>);
(iii) <u>Computer-assisted instruction</u> (body responsible, public catered for, type of computer, types of terminal, language used and objective).

In view of the abundant documentation available and the rapid changes in techniques, there appeared to be no point in including in this <u>Directory</u>, publications, meetings, research, etc. dating from before 1968. The reader must not of course expect to find exhaustive or precisely comparable information for each article under each heading. The development and progression of techniques do not keep the same pace in all countries.

Although there are fewer countries included than in the first version, it is hoped that this <u>Directory</u> will be of use to all who are concerned with improving educational techniques, now of recognized importance and that it will lead to increased exchanges between the various bodies concerned with the latest applications of these techniques.

INTRODUCTION

Le présent répertoire fait suite à l'ouvrage L'enseignement programmé : un répertoire international, publié conjointement, en 1967, par l'Unesco et l'Université de Pittsburgh. Cet ouvrage présentait des informations - assez fragmentaires, parfois - sur 67 pays. Dans cette nouvelle version, le lecteur trouvera des renseignements, généralement plus complets, sur les activités en matière d'enseignement programmé dans 31 pays. L'absence de certains pays qui figuraient dans le premier répertoire s'explique parce qu'ils n'ont pas répondu au questionnaire qui leur avait été adressé et parce que le CDEP n'a pu, de son côté, se procurer des renseignements les concernant.

Les informations recueillies ont été groupées, pour chaque pays, sous trois rubriques, subdivisées en un certain nombre de sous-sections :

STRUCTURES ET ACTIVITES

Cette rubrique rassemble les renseignements fournis sur :
(i)   Les centres s'occupant d'enseignement programmé (indication, dans chaque cas, du nom, de l'adresse et de la nature du centre : organisme privé, université, etc.).
(ii)   Les manifestations (conférences, colloques, séminaires, etc.). Les données figurant dans cette sous-section comportent généralement le titre de chaque manifestation, la mention de l'organisme responsable, les dates et le pays où a eu lieu la manifestation, le statut des participants, et l'indication des organismes chargés de la publication des Actes de cette manifestation.
(iii)   Les maisons d'édition spécialisées - avec mention de la raison sociale, de l'adresse et de la nature de l'entreprise.
(iv)   Les périodiques (titre, éditeur, adresse, périodicité et orientation).
(v)   Les organisations professionnelles utilisant l'enseignement programmé (raison sociale, adresse, public intéressé).
(vi)   Les fabricants de machines à enseigner (raison sociale, adresse, type de machines, caractéristiques).
(vii)   Les organismes assurant une formation (nom et nature, adresse, public auquel cette formation est destinée).
(viii) Les centres de documentation (adresse et nature des services qu'ils peuvent offrir).

PUBLICATIONS

Cette rubrique, particulièrement intéressante pour le lecteur désireux d'obtenir de plus amples informations sur les développements récents de l'enseignement programmé, énumère :
(i)   Les livres (auteur, titre, lieu de publication, nom et adresse de l'éditeur, année de parution, nombre de pages).

(ii) Les articles (auteur et titre de chaque article, périodique, où il a été publié, numéro de la livraison, année et mois de parution, nombre de pages, nature de l'article).
(iii) Les bibliographies.

REALISATIONS

Parmi les réalisations de ces dernières années, les plus importantes concernent :
(i) Les recherches (thème de chaque recherche, organisme qui la met en oeuvre, public intéressé).
(ii) Les cours programmés publiés (présentation identique à celle qui a été adoptée pour les livres, dans le cadre de la rubrique Publications).
(iii) Les activités d'enseignement assisté par ordinateur (organisme responsable, destinataires, type d'ordinateur, types de terminaux, langage utilisé et objet).

Etant donné l'abondance de la documentation existante et l'évolution rapide des techniques, il n'a pas paru utile de mentionner, dans ce répertoire, des publications, manifestations, recherches, etc., antérieures à 1968. D'autre part, le lecteur ne doit évidemment pas s'attendre à trouver, pour chaque article de chaque rubrique, des informations exhaustives ou exactement comparables : le développement et la progression des techniques ne suivent pas, en effet, le même rythme dans tous les pays.

En dépit du fait que le nombre des pays pris en considération est plus restreint que dans la première version, on peut espérer que ce répertoire constituera un utile instrument de travail pour tous ceux qui ont le souci d'améliorer des techniques d'enseignement dont l'intérêt n'est plus à démontrer et qu'il permettra, notamment, d'intensifier les échanges entre les divers organismes qui s'intéressent aux plus récentes applications de ces techniques.

ARGENTINA/ARGENTINE

I - ORGANIZATIONS AND ACTIVITIES / STRUCTURES ET ACTIVITES

   1 - CENTRES

   UNIVERSIDAD DE BUENOS AIRES, DIRECCION DE PEDAGOGIA UNIVERSITARIA,
   Grupo de instrucción programada
   Viamonte 430
   Buenos Aires

   3 - PUBLISHERS / MAISONS D'EDITION

   EDITORIAL ESTRADA
   Buenos Aires

   EDITORIAL KAPELUSZ
   Buenos Aires

   EDITORIAL PAIDÓS
   Buenos Aires

   EDITORIAL TROQUEL
   Buenos Aires

   UNIVERSIDAD NACIONAL DEL LITORAL, FACULTAD DE CIENCIAS DE LA EDUCACIÓN
   Paraná - Entre Ríos

   4 - PERIODICALS / PERIODIQUES

   BOLETÍN DE INSTRUCCIÓN PROGRAMADA
   Editeur: Universidad de Buenos Aires
   Adresse: Viamonte 430, Buenos Aires
   Périodicité: Semestriel
   Centres d'intérêt: Recherches. Réalisations. Actualité de l'enseignement
                      programmé

   5 - PROFESSIONAL ORGANIZATIONS / ORGANISATIONS PROFESSIONNELLES

   ARMADA ARGENTINA
   Comodoro Py y Corbeta Uruguay, 10° Piso, Buenos Aires
   Activité: Formation professionnelle

CENTRO MULTINACIONAL DE EDUCACIÓN DE ADULTOS
Calle Lamadrid 676, Buenos Aires
Activités: Cours d'enseignement programmé. Enseignement programmé par correspondance. Laboratoire.

FERROCARRILES ARGENTINOS
Av. Ramos Mejía 1302, Buenos Aires
Nature de l'organisme: Entreprise d'Etat
Activité: Formation professionnelle de base

7 - TRAINING ORGANIZATIONS / ORGANISMES ASSURANT UNE FORMATION

UNIVERSIDAD DE BUENOS AIRES, Grupo de instrucción programada,
Dirección de pedagogía universitaria
Viamonte 430. Buenos Aires
Nature de l'organisme: Université d'Etat
Public intéressé: Universitaires. Spécialistes

II - PUBLICATIONS

1 - BOOKS / LIVRES

CIRIGLIANO, Gustavo F.J. et al. La instrucción programada en la Argentina. Paraná - Entre Ríos, Universidad Nacional del Litoral, 1968, 105 p.

2 - ARTICLES

CIRIGLIANO, Gustavo F.J. "Prospectiva de la educación argentina", in Centenario (Editorial Estrada), 1969.

CODIANI; BUIGUES; KOHEN. "Enseñanza programada", in Didáctica (Codex), No. 3, 12 p.

3 - BIBLIOGRAPHIES

CIRIGLIANO, Gustavo F.J. et al. La instrucción programada en la República Argentina. Paraná - Entre Ríos, Universidad Nacional del Litoral, Facultad de Ciencias de la Educación, 1968.

DETERLINE, William A. Introducción a la enseñanza programada. Buenos Aires, Editorial Troquel, 1969.

FILEP, R.T. et al. Los métodos programados y audiovisuales en la escuela primaria. Buenos Aires, Editorial Paidós, 1969.

GARNER, Lee W. Instrucción programada. Buenos Aires, Editorial Troquel, 1968.

HINGUE, Françoise. La enseñanza programada. Buenos Aires, Editorial Kapelusz, 1969.

ZIELINSKI, Johannes; SCHOLER, Walter. <u>Fundamentos pedagógicos de la instrucción programada en su aspecto empírico</u>. Buenos Aires, Editorial Estrada, 1969.

III - RESEARCH AND APPLICATIONS / REALISATIONS

1 - RESEARCH / RECHERCHES

Thème: ELABORATION DE COURS PROGRAMMES EXPERIMENTAUX
Organisme: Dirección de Pedagogía Universitaria, Universidad de Buenos Aires
Public intéressé: Elèves des écoles secondaires

Thème: ELABORATION DE COURS PROGRAMMES EXPERIMENTAUX
Organisme: Dirección de Pedagogía Universitaria, Universidad de Buenos Aires
Public intéressé: Elèves de l'école primaire d'Avellaneda

AUSTRIA/AUTRICHE

I - ORGANIZATIONS AND ACTIVITIES / STRUCTURES ET ACTIVITES

1 - CENTRES

HOCHSCHULE FÜR BILDUNGSWISSENSCHAFT
A-9020 Klagenfurt
Nature of organization: University

INSTITUT FÜR ALLGEMEINE PÄDAGOGIK DER HOCHSCHULE FÜR WELTHANDEL WIEN
Türkenschanzstrasse 18, 1180 Wien
Nature of organization: University

INSTITUT FÜR BILDUNGS- UND ENTWICKLUNGSFORSCHUNG
Austrian study group for programmed instruction (API)
Schottenbastei 6, 1010 Wien
Nature of organization: non-profit making

INSTITUT FÜR WIRTSCHAFTSPÄDAGOGIK AN DER HOCHSCHULE FÜR WELTHANDEL
Franz-Klein-Gasse 1, 1190 Wien
Nature of organization: University

ÖSTERREICHISCHER BUNDESVERLAG
Schwarzenbergstrasse 5, 1010 Wien
Nature of organization: Business (publisher)

PÄDAGOGISCHES INSTITUT DES BUNDES FÜR OBERÖSTERREICH
Südtirolerstrasse 13-15, 4020 Linz
Nature of organization: Federal Institute of the State Ministry

VERLAG CARL UEBERREUTER
Alserstrasse 24, 1095 Wien
Nature of organization: Business

2 - ACTIVITIES / MANIFESTATIONS

(THE) ALPBACH EUROPEAN FORUM (International, national)
Place and date: Alpbach, annual
Participants: Research workers. School teachers. Vocational and university teachers. Adult educators

INTEGRATED TEACHING SYSTEM
Organized by: Institut für Bildungs- und Entwicklungsforschung
Austrian study group for programmed instruction (API)
Place and date: Wien, 14 February 1969
Participants: School teachers. Adult educators

PROGRAMMED INSTRUCTION (Regional conference)
Organized by: Institut für Bildungs- und Entwicklungsforschung
Place and date: Klagenfurt, 18-22 June 1969

PROGRAMMED LANGUAGE COURSES (Second language), (Regional conference)
Organized by: Institut für Bildungs- und Entwicklungsforschung (API)
Place and date: Wien, 28 March 1969
Participants: School teachers

3 - PUBLISHERS / MAISONS D'EDITION

VERLAG CARL UEBERREUTER
Alserstrasse 24, A-1095 Wien
Nature of organization: Commercial publisher

ÖSTERREICHISCHER BUNDESVERLAG
Schwarzenbergstrasse 5, 1010 Wien
Nature of organization: Commercial publisher

VERLAG HASLINGER
Klosterstrasse 6, 4020 Linz
Nature of organization: Commercial publisher

4 - PERIODICALS / PERIODIQUES

PU-PI (PROGRAMMIERTER UNTERRICHT - PROGRAMMIERTE INSTRUKTION)
Publisher: Study group for Programmed Instruction-Österreichischer Bundesverlag
Address: Schwarzenbergstrasse 5, 1010 Wien
Periodicity: Quarterly

7 - TRAINING ORGANIZATIONS / ORGANISMES ASSURANT UNE FORMATION

AUSTRIAN STUDY GROUP FOR PROGRAMMED INSTRUCTION
INSTITUT FÜR BILDUNGS- UND ENTWICKLUNGSFORSCHUNG
Schottenbastei 6, 1010 Wien
Nature of organization: Non-profit making
Public concerned: School teachers. University teachers. Vocational teachers. Adult educators

Austria/Autriche

HOCHSCHULE FÜR BILDUNGSWISSENSCHAFTEN
A-9020 Klagenfurt
Nature of organization: University
Public concerned: University students. Teachers. Adult educators

INSTITUT FÜR WIRTSCHAFTSPÄDAGOGIK AN DER HOCHSCHULE FÜR WELTHANDEL
Franz-Klein-Gasse 1, 1190 Wien
Nature of organization: University
Public concerned: University students. Vocational school teachers.
                  Adult educators

8 - DOCUMENTATION CENTRES / CENTRES DE DOCUMENTATION

AUSTRIAN STUDY GROUP FOR PROGRAMMED INSTRUCTION (API)
INSTITUT FÜR BILDUNGS- UND ENTWICKLUNGSFORSCHUNG
Schottenbastei 6, 1010 Wien

ÖSTERREICHISCHES LEHRMASCHINENLABOR
Gersthoferstrasse 22, 1180 Wien
Nature of organization: Non-profit making
Type of services: Exhibition of teaching machines, programmes, etc.

II - PUBLICATIONS

1 - BOOKS / LIVRES

VOLKL, I. Lerngewinn und Behalten bei verschiedenen Formen des programmierten Lernens. Wien-München, Österreichischer Bundesverlag, 1970.

III - RESEARCH AND APPLICATIONS / REALISATIONS

1 - RESEARCH / RECHERCHES

Theme: APPLICATION OF PROGRAMMED INSTRUCTION IN DRIVING SCHOOL
Organized by: Berufsförderungsinstitut, Wien
Public concerned: Driving schools

Theme: APPLICATION OF PROGRAMMED INSTRUCTION IN UNIVERSITIES
          (BUSINESS ACCOUNTING)
Organized by: Institut für Wirtschaftspädagogik
Public concerned: University students

Theme: CYBERNETICS AND PROGRAMMED INSTRUCTION
Organized by: Hochschule für Sozial- und Wirtschaftswissenschaften
              Institut für Kybernetik, Eslenweg 18, 4045 Linz

2 - PUBLISHED PROGRAMMED COURSES / COURS PROGRAMMES PUBLIES

Dr. SCHNEIDER, Wilfried; HAGEMANN, W. Mehrwertsteuer. Wien, Österreichisches Produktivitätszentrum, October 1969.
Adult education

Dr. SCHNELL, H.; GRATZENBERGER, F.; Dr. SRETENOVIC, K. Fundamental principles of economics. Wien, München, Verlag für Jugend und Volk, October 1969. 1000 p., 4 vol.
Adult education

BELGIUM/BELGIQUE

I - ORGANIZATIONS AND ACTIVITIES / STRUCTURES ET ACTIVITES

1 - CENTRES

AVINTER
Lamorinierestraat 236, Anvers 2000
Nature de l'organisme: Entreprise

LABORATOIRE DE PEDAGOGIE EXPERIMENTALE, UNIVERSITE DE LIEGE
Place Cockerill, Liège 4000
Nature de l'organisme: Université

LABORATOIRE DE PEDAGOGIE EXPERIMENTALE, UNIVERSITE DE LOUVAIN
Tiensestraat 100, Louvain 3000
Nature de l'organisme: Université

SEMINARIE EN LABORATORIUM VOOR DIDACTIEK, RIJKSUNIVERSITEIT GENT
Universiteitstraat, Gand 9000
Nature de l'organisme: Université

SERVICE D'ETUDES ET D'INFORMATIONS SUR LES TECHNIQUES D'ENSEIGNEMENT (SITE)
INSTITUT SUPERIEUR DE PEDAGOGIE
24, rue Ferrer, Mons 7000
Nature de l'organisme: Université

SERVICE DE MATHEMATIQUES APPLIQUEES ET DE TRAITEMENT DE L'INFORMATION (SMATI)
15, avenue des Tilleuls, Liège 4000
Nature de l'organisme: Université

2 - ACTIVITIES / MANIFESTATIONS

INFORMATION DES MILIEUX INDUSTRIELS ET ECONOMIQUES SUR LES POSSIBILITES
OFFERTES PAR LES TECHNIQUES DE L'ENSEIGNEMENT PROGRAMME

Organisateur: Association des ingénieurs diplômés de l'Université de
               Liège (AILg), 22 rue Forgeur, Liège
Lieu et dates: Liège, 1968 (L'enseignement programmé au service de
               l'industrie); 1969 (Ordinateurs et enseignement programmé)
Participants: Chercheurs. Universitaires. Spécialistes

INFORMATION DU PERSONNEL ENSEIGNANT (Conférence nationale)

Organisateur: Office belge pour l'accroissement de la productivité (OBAP)
Lieux et date: Bruxelles, Liège, Mons, Libromont, Namur, 1968
Participants: Enseignants scolaires. Universitaires
Actes publiés par: OBAP, Programme enseignement, 60 rue de la Concorde,
               Bruxelles 5

INFORMATION DU PERSONNEL ENSEIGNANT DANS LES PAYS FRANCOPHONES EN VOIE
DE DEVELOPPEMENT

Organisateur: Ministère des affaires étrangères et du commerce extérieur,
               Office de coopération et de développement, 5 place du
               Champ-de-Mars, 1050 Bruxelles
Lieu et date: Bruxelles, 1970
Objet: L'enseignement programmé (montage audio-visuel)

INFORMATION ET FORMATION ELEMENTAIRE SUR LES TECHNIQUES DE PROGRAMMATION (Conférence régionale, annuelle)
Organisateur: Direction générale des études, Ministère de l'éducation nationale
Lieux et dates: Liège 1968, Lierre 1968
Participants: Enseignants scolaires

INITIATION DES PROFESSEURS DE L'ENSEIGNEMENT SECONDAIRE A L'ENSEIGNEMENT PROGRAMME EN VUE DE COURS DE RATTRAPAGE SCOLAIRE (Conférence nationale, annuelle)

Organisateur: Ministère de l'éducation nationale
Lieu et dates: Partie francophone: Université de Liège, 1968, 1969, 1970, 1971
Participants: Chercheurs. Enseignants scolaires et universitaires
Actes publiés par: T. Decaigny, Inspecteur, Ministère de l'éducation nationale et de la culture française, Cité administrative de l'Etat, quartier Arcades, 3ème étage, 1010 Bruxelles

PRESENTATION D'EXPERIENCES ET DE MATERIEL (notamment MITSI) (Conférence semestrielle)
Organisateur: Groupement des utilisateurs de l'instruction programmée (GUIP)
Participants: Chercheurs. Universitaires. Spécialistes
Actes publiés par: GUIP, 31 avenue des Arts, Bruxelles 4

RECYCLAGE DU PERSONNEL ENSEIGNANT BELGE EN POSTE DANS LES PAYS EN VOIE DE DEVELOPPEMENT (Conférence internationale, annuelle)

Organisateur: Office de coopération et de développement
Lieu et date: Bruxelles, septembre 1968
Participants: Enseignants scolaires

3 - PUBLISHERS / MAISONS D'EDITION

AVINTER
Lamorinierestraat, Antwerpen 2000
Nature: Société de services

GAMMA
9 rue B. Frison, Tournai
Nature: Editions scolaires

Ad. WESMAEL-CHARLIER S.A.
rue de Fer 69, Namur 5000
Nature: Editions scolaires

4 - PERIODICALS / PERIODIQUES

BULLETIN D'INFORMATION DE LA DIRECTION GENERALE DE L'ORGANISATION DES ETUDES
Editeur: Ministère de l'éducation nationale et de la culture française
Adresse: Cité Administrative de l'Etat, Quartier Arcades, Bruxelles 1010
Périodicité: Mensuel
Centre d'intérêt: Actualités pédagogiques

EDUCATION - TRIBUNE LIBRE
Editeur: M. Missaire
Adresse: 13, rue Wollés, Bruxelles 3
Périodicité: Bimestrielle
Centre d'intérêt: Actualités. Réalisations pédagogiques

5 - PROFESSIONAL ORGANIZATIONS / ORGANISATIONS PROFESSIONNELLES

GROUPEMENT DES UTILISATEURS DE L'INSTRUCTION PROGRAMMEE (GUIP)
31, avenue des Arts, Bruxelles 4
Nature de l'organisation: Patronale, association d'enseignants
Activités: Echanges d'informations entre utilisateurs de l'enseignement programmé

6 - MANUFACTURERS OF TEACHING MACHINES / FABRICANTS DE MACHINES A ENSEIGNER

PROFAID INTERNATIONAL
6/8, square Albert-Ier, Bruxelles 7
Caractéristiques: Conservation des réponses; dispositif audio-visuel adaptable. Utilisation collective
Objet: Contrôle des réponses

7 - TRAINING ORGANIZATIONS / ORGANISMES ASSURANT UNE FORMATION

FACULTE DES SCIENCES APPLIQUEES
15 avenue des Tilleuls, Liège 4000
Nature de l'organisme: Université
Public intéressé: Enseignants scolaires. Universitaires

INSTITUT SUPERIEUR DE PEDAGOGIE, UNIVERSITE DE L'ETAT
18, rue du Parc, Mons 7000
Nature de l'organisme: Université
Public intéressé: Enseignants scolaires

LABORATOIRE DE PEDAGOGIE EXPERIMENTALE, UNIVERSITE DE LIEGE
Place Cockerill, Liège 4000
Nature de l'organisme: Université
Public intéressé: Enseignants scolaires

O.B.A.P.
60, rue de la Concorde, Bruxelles 5
Nature de l'organisme: Etablissement d'utilité publique
Public intéressé: Enseignants scolaires

SEMINARIE EN LABORATORIUM VOOR DIDACTIEK, RIJKSUNIVERSITEIT GENT
Universiteitstraat, Gand 9000
Nature de l'organisme: Université
Public intéressé: Enseignants scolaires. Universitaires

SERVICE DE MATHEMATIQUES APPLIQUEES ET DE TRAITEMENT DE L'INFORMATION
15, avenue des Tilleuls, Liège 4000
Nature de l'organisme: Université
Public intéressé: Enseignants scolaires. Universitaires

8 - DOCUMENTATION CENTRES / CENTRES DE DOCUMENTATION

CENTRE AUDIO-VISUEL DE L'ECOLE NORMALE DE LIERRE
Lierre
Nature des services: Documentation générale sur l'enseignement programmé
Liaison avec l'Université de Gand

CENTRE REGIONAL AUDIO-VISUEL DE L'ETAT
6, rue des Rivageois, Liège 4000
Nature des services: Documentation générale sur l'enseignement programmé.
Liaison avec l'Université de Liège

FONDATION DU CENTRE TECHNIQUE AUDIO-VISUEL INTERNATIONAL (AVINTER)
Lamorinierestraat 236, Anvers 2000
Nature de l'organisme: Etablissement d'utilité publique, créé avec le
concours du Ministère de l'Education nationale
Nature des services: Promotion de l'enseignement programmé. Réunions
et colloques. Bibliographies sur les auxiliaires
audio-visuels et l'enseignement des langues

GROUPEMENT DES UTILISATEURS DE L'INSTRUCTION PROGRAMMEE (GUIP)
Avenue des Arts 31, Bruxelles 4
Nature des services: Fichier des cours programmés en langue française.
Promotion de l'enseignement programmé (dans
l'industrie surtout)

SERVICE D'ETUDES ET D'INFORMATION SUR LES TECHNIQUES D'ENSEIGNEMENT (SITE)
Institut supérieur de pédagogie, 24, rue Ferrer, Mons 7000
Nature des services: Conseil et information à l'intention des enseignants
et des entreprises

II - PUBLICATIONS

1 - BOOKS/LIVRES

BERTEN, A. *L'instruction programmée.* Anvers, AVINTER, 1968, 53 p.
Généralités sur l'enseignement programmé. Elaboration et
application des cours programmés

————— ; VAN DEN BIJLLAARDT, J.G. *Lexique des termes usuels en instruction programmée.* Anvers, AVINTER, 1968, 40 p.
Lexique anglais-français-néerlandais

D'HAINAUT, L. *L'enseignement de concepts scientifiques et techniques à l'aide de cours programmés.* Bruxelles, Université libre de Bruxelles
(Faculté des sciences psychologiques et pédagogiques), 1971,
506 p. (Distribué par l'auteur)

—————. *Enseignement programmé Rapport d'expérience.* Bruxelles, O.B.A.P.,
1971, 393 p.

DE BLOCH, A. *Geprogrammeerde Instructie.* Anvers, Ed. Standaard, 1968, 220 p.
Ouvrage de synthèse

HOUZIAUX, M.O. *Vers l'enseignement assisté par ordinateur.* Préface de S. Roller.
Paris, Presses Universitaires de France, Collection "SUP-L'éducateur",
1972.

SKINNER, B.F. *La révolution scientifique de l'enseignement* (traduction de
R. Richelle). Bruxelles, Ed. I.C. Dessart (2, Galerie des Princes),
1969, 316 p.

2 - ARTICLES

BARTHOLOME, M. "Terminaux pour enseignement et anamnèse assistés par ordinateur", in Revue Universelle des Mines (Liège), décembre 1971, 8 p.
Rapport de recherche

BERTEN, A. "Une technologie du "Faire apprendre": l'instruction programmée in Revue Industrie, août-septembre-octobre 1968, 27 p.
Panorama

D'HAINAUT, L. "Les problèmes de l'élaboration d'un cours programmé", in Bulletin d'information (Bruxelles, Direction générale de l'Organisation des études), No.7, septembre 1968, 16 p.
Panorama. Rapport d'expérience

_____. "L'opportunité et le coût d'implantation d'un système d'enseignement programmé pour la formation dans l'entreprise", in Bulletin de la Société Royale des Ingénieurs et des Industriels, No.12, 1970, pp. 573-583

_____. "Techniques d'analyse d'un contenu d'enseignement", in Bulletin de la Fédération des Industries Belges, No.19, juillet 1970, pp. 37-54

_____. "Technologie de l'enseignement et programmation didactique", in Enseignement programmé, No.8, décembre 1969, pp. 9-20.

_____. "Un modèle pour la détermination et la sélection des objectifs pédagogiques du domaine cognitif", in Enseignement programmé, No.11, septembre 1970, pp. 21-38.

_____. "Une tentative de perfectionnement des cours programmés par adjonction d'une mémoire et rédaction à l'aide de séquences fonctionnelles", in Enseignement programmé (Paris, Ed. Dunod), No.3, 1968, 12 p.
Rapport d'expérience

HOUZIAUX, M.O. "La programmation intrinsèque au service du cours de langue française", in Marche Romane (Liège), XXI, No.2, 1972.
Rapport de recherche et d'expérience

_____. "L'ordinateur au service de l'enseignement de la médecine", in Revue médicale de Liège, XXV, No.10, pp. 337-342.
Panorama

_____. "Note sur l'enseignement programmé en Belgique", in Education, Tribune libre, No.114, novembre 1968, pp. 45-69.

_____. "Panorama critique de divers types d'enseignement programmé", in Bulletin d'Information (Bruxelles, Direction générale de l'organisation des études), avril-mai 1968, 44 p.
Panorama. Rapport d'expérience

LANDSHEERE, G. de "Enseignement programmé et psychopédagogie", in Bulletin d'Information (Bruxelles, Direction générale de l'organisation des études), No.8-9-10, 1968, 57 p.
Panorama

LEFEBVRE, P.; HOUZIAUX, M.O. "Anamnèse assistée par ordinateur en diabétologie. Résultats préliminaires", in Revue Médicale de Liège, XXIV, No. 22, novembre 1969, pp. 803-809.
Rapport d'expérience

VANDERVELDE, L. "La technique de la question à choix multiple", in Bulletin d'information, (Bruxelles, Direction générale de l'organisation des études), février 1969, 6 p.
Panorama. Rapport d'expérience

3 - BIBLIOGRAPHIES

Instruction programmée et machines à enseigner. Anvers, AVINTER, env. 120 p. (publication annuelle, 6 volumes et 3 études déjà parus)

III - RESEARCH AND APPLICATIONS / REALISATIONS

1 - RESEARCH / RECHERCHES

Thème: COMPARAISON ENTRE L'ENSEIGNEMENT PROGRAMME ET LES METHODES TRADITIONNELLES POUR L'APPRENTISSAGE DU TRAVAIL ADMINISTRATIF D'UNE VENDEUSE
Organisme: Laboratoire de pédagogie expérimentale, Université de Louvain
Public intéressé: Personnel de vente d'un grand magasin

Thème: ESSAI D'EXERCICES CORRECTIFS PROGRAMMES SELON UNE METHODE ORIGINALE ET PORTANT SUR LA NOTION DE POURCENTAGE
Organisme: Laboratoire de pédagogie expérimentale, Université de Liège
Public intéressé: Elèves de l'enseignement secondaire

Thème: ETUDE CRITIQUE DE L'ENSEIGNEMENT PROGRAMME
Organisme: Laboratoire de pédagogie expérimentale. Université de Louvain

Thème: ETUDE DE L'APPLICATION DES COURS PROGRAMMES A L'ENSEIGNEMENT DES CONCEPTS SCIENTIFIQUES ET TECHNIQUES
Organisme: Institut supérieur de pédagogie, Université de l'Etat Mons
Public intéressé: Elèves de l'enseignement secondaire général et technique

Thème: ETUDE DE L'EFFICACITE D'UN MATERIEL PROGRAMME POUR L'ETUDE DE LA NUMERATION DECIMALE ET DU CALCUL DECIMAL
Organisme: Laboratoire de pédagogie expérimentale, Université de Louvain
Public intéressé: Elèves de l'enseignement primaire

Thème: ETUDE DE L'EFFICACITE DE CARNETS PROGRAMMES POUR L'APPRENTISSAGE DE L'ORTHOGRAPHE
Organisme: Institut supérieur de pédagogie
Public intéressé: Elèves de l'enseignement primaire ou de la première année de l'enseignement secondaire

Thème: ETUDE DE L'EFFICACITE DE DIFFERENTES MODALITES D'APPLICATION DE COURS PROGRAMMES DANS LES STRUCTURES SCOLAIRES NORMALES
Organisme: Office belge pour l'accroissement de la productivité
Public intéressé: Elèves de l'enseignement technique, 15-18 ans

Thème: ETUDE SUR L'OPPORTUNITE D'UTILISER DES COURS PROGRAMMES POUR L'ENSEIGNEMENT DES SCIENCES PHYSIQUES, CONJOINTEMENT AVEC DES EXPERIENCES REALISEES PAR LE PROFESSEUR OU LES ELEVES
Organisme: Athénée provincial du Centre, Morlanwelz
Public intéressé: Elèves de l'enseignement secondaire général

Thème: MISE AU POINT D'UNE NOUVELLE TECHNIQUE D'EXPLOITATION DE LA PROGRAMMATION CROWDERIENNE (POUR L'ENSEIGNEMENT DE LA GRAMMAIRE FRANÇAISE)
Organisme: SMATI, Université de Liège
Public intéressé: Elèves de l'enseignement secondaire

Thème: REALISATION D'UNE MACHINE A ENSEIGNER AUDIO-VISUELLE POUR LA PRESENTATION DE PROGRAMMES INTRINSEQUES ET DOTEE DE CERTAINES FONCTIONS LOGIQUES (CIRCUITS INTEGRES): SAVA 6/35
Public intéressé: Etudiants universitaires (Département d'astrophysique de l'Université de Mons)

Thème: RECHERCHE OPERATIONNELLE SUR L'OPPORTUNITE D'UTILISATION DE COURS PROGRAMMES DANS L'ENSEIGNEMENT TECHNIQUE ET SUR LES MODES POSSIBLES D'UTILISATION DE CE MOYEN PEDAGOGIQUE
Organisme: Office belge pour l'accroissement de la productivité.

Public intéressé: Elèves de l'enseignement technique (première année A.2 - Electricité, mécanique, electromécanique)

Thème: TENTATIVE DE PERFECTIONNEMENT DES COURS PROGRAMMES A REPONSE CONSTRUITE PAR ADJONCTION D'UNE "MEMOIRE" ET DIVISION EN VOIES MULTIPLES
Organismes: Ecole de formation générale de la SNCF à Louvre (France).
Service de recherche pédagogique de la librairie Hachette
Public intéressé: Elèves de l'enseignement secondaire général ou technique

2 - PUBLISHED PROGRAMMED COURSES / COURS PROGRAMMES PUBLIES

D'HAINAULT, L. Arrondir et estimer. Paris, Bruxelles, Librairie Hachette, 1968.
Niveau secondaire. Enseignement technique

_____. Puissances de dix. Paris, Bruxelles, Librairie Hachette, 1968.
Niveau secondaire. Enseignement technique

_____. La règle à calcul. Paris, Bruxelles, Librairie Hachette, 1969.
Education des adultes. Niveau secondaire. Enseignement technique. Formation professionnelle

_____. Les incertitudes de mesure. Parus, Bruxelles, Librairie Hachette, 1970.
Niveau secondaire. Enseignement général et technique

_____. L'utilisation des cahiers programmés. Paris, Bruxelles, Librairie Hachette, 1971.
Livre du maître.

FRANÇOIS, L. Comment extraire une racine carrée. Tournai, GAMMA, 1969, 300 items.
      Education des adultes. Niveau secondaire. Formation professionnelle

_____. Premières notions de la théorie des ensembles. Tournai, 1969, 500 items.
      Education des adultes. Niveau secondaire

GOUREVITCH, G. Cours programmé d'algèbre. Tournai, GAMMA, 1969, 700 items.
      Niveau secondaire. Enseignement technique. Formation professionnelle

HOUZIAUX, M.O. Leçons programmées de grammaire française. Le complément d'objet direct (fasc.1). Namur, Ad. Wesmael-Charlier, 1972.
      Niveau secondaire

HUGUGES, R.J.; PIPE. Introduction à l'électronique. Tournai, GAMMA, 1968, 450 items.
      Niveau secondaire. Enseignement technique. Formation professionnelle

LEACH, R.B.; EWING, G.W. Chimie. Tournai, GAMMA, 1969, 500 items.
      Niveau secondaire. Enseignement technique

SCOTT. Techniques de programmation. Tournai, GAMMA, 1968, 600 items.
      Niveau secondaire supérieur. Formation professionnelle

SLATTERY, J. Correspondance commerciale. Tournai, GAMMA, 1969.
      Niveau secondaire. Enseignement technique. Formation professionnelle

3 - COMPUTER ASSISTED INSTRUCTION / ENSEIGNEMENT ASSISTE PAR ORDINATEUR

ANAMNESE ASSISTEE PAR ORDINATEUR EN MEDECINE INTERNE
Organisme: Université de Liège et Fonds de la recherche scientifique médicale
Destinataires: Patients (diabète, neurologie, néphrologie, hématologie, etc.)
Type de l'ordinateur: PDP 8-E
Type des terminaux: Consoles audio-visuelles conçues et réalisées au SMATI et télétypes
Langage utilisé: LPA II (Interpréteur) et 8K PAL D

ENSEIGNEMENT
Organisme: Ecole Singelijn
Destinataires: Elèves de l'enseignement primaire, degré supérieur
Type de l'ordinateur: Bull General Electric 265 (Time sharing)
Type des terminaux: Télétypes

ENSEIGNEMENT MEDICAL ASSISTE PAR ORDINATEUR (DOCEO II)
Organisme: Université de Liège et Fonds de la recherche scientifique médicale
Destinataires: Médecins et personnel para-médical
Type de l'ordinateur: PDP 8-E
Type des terminaux: Consoles audio-visuelles conçues et réalisées au SMATI et télétypes
Langage utilisé: LPD II (Interpréteur) et 8K PAL D

SYSTEME DE CONTROLE DES CONNAISSANCES EN PROGRAMMATION
Organisme: Service de mathématiques appliquées et de traitement de l'information. Université de Liège
Destinataires: Etudiants en sciences appliquées
Type de l'ordinateur: PDP II
Type des terminaux: Consoles audio-visuelles conçues et réalisées au SMATI et consoles alpha-numériques du type écran cathodique

SYSTEME DE CONTROLE POUR LES TRAVAUX PRATIQUES EN PROGRAMMATION COMPATIBLE AVEC LE SYSTEME D'EXPLOITATION 360
Organisme: Service de mathématiques appliquées et de traitement de l'information. Université de Liège
Destinataires: Etudiants en sciences appliquées
Type de l'ordinateur: IBM 360/65 MVT-ASP

UN SYSTEME D'INSTRUCTION MULTIMEDIA ASSISTE ET GERE PAR ORDINATEUR
Organisme: Université de Louvain, Centre IMAGO
Destinataires: Etudiants de l'enseignement supérieur (cours de physique, zoologie, micro-économie, gestion financière)
Type de l'ordinateur: Honeywell-1642 (Time-sharing) et Bull General Electric 265 (Time-sharing)
Type des terminaux: Télétypes
Langage utilisé: FORTRAN
Objet: Enseignement et contrôle des connaissances et des aptitudes

BULGARIA/BULGARIE

I - ORGANIZATIONS AND ACTIVITIES / STRUCTURES ET ACTIVITES

1 - CENTRES

CENTRE DE DOCUMENTATION ET D'INFORMATION PEDAGOGIQUES
125, boulevard Lénine, Bloc V, Sofia
Nature de l'organisme: Gouvernemental

INSTITUT SUPERIEUR D'ECONOMIE KARL MARX
20, rue Stéphane Karadja, Sofia
Nature de l'organisme: Universitaire

INSTITUT SUPERIEUR DE FINANCES ET D'ECONOMIE
Svichtov
Nature de l'organisme: Universitaire

INSTITUT SUPERIEUR DE MACHINES ELECTROTECHNIQUES
1, rue du 19 février, Sofia
Nature de l'organisme: Universitaire

INSTITUT SUPERIEUR DE MEDECINE
Plovdiv
Nature de l'organisme: Universitaire

INSTITUT SUPERIEUR DE MEDECINE
1, rue Gueorgui Sofiiski, Sofia
Nature de l'organisme: Universitaire

INSTITUT SUPERIEUR DE MEDECINE
55, rue Marine Drinov, Varna
Nature de l'organisme: Universitaire

INSTITUT SUPERIEUR DE TECHNOLOGIE CHIMIQUE
Bourgas
Nature de l'organisme: Universitaire

UNIONS DES SCIENCES TECHNIQUES,
Section "Moyens d'éducation technique"
108, rue Rakovski, Sofia

UNIVERSITE DE SOFIA "CLEMENT D'OKHRID"
15, boulevard Rouski, Sofia
Nature de l'organisme: Universitaire

2 - ACTIVITIES/ MANIFESTATIONS

COLLOQUE SUR LA SITUATION ET LES PERSPECTIVES DE L'ENSEIGNEMENT
PROGRAMME (Manifestation internationale)

Organisateur: UNESCO
Lieu et date: Varna, 1968
Participants: Chercheurs. Universitaires. Professionels.
Actes publiés par: UNESCO. Place de Fontenoy, 75 Paris 7e

COLLOQUE SUR LES PROBLEMES D'ORDRE DIDACTIQUE ET PSYCHOLOGIQUE DE
L'ENSEIGNEMENT PROGRAMME (Manifestation régionale, annuelle)

Organisateurs: Chaires de Pédagogie et de psychologie de l'Université
      d'Etat de Sofia
Lieu : Université de Sofia.
Participants: Enseignants scolaires. Universitaires. Professionnels

COLLOQUE SUR LES THEORIES PEDAGOGIQUES CONTEMPORAINES (Colloque national)

Organisateurs: Institut de théories sociales contemporaines,
      Université de Sofia, Institut de recherches scientifiques
      sur l'éducation "T. Samodoumov"
Lieu et date: Sofia, colloque permanent
Participants: Chercheurs. Enseignants scolaires. Universitaires.
      Professionnels

CONFERENCE SUR LES METHODES CONTEMPORAINES ET MOYENS DIDACTIQUES TECHNIQUES,
EMPLOYES DANS LES ETABLISSEMENTS D'ENSEIGNEMENT SUPERIEUR (Conférence
internationale)

Organisateurs: Comité pour la science, le progrès technique et l'enseigne-
      ment supérieur; Ministère de l'instruction publique
Lieu et date: Sofia, octobre 1971
Participants: Enseignants universitaires et directeurs d'entreprises
      de production de moyens didactiques techniques

CONFERENCE SUR LES PROBLEMES DE L'ENSEIGNEMENT PROGRAMME DANS LES
ETABLISSEMENTS SUPERIEURS DE MEDECINE

Organisateurs: Ministère de la santé publique, Institut supérieur de
      Médecine de Plovdiv (avec participation internationale)

Lieu et date: Plovdiv, novembre 1970
Participants: Enseignants des instituts supérieurs de médecine de Bulgarie et spécialistes de l'Organisation mondiale de la santé

3 - PUBLISHERS / MAISONS D'EDITION

SERVICE D'IMPRESSION DE L'INSTITUT DE RECHERCHES SCIENTIFIQUES SUR L'EDUCATION "T. SAMODOUMOV"
125, boulevard Lénine, bloc V, Sofia
Nature: Editeur scolaire

SERVICE D'IMPRESSION DU MINISTERE DE L'EDUCATION NATIONALE
18, boulevard "Al. Stamboliiski", Sofia
Nature: Editeur scolaire

NARODNA PROSVETA (Instruction publique)
37, V. Droumev, Sofia
Nature: Editeur scolaire

4 - PERIODICALS / PERIODIQUES

BULLETIN DE L'INSTITUT DE RECHERCHES SCIENTIFIQUES SUR L'EDUCATION
Adresse: 125, boulevard Lénine, Bloc V, Sofia
Périodicité: Annuel

HISTOIRE ET GEOGRAPHIE (L'ENSEIGNEMENT DE LA GEOGRAPHIE DEPUIS 1969)
Adresse: 5, Boulevard Vitocha, Sofia
Périodicité: Bimensuel

L'ENSEIGNEMENT PRIMAIRE
Adresse: 5, Boulevard Vitocha, Sofia
Périodicité: Mensuel

L'ENSEIGNEMENT PROFESSIONNEL
Adresse: 5, Boulevard Vitocha, Sofia
Périodicité: Mensuel

MATHEMATIQUES ET PHYSIQUE
Adresse: 5, Boulevard Vitocha, Sofia
Périodicité: Bimensuel

NARODNA PROSVETA (Instruction publique)
Adresse: 5, Boulevard Vitocha, Sofia
Périodicité: Mensuel

PROBLEMES DE L'ENSEIGNEMENT SUPERIEUR
Adresse: 125, Boulevard Lénine, Bloc V, Sofia
Périodicité: Bimensuel

7 - TRAINING ORGANISATIONS / ORGANISMES ASSURANT UNE FORMATION

INSTITUTS POUR LE PERFECTIONNEMENT DES PROFESSEURS
220 boulevard du "9 septembre", Sofia; Varna et Stara-Zagora
Nature des organismes: Gouvernementaux

INSTITUT DE RECHERCHES SCIENTIFIQUES SUR L'EDUCATION "T. SAMODOUMOV"
125 boulevard Lénine, Bloc V, Sofia
Nature de l'organisme: Gouvernemental
Public intéressé: Enseignants scolaires et universitaires. Spécialistes

UNIVERSITE DE SOFIA "CLEMENT D'OKHRID"
15 boulevard Rouski, Sofia
Nature de l'organisme: Universitaire

8 - DOCUMENTATION CENTRES / CENTRES DE DOCUMENTATION

CENTRE DE DOCUMENTATION ET D'INFORMATION PEDAGOGIQUES DE L'INSTITUT
DE RECHERCHES SCIENTIFIQUES SUR L'EDUCATION "T. SAMODOUMOV"
125, boulevard Lénine, Bloc V, Sofia
Nature de l'organisme: Gouvernemental

II - PUBLICATIONS

1 - BOOKS / LIVRES

KOSTOV, G.   La cybernétique et le processus d'apprentissage. Sofia, Editions OF, 1971, 44 pages plus tableaux

————.   Cybernétique et réflexion (étude). Sofia, 1969, 120 pages plus tableaux. Bibliographie p. 114-117

La cybernétique et le processus d'apprentissage (Recueil de traductions). Sous la direction de D. Tzvetkov. Sofia, 1969, 252 p.

YANAKIEV, M.; TODORKA, V.   Un essai de programmer l'enseignement de l'orthographe. Sofia, Narodna Prosveta, 1971, 267 p.

2 - ARTICLES

DIMOVA-AVRAMOVA, N.   "Possibilités d'application de la programmation en matière d'enseignement de la langue allemande", in Annuaire de l'Université de Sofia, Faculté des philologies occidentales, t. LXIII, No. 1.2, 1970, p. 171-202. Résumé en allemand plus bibliographie.

GUEORGUIEV-BIJKOV, G.   "De quelle manière se crée un matériel programmé", in Enseignement professionnel, No. 8, 1971, p. 9-15.

————.   "Méthodes de programmation du contenu de l'enseignement", in Enseignement professionnel, No. 8, 1971, p. 5-10.

MATEEVA, N.   "Essai de programmation des connaissances en culture physique en classe de Vème", Oeuvres de l'Institut supérieur de culture physique "G. Dimitrov", v. XIII, 1970, No. 1.2, première partie, p. 129-137. Résumé en langue française.

PIRIOV GUENTCHO, D.   "Problèmes psychologiques de l'enseignement programmé", in Narodna prosveta, Sofia, No. 7, 1969, p.24-35.

STAMBOLIEV, S. "Aspects psychologiques contemporains dans l'algorithmisation de l'éducation", in <u>Narodna prosveta</u>, No. 4, Sofia, 1969, p.28-37.

—————————, et BONEV, Tz. "Tendances contemporaines dans l'éducation programmée et l'emploi de moyens techniques", in <u>Enseignement professionnel</u>, No. 12, 1969, p.16-17.

TZVETKOV, D. "Contribution à la théorie de l'expérimentation didactique", in <u>Narodna prosveta</u>, No. 11, Sofia, 1970, p.84-93.

—————————, TOUROULEIKOVA, H. "Une expérience d'étude constructive de théorèmes géométriques à l'aide d'un texte programmé", in <u>Bulletin d'information de l'Institut de recherches scientifiques sur l'éducation "T. Samodoumov"</u>, No. 1.24, 1971, p.224-26 Résumés en russe et en français; bibliographie.

—————————, —————————. "Un modèle de texte ramifié programmé sans choix de la réponse", in <u>Bulletin d'information de l'Institut de recherches scientifiques sur l'éducation "T. Samodoumov"</u>, No. 1.22, 1969, p.227-271, 18 fig. Bibliographie de 25 titres, résumés en russe et en anglais.

VEKILSKA, P. "Le rôle de l'enseignement programmé dans le développement de la réflexion chez les élèves étudiant la géographie, in <u>L'enseignement de la géographie</u>, No. 3, 1969, p.8-12.

—————————, STAMBOLIEV, S. "Modèle de texte programmé linéaire en géographie. Géographie physique générale. Chapitre "Climatologie" in <u>Bulletin d'information de l'Institut de recherches scientifiques sur l'éducation "T. Samodoumov"</u>, No. 1.22, 1969, p.273-31 16 tabl. Bibliographie de 18 titres, résumés en russe et en anglais.

3 - BIBLIOGRAPHIES

KOLEVA, S. <u>Littérature sur l'enseignement programmé</u> (publiée en langue bulgare de 1963 à 1968). Sofia, 1969, 20 p.

III - RESEARCH AND APPLICATIONS / REALISATIONS

2 - PUBLISHED PROGRAMMED COURSES / COURS PROGRAMMES PUBLIES

GALANOV, P. <u>Recueil de textes programmés pour le contrôle objectif et l'appréciation des connaissances des élèves en physique.</u> Sofia, Ministère de l'instruction publique, 1970. Première partie: Mécanique, 137 p.; Deuxième partie: Physique moléculaire et chaleur, 82 p.; Troisième partie: Electricité, 135 p.

—————————. <u>Manuel méthodique pour utiliser le Recueil de textes programmés pour le contrôle objectif et l'appréciation des connaissances des élèves en physique.</u> Sofia, Ministère de l'instruction publique, 1970. Première partie: Mécanique, 133 p.; Deuxième partie: Physique moléculaire et chaleur, 86 p.; Troisième partie: Electricité, 109 p.

KANTCHEV, N.   L'enseignement programmé et les problèmes de géométrie. Recueil de problèmes de géométrie avec solutions. (Manuel destiné aux professeurs et aux élèves des écoles secondaires). Sofia, 1970, 208 p.

TOUROULEIKOVA, E.; TZVETKOV, D.   Algèbre, nombres rationnels. 1968. 133 p. Niveau secondaire.

————————————————————. Inégalités de premier degré. Déterminantes. Cercle. (Manuel programmé) Sofia, Institut de recherches scientifiques sur l'éducation "T. Samodoumov", 1968, 79 p. Offset.

VEKILSKA, P.; STAMBOLIEV, S.   Textes programmés sur la climatologie. Sofia, 1969, 52 p. (Deuxième édition 1970).

YANAKIEV, M.; TODORKA, V.   Manuel programmé sur l'orthographe de la langue bulgare. Première partie, Sofia, Institut de recherches scientifiques sur l'éducation "T. Samodoumov", 1970, 484 p. Offset.

CZECHOSLOVAKIA/TCHECOSLOVAQUIE

I - ORGANIZATIONS AND ACTIVITIES / STRUCTURES ET ACTIVITES

1 - CENTRES

DEPARTMENT OF AUDIO-VISUAL AND PROGRAMMED INSTRUCTION,
PRAGUE SCHOOL OF ECONOMICS
Prague 3, náměstí G. Klimenta 4
Nature of organization: University

DEPARTMENT OF EDUCATIONAL TECHNOLOGY, FACULTY OF EDUCATION,
CAROLINE UNIVERSITY
Prague I, Rettigové 4
Nature of organization: University

DEPARTMENT OF PROGRAMMED INSTRUCTION, RESEARCH INSTITUTE OF EDUCATION
Bratislava, Štúrova 5,
Nature of organization: Governmental

DEPARTMENT OF PROGRAMMED INSTRUCTION AND EDUCATIONAL TECHNOLOGY,
POST-GRADUATE MEDICAL AND PHARMACEUTICAL INSTITUTE
Prague 8, Bohnice, Ústavní 91,
Nature of organization: Governmental

LABORATORY FOR PROGRAMMED LEARNING RESEARCH, COMENIUS INSTITUTE, THE
CZECHOSLOVAK ACADEMY OF SCIENCES
Prague 4, Jeremenkova 70,
Nature of organization: Governmental

RESEARCH CENTRE OF INSTRUCTIONAL METHODS AND AIDS
Olomouc
Nature of organization: Governmental

RESEARCH CENTRE OF EDUCATIONAL METHODS AND AIDS
Brno, P. S. 545,
Nature of organization: Governmental

2 - ACTIVITIES / MANIFESTATIONS

CONFERENCE ON PROGRAMMED INSTRUCTION AND EDUCATIONAL TECHNOLOGY
(International conference)
Organized by: The Czechoslovak Academy of Sciences
Place and date: Liblice, annual
Participants: Research workers; school and university teachers; adult educators
Purpose: Evaluation of research; exchange of experience; planning of research

FIRST CONFERENCE ON CYBERNETIC PEDAGOGY (International conference)
Organized by: The Czechoslovak Academy of Sciences, Caroline University and other institutions
Place and date: Prague, May 1969 (annual or biennial)
Participants: School, university and vocational teachers; adult educators
Purpose: Cybernetic pedagogy and cybernetic teaching devices
Proceedings: In print

INTERPROGRAMMA III (International conference)
Organized by: The Czechoslovak Academy of Sciences
Place and date: Liblice (every two or three years)
Participants: Research workers; school, university and vocational teachers; adult educators and others
Purpose: Theory and methods of Programmed Learning
Proceedings: Programmed Instruction III: Proceedings from the Third Liblice Conference, Prague 1969, vol. 1, 2, 3

THE CZECHOSLOVAK-HUNGARIAN-POLISH SEMINAR ON PROGRAMMED LEARNING
(International Conference)
Organized by: The Czechoslovak Academy of Sciences
Place and date: Tupadly (near Prague), January 1968
Participants: Research workers
Purpose: Exchange of information and agreement on an international trilateral research co-operation
Proceedings: In: Kwartalnik pedagogiczny, XIII, 1968, 3, p. 289-290. (Polish)

THE CZECHOSLOVAK-HUNGARIAN SEMINAR ON PROGRAMMED LEARNING (International)
Organized by: The Czechoslovak Academy of Sciences, The Hungarian Institute for Educational Research
Place and date: Budapest (irregular)
Participants: School, university and vocational teachers; adult educators
Proceedings: Published in Szakmunkásnevelés, XVIII, 1967 (Hungarian)

3 - PUBLISHERS/MAISONS D'EDITION

THE SLOVAK EDUCATIONAL PUBLISHING HOUSE
Bratislava, Sasínkova 5
Nature of organization: Governmental publisher of textbooks, educational journals and monographs in Slovak

THE STATE EDUCATIONAL PUBLISHING HOUSE
Prague 1, Ostrovní 30
Nature of organization: Governmental publisher of textbooks, educational journals and monographs in Czech

4 - PERIODICALS/PERIODIQUES

JEDNOTNÁ ŠKOLA (Unified School)
Publisher: The Slovak Educational Publishing House
Address: Bratislava, Sasínkova 5
Periodicity: Monthly
Field of interest: Research; application

ODBORNÁ VÝCHOVA (Vocational Education)
Publisher: The State Educational Publishing House
Address: Prague 1, Lazarská 8
Periodicity: Monthly (but not only on programmed instruction)
Field of interest: Application; topical events

PEDAGOGIKA (Pedagogy)
Publisher: Academia, The Publishing House of the Czechoslovak Academy of Sciences
Address: Prague 1, Vodičkova 40
Periodicity: Bi-monthly
Field of interest: Research

PROGRAMOVANÉ UČENÍ (Programmed Learning)
Publisher: The Comenius Institute of the Czechoslovak Academy of Sciences in co-operation with the Research Centre of Educational Methods and Aids
Address: Prague 4, Jeremenkova 70; Brno P.S.545
Periodicity: Bi-monthly
Field of interest: Topical events; international news

6 - MANUFACTURERS OF TEACHING MACHINES / FABRICANTS DE MACHINES A ENSEIGNER

AOZ
OLOMOUC
Type of machine: MODIFIKA - Teaching machine, teacher's desk for remote control and evaluation, light blackboard, automated classroom
Characteristics: Linear programming, storage and analysis of replies, collective use
Code language used: Number code
Purpose: Evaluation; teaching; application exercises

AOZ
Olomouc
Type of machine: DRIVER-TRAINING - Trainer, teacher's desk for remote control and evaluation, device for shadow-projection, automated classroom
Characteristics: Linear programming and other; storage and analysis of replies; integrated and adaptable audio-visual device; individual and collective use (5 students)
Code language used: Number code, light code
Purpose: Evaluation; teacher-training; application exercises

AOZ
Olomouc
Type of machine: K 121 - Teaching machine, remote control device, teacher's directing counter for the K 121 automated classroom
Characteristics: Linear programming and other; storage and analysis of replies; integrated audio-visual device; individual and collective use (16 students)
Code language used: Number code
Purpose: Evaluation; teaching; application exercises

OKR
Ostrava
Type of machine: METAL SAW TRAINER - A feed-back light signal device with individual achievement recorder; automated classroom
Characteristics: Storage and analysis of individual replies; individual use
Code language used: Light code
Purpose : Evaluation; application exercises; training

TESLA
Vráble, okr. Nitra
Type of machine: REPEX - Teaching machine, remote control and evaluation device, automated classroom
Characteristics: Linear programming and other; storage of replies; individual and collective use
Code language used: Number code
Purpose : Evaluation; teaching; application exercises

TESLA
Praha 3 - Žižkov Strašnice
Type of machine: UNITUTOR - Teaching machine
Characteristics: Linear programming, branching and other; storage and analysis of replies; integrated audio-visual device; individual use
Code language used: Light code
Purpose : Evaluation; teaching; application exercises.

7 - TRAINING ORGANIZATIONS / ORGANISMES ASSURANT UNE FORMATION

DEPARTMENT OF AUTOMATION
Technical University, Brno
Nature of organization: University
Public concerned: School, university and vocational teachers

DEPARTMENT OF PROGRAMMED INSTRUCTION AND EDUCATIONAL TECHNOLOGY,
POST-GRADUATE MEDICAL AND PHARMACEUTICAL INSTITUTE
Prague 8, Bohnice, Ústavní 91
Nature of organization: Governmental
Public concerned: Health professionals

LABORATORY FOR PROGRAMMED LEARNING RESEARCH, COMENIUS INSTITUTE
OF THE CZECHOSLOVAK ACADEMY OF SCIENCES
Prague 4, Jeremenkova 70,
Nature of organization: Governmental
Public concerned: School, university, vocational and adult teachers

RESEARCH INSTITUTE OF EDUCATION
Bratislava, Štúrova 5,
Nature of organization: Governmental
Public concerned: School teachers

REGIONAL INSTITUTE OF EDUCATION
Prague 1, Týn 3
Nature of organization: Governmental
Public concerned: School and vocational teachers

RESEARCH CENTRE OF INSTRUCTIONAL METHODS AND AIDS
Brno P.S.545,
Nature of organization: Governmental
Public concerned: University and vocational teachers;   adult educators

II - PUBLICATIONS

1 - BOOKS/LIVRES

MALACH, A. *Metodika trenažérového výcviku* (Technology of Driver-trainer Training). Brno, The Research Centre of Instructional Methods and Aids, 1968, Vol. I, 73 p.; Vol. 2, 72 p.
Description and analysis of results of long-term experimental programmed training, using a driver-trainer automated classroom. Project of curriculum and strategy of driver-training, understood as an integration of the traditional and programmed instructional system.

NOVÁKOVÁ, M. *Programované učení z hlediska didaktiky* (Programmed learning in view of didactics). Prague, State Educational Publishing House, 1969, 83 p.
Programmed learning treated as objective instruction (based on the analysis of educational objectives), as an effective method of activating pupils, as a way of directing human learning, as individualized instruction.

SATÁNEK, A. *Programovaná výuka ve zdravotnictví* (Programmed instruction in medicine). Prague, Avicenum - The State Health Publishing House, 1972, 156 p.
New view on using the programmed learning at university level, in nursing schools and in public health education with several examples.

STEJSKAL, B. Producing programmes for the UNITUTOR teaching machine (Part I, Text, Part II, Illustrations). Prague, ARTIA - Foreign Trade Corporation, 1971, 61 and 106 p.
The publication deals with the work of the author of a programme, i.e. with didactic possibilities, and with aspects of programme writing.
(Russian, German.)

_____. a kol. Základy programování pro vyučovací automat UNITUTOR (Elements of programming of the UNITUTOR Teaching Machine). Prague, TESLA, 1971, 166 p.
Description of programming (coding).
(Russian and German).

TOLLINGEROVÁ, D. Úvod do teorie a praxe programovaného učení. (Introduction to the theory and practice of programmed learning). Brno, Research Centre of Instructional Methods and Aids, 1969, Vol.1, 89 p.
Explanation of the most important concepts and laws of programmed learning.

TŮMA, J.; KREČAN, Z. Vyučovací stroje (Teaching Machines). Prague, State Technical Publishing House, 1967, 205 p.
A richly illustrated technical description and theoretical explanation of the most important foreign and home-made machines and their educational application.

2 - ARTICLES

ŠATÁNEK, A. "Programovaná výuka při specializaci lékařů a v postgraduálním studiu" (Use of Programmed Instruction in specialization of Physicians and in Continuing Education) in Lekársky obzor Bratislava, 1968, p.223-224.

_____. "Programmed learning in the teaching of medicine in Czechoslovakia", in Aspects of Educational Technology. London, 1968, p.462-463.

_____. "Některé otázky programované výuky v postgraduálním studiu lékařů a farmaceutů" (Several important questions of Programmed Instruction in continuing study of Physicians and Pharmacists) in Československé zdravotnictví. Prague, 1968, p.132-138.

_____. "Einige Probleme des Programmierten Unterrichts in der Erwachsenen-Fortbildung an Hand von Beispielen aus der ärztlichen Weiterbildung" (Some problems concerning Programmed Instruction for advanced studies in light of examples drawn from post-graduate medical education), in Kommunikation. Quickborn, 1969, p.1-18.

_____. "K teoretickým otázkám programované didaktiky" (Theoretical questions of programmed didactics) in Vysoká škola, Prague, 1970, p.468-476.

──────.	"Programované učení v týmu" (Team programmed learning) in Praktický lékař, Prague, 1970, p.515-518.
──────.	"Podíl vědeckého řízení výukového procesu na efektivitě postgraduálního studia" (The influence of scientific control of the educational process on the effectivity of continuing study) in Praktický lékař. Prague, 1970, p.850-853.
──────.	"Programmierter Unterricht bei des Spezialisierung der Arzte in der ČSSR" (Programmed instruction in the spécialization of physicians in Czechoslovakia), in Praxis und Theorie des Programmierten Unterrichtes. München, 1970, p.84-88.
──────.	"Vyučovací stroje v pedagogickém procesu" (Teaching machines in the educational process), in Osveta, Bratislava, 1970, p. 19-30.
SOUKUP, F.	"Können komplexe Sprachfertigkeiten durch Lehr-programme entwickelt werden ?" (Can teaching programmes form complex language skills ?), in Neue Unterrichtspraxis. Köln, 1971, No.3, p.161-167.
STEJSKAL, B.	"The programme as a stockpile of educational work" in Aspects of Educational Technology III. London, Pitman and Sons, 1969, p.92-96.
──────.	"On classification of programmes presented by teaching machines and computers", in Aspects of Educational Technology, IV. Pitman and Sons, 1970, p.155-157.
──────.	"Tvorba vyvčovacich programů pro samočinné počitace a některé vyvčovací automaty" (Formation of teaching programmes for automatic computers and some teaching machines). Prague, Tesla Strasnice, 1970, Vol. 1, 106 p., Vol. II, 59 p.
──────.	"Základy programování pro vyvčovací automat UNITUTOR" (Basis of programming for the teaching machine UNITUTOR). Prague, Tesla Strasnice, 1971, 166 p.
──────.;	Gottheiner, T.; Soukup, F. "Teaching conversation on a teaching machine" in Aspects of Educational Technology, IV. London, Pitman and Sons, 1970, p.146-157.
ŠTĚPAN, V.	"The university of a teaching machine - the basic prerequisite for satisfying higher pedagogic demands" in Aspects of Educational Technology, III. London, Pitman and Sons, 1969, p. 97-104.
──────.	"Zur integration von Programmiertem Unterricht in die derzeitige Praxis in der CSSR" (On integration of Programmed Instruction in contemporary practice in Czechoslovakia in Neue Unterrichtspraxis, No.2. Köln, 1971, p.75-77.

TOLLINGEROVA, D. "Programované učení v ČSSR" (Programmed learning in the CSSR) in <u>Modern conception of primary general education</u>. Prague, 1968, p. 221-230. Research survey

3 - BIBLIOGRAPHIES

MAREŠ, J.; TOLLINGEROVÁ, D. <u>Programované učení a vyučovací stroje II</u> (Bibliography of programmed learning and teaching machines 1965-1969). Prague, The State Library of the CSSR, 1970, 4100 items.

4 - AUDIO-VISUAL PRODUCTIONS/PRODUCTIONS AUDIO-VISUELLES PROGRAMMEES

FILMS

PROGRAMOVÁNÍ NA UČILIŠTÍCH OKR (Programmed learning in minor vocational training), 15 minutes, 16 mm. Colour.
Producer: J. Kulendík

PROGRAMMED PROBLEM SOLVING METHOD
Producer: National Medical Audiovisual Center, Atlanta, USA., 1971

SCHOLA LUDUS. 20 minutes, 35 mm. Black and white
Producer: R. Obdržálek

TRENAŽÉROVÍ JEZDCI (Driver-trainer). 25 minutes, 35 mm. Colour
Producer: F. Karásek

VYUČOVACÍ STROJE (Teaching Machines). 25 minutes, 35 mm. Colour
Producer: F. Karásek

SLIDES / DIAPOSITIVES

ŠVÁBOVÁ, Z.   Programovaná intonace (Programmed intonation). Olomouc 1968. Audio-visual montage for the teaching of singing

PROGRAMMES FOR THE TEACHING MACHINE UNITUTOR
PRAGUE SCHOOL OF ECONOMICS PROGRAMMES

BORÁKOVÁ, a kol.   Zásobování materiálem (supplies of materials)

EICHLER   Formulace úlohy lineárního programování (linear programming)

GOTTHEINEROVÁ; STEJSKAL. <u>A brief guide to telephone conversations</u>. Part I: Introduction. Part II: A morning on the 'phone

KRUKA, V.; KRYKOVÁ; STEJSKAL, B. <u>V sázce je čest</u> (Honour at stake), Prague, Tesla-Strašnice, 1968. Audio-visual montage; 380 frames. Programmed crime story for the teaching machine UNITUTOR

MALÝ, a kol.	Horizontální organizace podniku (Horizontal Enterprise Organization)
MATOUŠEK.	Hospodářská geografie ČSSR (Economic geography of Czechoslovakia). I. díl - Přírodní podmínky (Natural conditions); II. díl - Obyvatelstvo (Population); III. díl, 1. část - Hospodářství (Economy); III. díl, 2. část - Hospodářství (Economy)
MISTERKOVA, a kol.	Třídění hospodářských prostředků a zdrojů (Classification of means and resources)
PUŠ, a kol.	Short stories
SOUKUP:	Silná slovesa v němčině (Přítomný čas) (Strong verbs in German - the present tense). 1. lekce (lesson 1); 2. lekce (lesson 2).
——————.	Strong verbs in German (The present tense) - English version. Lesson 1 and II.
SPINKOVA.	Il faut semer pour recolter. (Pravopisné zmeny ve francouzstine)
STEJSKAL, B.; KRYKA, V.	Patnáct zápalek (Fifteen matches). Prague, Tesla-Strasnice, 1968. Audio-visual montage: 90 frames. A programmed game for the teaching machine UNITUTOR.
VIHAN, a kol.	Zobrazení hospodářských operací v účetnictví (Survey of accountancy transactions)

OTHER UNITUTOR PRODUCERS

ARTIA.	Foreign Trade Corporation, Ve Smeckách 30, Prague 1
ISA	Institute of Social Analysis, Section of Labour Rationalization, Division OLOMOUC, Krízkovského 12.
KOMENIUM	tř. Obránců míru 4, Prague 7.

III - RESEARCH AND APPLICATIONS / REALISATIONS

1 - RESEARCH / RECHERCHES

Theme: AN EXPERIMENTAL STUDY OF ERROR ACHIEVEMENT IN LEARNING AND PROBLEM SOLVING
Organized by: The Laboratory for Programmed Learning Research, Prague
Public concerned: Laboratory research

Theme: AN EXPERIMENTAL STUDY OF THE INFLUENCE OF INFORMATION FEED-BACK OF DIFFERENT QUALITY AND LEVEL UPON LEARNING ACHIEVEMENT

Organized by: The Laboratory for Programmed Learning Research, Prague
Public concerned: Laboratory research

Theme: FOLLOWING EFFECTIVENESS OF VARIOUS FORMS OF CONTROL IN THE INSTRUCTION IN SELECTED SPECIALIZATIONS AND SUBSPECIALIZATIONS
Organized by: Department of Programmed Instruction and Educational Technology, Post-graduate Medical and Pharmaceutical Institute, Prague
Public concerned: Physicians and pharmacists

Theme: INTEGRATION OF PROGRAMMED AND CONVENTIONAL INSTRUCTION IN THE CZECH PRIMARY SCHOOL
Organized by: Regional Institute of Education, Brno. Co-ordinated by the Laboratory for Programmed Learning Research, Prague.

Theme: INTEGRATION OF PROGRAMMED AND CONVENTIONAL INSTRUCTION IN THE SLOVAK PRIMARY SCHOOL
Organized by: The Research Institute of Education, Bratislava
Public concerned: Primary schools (6-15 years)

Theme: PROGRAMMED INSTRUCTION IN MINOR VOCATIONAL EDUCATION AND TRAINING
Organized by: O.K.R., Ostrava. Co-ordinated by the Laboratory for Programmed Learning Research, Prague

Theme: PROGRAMMED INSTRUCTION IN SMALL GROUPS (PHYSICS)
Organized by: Primary School Šternberk (near Olomouc). Co-ordinated by the Laboratory for Programmed Learning Research, Prague.

Theme: PROGRAMMED INSTRUCTION IN UNIVERSITY MATHEMATICS
Organized by: Prague Technical University. Co-ordinated by the Laboratory for Programmed Learning Research, Prague
Public concerned: Technical university

Theme: PROGRAMMED LEARNING IN ECONOMIC HIGH SCHOOLS
Organized by: The Prague School of Economics. Co-ordinated by the Laboratory for Programmed Learning Research, Prague.

Theme: USE OF CONCEPTIONS AND METHODS OF THE INFORMATION THEORY AND OF OTHER SYSTEM THEORIES (INTERNATIONAL RESEARCH)
Organized by: Department of Programmed Instruction and Educational Technology, Post-graduate Medical and Pharmaceutical Institute, Prague.
Public concerned: Physicians and pharmacists

2 - PUBLISHED PROGRAMMED COURSES / COURS PROGRAMMES PUBLIES

BALCAR, L. Dějiny antiky (History of the Antique). Ustí n. Labem, Faculty of Education, 1969, 113 p.
Summarization and repetition of subject matter. Suitable for pupils' homework. Primary schools (6-15 years)

BEDNAŘIK, M.　　Gravitační pole (Field of gravity). Prague, Comenius Institute, 1967, 92 p. Basic astronomical concepts, formulas and quantities. Basic mathematical calculations with those quantities.
Secondary schools (15-18 years)

BERNATH, P.　　Programovaná učebnica slovenského jazyka (Programmed textbook of the slovak language). Bratislava, S.P.N., 1969, 122 p. 357 basic grammar problems adapted for children in the 2nd form of primary schools.
(6-15 years).

BROŽA, J.　　Voda a užitečné nerosty. (Water and useful minerals) Brno, K.P.U., 1969.
299 items concerning water: its occurrence, circulation, nature and use; useful minerals. Primary schools (6-15 years)

DOLEJŠÍ, I.　　Učíme se popsat rostlinu (We are learning to describe a plant). Prague, Comenius Institute, 1968, 148 p. Training and introduction to plant morphology.
Primary schools (6-15 years)

FISNER, B.; MILNERA, S. Základy obecné a fyzikální chemie (Outlines of general and physical chemistry). Prague, S.P.N., 1968, 306 p. Introduction to university chemistry.

GESCHWINDER, J.　　Fyzika (Physics). Faculty of Education, Ustí n. Labem, 1968, 70 p.
Electrical circuit, conducting power of fluids, magnetism.
Adapted for 8th form primary school (6-15 years)

GOTTHEINEROVÁ, T. et al.　　Angličtina pro zahraniční obchod (English for Foreign Trade). Prague, S.P.N., 1969, 1030 p. Programmed English adapted for use at the Foreign Trade Faculty of the Prague School of Economics.
Universities; adult education.

MELEZINEK, A.　　Základní elektronické součástky a obvody. (Basic electronic parts and circuits). Prague, Technical University, 1968, 251 p.
Universities; technical education (15-18 years)

NEDĚLIK, I.　　Škůdci řepy. (Parasites of Beet). Kojetín; School of Agriculture, 1969, 65 p.
Description of parasites of sugar beet and some methods of extermination. Vocational education (15-18 years)

NOVAKOVA, M.　　Skladebné dvojice. (Syntactical couples). Olomouc, Faculty of Education.
Instructions for making a syntactical analysis of a Czech sentence.
Adapted for 6th form primary schools (6-15 years)

PALOUŠ, R.; PACHMAN, E.   Obecná chemie (General chemistry). Prague,
 Socialistic Academy, 1968, 800 items.
 Teaching machine. Summarization of high school chemistry;
 suitable for university beginners.
 University. Secondary schools (15-18 years)

PRŮCHA, J.   Atomistika. (Atomistics). Prague, Tesla-Strasnice, 1969,
 520 items.
 Teaching machine; introduction to atomistics for
 chemistry beginners.
 Technical education (15-18 years)

ŠTÁHLAVSKÁ, D.   Farmaceutická analýza (Pharmaceutical Analysis(I, II, III,
 IV. Prague, Department of Programmed Instruction and
 Educational Technology, Post-graduate Medical and
 Pharmaceutical Institute, 1971/1972.
 Pharmacists.

STANĚK, E.   Technické kreslení. (Technical drawing). Ostrava,
 O.K.R., 1969, 90 p.
 Theoretical topics needed in minor training.
 Adult education.

ZLATNÍK, Č. et al.   Matematika I. (Mathematics, vol. 1). Prague,
 Technical University, 1969, 276 p.
 Programmed introduction to university mathematics.
 Introduction to the theory of Sets, linear algebra,
 functions and other topics.
 University.

3 - COMPUTER ASSISTED INSTRUCTION / ENSEIGNEMENT ASSISTE PAR ORDINATEUR

EVALUATION OF VARIOUS EXPERIMENTAL TOPICS
Organization: Department of Mathematical Machines
                   Technical University of Bratislava, Vazovova 1/b
Public concerned: University
Type of computer: MSP-2a (made in the CSSR)
Type of terminals: Teletyp Consul (adapted)
Type of language: Experimental

USING COMPUTER IN EDUCATION (FOR TEACHING AND DIAGNOSTIC OF KNOWLEDGE
Organization: Department of Programmed Instruction and Educational
                   Technology, Post-graduate Medical and Pharmaceutical
                   Institute, Prague 8, Ustavní 91
Public concerned: Post-graduate Medical and Pharmaceutical Institute
Type of computer: 1) AP Tesla
                   2) Portable digital computer
Type of language: Experimental

FINLAND/FINLANDE

I - ORGANIZATIONS AND ACTIVITIES / STRUCTURES ET ACTIVITES

1 - CENTRES

DEPARTMENT OF EDUCATION, UNIVERSITY OF TURKU
Turku
Nature of organization: University

DEPARTMENT OF EDUCATION, UNIVERSITY OF TAMPERE
Tampere
Nature of organization: University

DEPARTMENT OF PSYCHOLOGY, UNIVERSITY OF TAMPERE
Tampere
Nature of organization: University

INSTITUTE FOR EDUCATIONAL RESEARCH, DEPARTMENT OF EDUCATION, UNIVERSITY OF JYVÄSKYLÄ
Jyväskylä
Nature of organization: University

2 - ACTIVITIES / MANIFESTATIONS

DIE ERSTE NORDEUROPÄISCHE TAGUNG DER GESELLSCHAFT FÜR PROGRAMMIERTE INSTRUKTION
Organized by: Deutsches Institut Helsinki and the University of Turku
Place and date: University of Turku, 2-4 October 1970.
Participants: Research workers. University teachers
Purposes: Programmed learning in schools providing general education.
                   Research on programmed learning
Proceedings: Werkhefte für technische Unterrichtsmittel. Heft 5.
                   Lehren und Lernen nach 1970. München, Goethe-Institut.

SEMINAR OF PROGRAMMED LEARNING
Organized by: Unesco Committee of Finland
Place and date: University of Tampere, 1968
Participants: Research workers. School and vocational teachers.
                   Adult educators
Purposes: Programmed learning in schools providing general education.
                   Programmed learning in adult education. Programmed
                   language teaching. Research on programmed learning.
Proceedings: Peltonen et al. Ohjelmoidun Opetuksen Perusteet
                   (Principles of programmed learning), Tapiola, Weilin
                   and Göos Ed., 1969.

3 - PUBLISHERS/MAISONS D'EDITION

KUSTANNUSOSAKEYHTIÖ OTAVA
Uudenmaankatu 10, Helsinki 10
Nature of organization: Commercial publisher

TAMMI KUSTANNUS OY
Hämeentie 15, Helsinki 50
Nature of organization: Commercial publisher

WEILIN & GÖÖS OY
Mannerheimintie 40, Helsinki 10
Nature of organization: Commercial publisher

WERNER SÖDERSTRÖM OSAKEYHTIÖ (WSOY)
Bulevardi 12, Helsinki 12
Nature of organization: Commercial publisher

7 - TRAINING ORGANIZATIONS/ORGANISMES ASSURANT UNE FORMATION

/ Only to a small degree in the following teacher training colleges /

JYVÄSKYLÄN NORMAALILYSEO (NORMAL SCHOOL OF JYVÄSKYLÄ)
Jyväskylä
Nature of organization: Governmental
Public concerned: School teachers

KAJAANIN SEMINAARI (TEACHER TRAINING SCHOOL OF KAJAANI)
Kajaani
Nature of organization: Governmental
Public concerned: School teachers

II - PUBLICATIONS

1 - BOOKS / LIVRES

PELTONEN et al. Ohjelmoidun opetuksen Perusteet (Principles of programmed learning). Tapiola, Weilin and Göos, 1969. Lectures and reports of working groups given at the seminar of Programmed learning in Tampere (1968).

III - RESEARCH AND APPLICATIONS / REALISATIONS

2 - PUBLISHED PROGRAMMED COURSES / COURS PROGRAMMES PUBLIES

DAHLKVIST, Ragnar; HILDING, Sven. Prosenttilaskun alkeet (Elements of mathematics). Helsinki, Werner Söderström, 1969, 63 p., 155 items.
Primary and secondary levels.

HELLA, Atso. Orgaanisten yhdistysten nimet ja kaavat (Chemistry names and formulae of organic compounds). Helsinki, Werner Söderström, 1969, 50 p., 226 items.
Secondary level.

HUOPIO, Erkki. Paikkajärjestelmä, kymmenjärgestelmä ja viisijärjestelmä (Mathematics on various systems of numbers). Helsinki, Kustannusosakeyhtiö Otava, 1969, 30 p., 47 items.
Primary level.

SUOMALAINEN, Markku. Opetusteknologisen mallin sovellus lineaarisen opetusohjelman laadintaan (Application of educational technological model linear programmed instruction. Evaluation of the applicability of the model, and experiment on the effects of reinforcement on the effectiveness of grammar instruction). Reports of the Institute of Educational Research, 1972, 35 p., 244 items.
Primary and secondary levels.

FRANCE

I - ORGANIZATIONS AND ACTIVITIES / STRUCTURES ET ACTIVITES

1 - CENTRES

CENTRE D'ETUDES ET DE RECHERCHES PSYCHOLOGIQUES DE L'ARMEE DE L'AIR
(C.E.R.P.A.I.R.)
Base 272, 78 Saint Cyr.   Tél: 950.00.68
Nature de l'organisme: Gouvernemental

CENTRE D'ETUDES ET RECHERCHES PSYCHOTECHNIQUES (C.E.R.P.)
13, Place de Villiers, 93 Montreuil
Nature de l'organisme: Gouvernemental

CENTRE DE DOCUMENTATION
Quartier Augereau, 77.010 Melun
Nature de l'organisme: Gouvernemental

CENTRE NATIONAL D'ETUDES DES TELECOMMUNICATIONS
Route de Trégastel, 22 Lannion.   Tél: (96) 38.11.11
39/41 rue Gambetta, 38 Grenoble
34 rue Jean-Bart, 59 Lille
100 bis, rue Hénon, 69 Lyon
Cedex 3022, 76 Rouen St. Clément
B.P. 3203, 31 Toulouse
Nature de l'organisme: Gouvernemental

CENTRE NATIONAL DE TELE-ENSEIGNEMENT
60, Boulevard du Lycée, 92 Vanves
Nature de l'organisme: Gouvernemental

CENTRE UNIVERSITAIRE DE COOPERATION ECONOMIQUE ET SOCIALE (C.U.C.E.S.)
Rue de Saurupt, 54 Nancy
Nature de l'organisme: Association (loi de 1901)

COMPAGNIE I.B.M. (France)
5, Place Vendôme, 75 Paris 1°
Nature de l'organisme: Compagnie privée

ECOLE NORMALE SUPERIEURE DE SAINT-CLOUD (C.R.E.F.E.D.)
Avenue Pozzo di Borgo, 92 Saint-Cloud. Tél: 603.18.00
Nature de l'organisme: Gouvernemental

E.D.F. - G.D.F., Service PROFOR
23 bis, Avenue de Messine, 75 Paris 8e.
Nature de l'organisme: Entreprise nationale

E.L.F. - E.R.A.P.
7, rue Nélaton, 75 Paris 15°
Nature de l'organisme: Compagnie privée

INSTITUT DE MATHEMATIQUES APPLIQUEES (I.M.A.G.)
Université scientifique et médicale de Grenoble
Cedex 53, 38041   Saint Martin d'Hères.   Tél: 87.45.61
Nature de l'organisme: Université

INSTITUT DE RECHERCHES D'INFORMATIQUE ET D'AUTOMATIQUE (I.R.I.A.)
Domaine de Voluceau, 78 Rocquencourt.   Tél: 954.90.20
Nature de l'organisme: Gouvernemental

INSTITUT DE RECHERCHE EN MATHEMATIQUES AVANCEES
Université scientifique et médicale de Grenoble
Cedex 53, 38 Grenoble-Gare.   Tél: 87.45.61

INSTITUT NATIONAL DE RECHERCHE ET DE DOCUMENTATION PEDAGOGIQUES (I.N.R.D.P.)
29, rue d'Ulm, Paris 5°.   Tél: 325.41.64
    Centres régionaux de recherche et de documentation pédagogiques:
    75 Cours d'Alsace-Lorraine, 33 Bordeaux.   Tél: 44.12.92
    11, Avenue du Général Champon, 38 Grenoble.   Tél: 87.77.62
    99, rue de Metz, 54 Nancy.   Tél: 52.85.14
     3, rue Roquelaine, Toulouse-Cedex.   Tél: 625454-31068
Nature de l'organisme: Gouvernemental

INSTITUT NATIONAL POUR LA FORMATION DES ADULTES (I.N.F.A.)
Rue de Saurupt, 54 Nancy.   Tél: 53.72.36
Nature de l'organisme: Gouvernemental

I.R.E.M.
Tour de Mathématiques - Domaine Universitaire
B.P.41, 38041 Saint Martin d'Hères
Nature de l'organisme: Université

LABORATOIRE D'INFORMATIQUE, FACULTE DES SCIENCES
118, route de Narbonne, 31 Toulouse.   Tél: 52.12.12
Nature de l'organisme: Université

LABORATOIRE DE PSYCHOLOGIE DU TRAVAIL
41, rue Gay Lussac, 75 Paris 5°
Nature de l'organisme: Gouvernemental

MAISON DES SCIENCES DE L'HOMME
Centre de mathématiques appliquées et de calcul
54, Boulevard Raspail, 75 Paris 6°.   Tél: 222.02.18
Nature de l'organisme: Gouvernemental

France

MINISTERE DES POSTES ET TELECOMMUNICATIONS
Services de Formation
46, rue Barrault, 75 Paris 13°
Nature de l'organisme: Gouvernemental

OFFICE FRANCAIS DES TECHNIQUES MODERNES D'EDUCATION (O.F.R.A.T.E.M.E.)
29, rue d'Ulm, 75 Paris 5°
    Département de la recherche et de la formation
    35, rue Maurice Arnoux, 92 Montrouge.   Tél: 735.18.10
Nature de l'organisme: Gouvernemental

ORGANISATION ET INSTRUCTION PROGRAMMEE (OIP)
4, rue de Stockholm, 75 Paris 1°
Nature de l'organisme: Société privée

ORGANISME NATIONAL DE SECURITE ROUTIERE (O.N.S.E.R.)
Autodrome de Linas-Montlhéry, 91 Montlhéry
Nature de l'organisme: Gouvernemental

PRINTEMPS-PRISUNIC
Service de formation
22, rue Joubert, 75 Paris 9°
Nature de l'organisme: Compagnie privée

S.E.M.A. (Département Enseignement Programmé)
9, rue Georges Pitard, 75 Paris 15°   Tél: 842.68.00
Nature de l'organisme: Société privée

SOCIETE DE PEDAGOGIE CYBERNETIQUE ET D'INFORMATIQUE (S.P.C.I.)
31, rue des Francs-Bourgeois, 75 Paris 4°.   Tél: 277.43.20
Nature de l'organisme: Société privée

SOCIETE PHILIPS
162, rue St. Charles, 75 Paris 15°.   Tél: 532.21.19: 828.62.72
Nature de l'organisme: Société privée

SOCIETE SINTRA (Machines MITSI)
26, rue de Malakoff, 92 Asnières.   Tél: 783.69.80
Nature de l'organisme: Société privée

SODETEG (Systèmes et moyens d'éducation)
9, avenue Réaumur, 92 Le Plessis Robinson. Tél: 736.43.21
Nature de l'organisme: Société privée

THOMSON-HOUSTON (France)
55, rue des Orteaux, 75 Paris 20°
Nature de l'organisme: Compagnie privée

UNITE D'ENSEIGNEMENT ET DE RECHERCHE, DIDACTIQUE DES DISCIPLINES
SCIENTIFIQUES (DDS)
Ordinateur pour étudiants, Université de Paris VII
  2, place Jussieu, 75 Paris 5° Tél: 336.25.25
Nature de l'organisme: Université

France

UNITE D'ENSEIGNEMENT ET DE RECHERCHE, SCIENCES DE L'EDUCATION
Route de la Tourelle, 75 Vincennes
Nature de l'organisme: Université

UNITE D'ENSEIGNEMENT ET DE RECHERCHE, SCIENCES DE L'EDUCATION
Rue Albert-Lautman, 31070 Cedex Toulouse
Nature de l'organisme: Académie

UNITE D'ENSEIGNEMENT ET DE RECHERCHE, SCIENCES DE L'EDUCATION, UNIVERSITE RENE DESCARTES
28, rue Serpente, 75 Paris 6°
Nature de l'organisme: Université

2 - ACTIVITIES/MANIFESTATIONS

Colloque OTAN - TENDANCES ACTUELLES DE LA RECHERCHE EN ENSEIGNEMENT PROGRAMME (Manifestation internationale)

Organisateur: OTAN (Groupe Facteurs Humains) et Centre de documentation sur l'enseignement programmé
Lieu et date: Nice, 13 - 17 mai 1968
Participants: Chercheurs
Objet: Faire le point sur la situation de la recherche en enseignement programmé
Actes publiés par: Editions Dunod, 92 rue Bonaparte, 75 Paris 6°

L'INFORMATIQUE AU SERVICE DE L'HOMME (Manifestation nationale)

Organisateur: Université de Grenoble, Faculté des Sciences 38041 Grenoble. Tél: 87.85.71
Participants: Chercheurs

LA PEDAGOGIE, BILAN DE 10 ANNEES D'EXPERIENCE (Manifestation régionale)

Organisateur: EUREQUIP, 177 Avenue du Roule, 92 Neuilly. Tél: 624.60.71
Lieu et date: Paris, 21 avril 1970

POURQUOI ET COMMENT UTILISER L'ENSEIGNEMENT PROGRAMME

Organisateur: A.I.D.E.R. - Organisations professionnelles de l'Isère
Lieu et date: Grenoble, février 1971
Participants: Formateurs d'adultes. Enseignants.

SEMINAIRE D'ENSEIGNEMENT PROGRAMME (Manifestation annuelle, régionale)

Organisateur: Ecole pratique des Hautes Etudes (6° section) Rue du Cherche-Midi, Paris 6°
Lieu et dates: Paris, 1968-1969-1970
Participants: Chercheurs

SEMINAIRE DE FORMATION A L'ENSEIGNEMENT PROGRAMME (Manifestation régionale, annuelle)

Organisateur: Institut national pour la formation des adultes
Lieu et dates: Paris, 1968-1969-1970
Participants: Enseignants scolaires, Formateurs d'adultes, Formateurs de chercheurs

SEMINAIRE EUROPEEN SUR L'ENSEIGNEMENT PROGRAMME (Manifestation internationale annuelle)
Organisateur: Institut européen pour la formation professionnelle
153 avenue Victor Hugo, 75 Paris 16°
Lieu et date: Château d'Artigny, mars 1969
Objet: Panorama des réalisations européennes en enseignement programmé. Définition d'une politique concertée
Participants: Responsables de formation

STAGE D'INITIATION A L'ENSEIGNEMENT PROGRAMME
Organisateur: Centre national de télé-enseignement (C.N.T.E.)
Lieu et dates: Vanves, 15-19 avril 1969; 11-12 décembre 1969
Objet: Confrontation des travaux des professeurs et résultats des expériences
Participants: Professeurs

3 - PUBLISHERS / MAISONS D'EDITION

BORDAS
37-39, rue Boulard, 75 Paris 14°. Tél: 734.85.57
24-26, boulevard de l'Hôpital, 75 Paris 5°

ARMAND COLIN
103, boulevard Saint-Michel, 75 Paris 5°. Tél: 633.49.70; 033.37.33

DUNOD
92, rue Bonaparte, 75 Paris 6°. Tél: 548.28.82
24-26, boulevard de l'Hôpital, 75 Paris 5°

EDITIONS D'ORGANISATION
7, rue Rousselet, 75 Paris 7°

EDITIONS HOMMES ET TECHNIQUES
91, rue Jean Jaurès, 92 Puteaux

ENTREPRISE MODERNE D'EDITION
4, rue Cambon, 75 Paris 1er. Tél: 073.51.01; 073.88.94

EYROLLES
61, boulevard Saint-Germain, 75 Paris 6°

FAYARD Arthème
75, rue des Saints-Pères, 75 Paris 6°. Tél: 222.84.50

FLAMMARION (MEDECINE - SCIENCES)
20, rue de Vaugirard, 75 Paris 6°. Tél: 033.94.10

GAMMA
rue Garancière, 75 Paris 6°. Tél: 633.29.30

GAUTHIER-VILLARS
55, quai des Grands-Augustins, 75 Paris 6°

HACHETTE
79, boulevard Saint-Germain, 75 Paris 6°. Tél: 325.22.11

LEARNING SYSTEMS INSTITUTE
55, avenue Kléber, 75 Paris 16°

PEDAGOGIE MODERNE
70, rue Michel-Ange, 75 Paris 16°.   Tél: 288.80.54

4 - PERIODICALS / PERIODIQUES

BULLETIN DE LIAISON ET D'INFORMATION PEDAGOGIQUE
Enseignement à distance, C.N.T.E. (OFRATEME)
Périodicité: Trimestriel
Centre d'intérêt: Liaison pédagogique des différents centres de
                  télé-enseignement

BULLETIN DE PSYCHOLOGIE
Editeur: Groupes d'études de psychologie de l'Université de Paris
Périodicité: 15 numéros par an
Centre d'intérêt: Etudes psychologiques

BULLETIN DU C.E.R.P. (Centre d'études et recherches psychologiques)
Editeur: Association nationale pour la formation professionnelle
            des adultes (A.F.P.A.)
Adresse: 13, Place de Villiers, 93 Montreuil
Périodicité: Trimestriel
Centres d'intérêt: Recherches et études psychologiques. Réalisations
            en enseignement automatisé

BULLETIN DU LABORATOIRE DE PEDAGOGIE
Editeur: Université de Paris, Faculté des Lettres et Sciences humaines
Adresse: 16, rue de la Sorbonne, 75 Paris 5°
Périodicité: 6 numéros par an
Centres d'intérêt: Techniques pédagogiques. Sciences de l'éducation

INFORMATIQUE ET GESTION
Editeur: Association pour l'informatique de gestion
Adresse: Centre universitaire Dauphine, 4, rue Charles Renouvier,
                                                    75 Paris 16°
Périodicité: Mensuel
Centres d'intérêt: Informatique. Enseignement automatisé. Gestion

JOURNAL DE L'AUDIOVISUEL
Editeur: Les Editions Techniques Spécialisées
Adresse: 41, rue de la Grange aux Belles, 75 Paris 10°
Périodicité: 10 numéros par an
Centres d'intérêt: Techniques audio-visuelles. Applications. Informations.

L'EDUCATION
Adresse: 91, avenue Ledru-Rollin, 75 Paris 11°
Centres d'intérêt: Action éducative. Evolution et perspectives. Actualités.

MEDIA
Editeur: Office français des techniques modernes d'éducation
Adresse: 29, rue d'Ulm, 75 Paris 5°
Périodicité: Mensuel
Centre d'intérêt: Techniques modernes d'éducation

01 INFORMATIQUE
Editeur: Les Editions Tests
Adresse: 41, rue de la Grange aux Belles, 75 Paris 10°
Périodicité: Hebdomadaire et mensuel
Centres d'intérêt: La vie professionnelle de l'informatique (hebdomadaire).
                   Etudes de référence pour les responsables des
                   services informatiques (mensuel).

REVUE FRANCAISE DE PEDAGOGIE
Editeur: Institut national de recherche et de documentation pédagogiques
Adresse: 29, rue d'Ulm, Paris 5°
Centre de vente: S.E.V.P.E.N., 13, rue du Four, 75 Paris 6°
Périodicité: Trimestriel
Centre d'intérêt: Technologie éducative

5 - PROFESSIONAL ORGANIZATIONS / ORGANISATIONS PROFESSIONNELLES

ASSOCIATION DES PROFESSEURS DE BIOLOGIE ET GEOLOGIE DE L'ENSEIGNEMENT
PUBLIC (ex. Union des Naturalistes)
29, rue d'Ulm, 75 Paris 5°

ASSOCIATION DES PROFESSEURS DE LANGUES VIVANTES (A.P.L.V.)
29, rue d'Ulm, R 75 Paris 5°

ASSOCIATION DES PROFESSEURS DE MATHEMATIQUES (A.P.M.)
29 rue d'Ulm, 75 Paris 5°

ASSOCIATION DES PROFESSEURS DE PHYSIQUE (Union des Physiciens)
Lycée Saint Louis, 44 Boulevard St. Michel, 75 Paris 6°.   Tél: 326.44.01
                                                                326.16.23

ASSOCIATION FRANCAISE POUR LA CYBERNETIQUE ECONOMIQUE ET TECHNIQUE (A.F.C.E.T.)
Centre Universitaire Dauphine
Place du Maréchal de Lattre de Tassigny, 75 Paris 16°.   Tél: 553.50.20
    Activité: Echange d'informations entre les équipes de recherche

ASSOCIATION INTERENTREPRISES POUR LE DEVELOPPEMENT DE
L'ENSEIGNEMENT PROGRAMME (A.I.D.E.P.)
20, rue d'Arcueil, 75 Paris 14°.   Tél: 589.10.02
Nature de l'organisation: Privée

INSTITUT EUROPEEN POUR LA FORMATION PROFESSIONNELLE
153, avenue Victor-Hugo, 75 Paris 16°
Nature de l'organisation: Privée

6 - MANUFACTURERS OF TEACHING MACHINES / FABRICANTS DE MACHINES A ENSEIGNER

NAVARIN, S.A.
4, rue Fromentin, 75 Paris 9°

PHILIPS
162, rue Saint Charles, 75 Paris 15°. Tél: 532.21.29
Type de machine: Projecteur pour P.I.P.
Caractéristiques: Programme à branchement. Conservation des réponses.
                        Dispositif audio-visuel intégré. Utilisation
                        individuelle ou pour petit groupe.

SINTRA
2, rue de Malakoff, 92 Asnières.   Tél: 783.69.80
Type de machine: MITSI
Caractéristiques: Programme à branchement. Analyse des réponses.
                        Dispositif audio-visuel intégré. Utilisation
                        individuelle.

SOCIETE DE PEDAGOGIE CYBERNETIQUE ET D'INFORMATIQUE
31, rue des Francs Bourgeois, 75 Paris 4°. Tél: 277.43.20
Type de machine: **Test O Matic**
Caractéristiques: **Dispositif de** disques avec voyants, coordonné
                        avec un cours programmé conçu ad hoc et permettant
                        le branchement à partir des réponses de l'élève.
                        Utilisation individuelle.

SODETEG
9, avenue Réaumur, 92 Le Plessis Robinson.   Tél: Mic: 59.00
Type de machine: Selfmaster, modèle A
Caractéristiques: Programme à branchement. Compteur de bonnes et
                        mauvaises réponses. Eléments logiques à base
                        de circuits intégrés. Types MOS. Clavier
                        identique à celui d'une machine à écrire.

STILLIT
62, rue de Ponthieu, 75 Paris 8°
Type de machine: Stillitron
Caractéristiques: Bloc à circuits imprimés signalant la bonne ou
                        la mauvaise réponse coordonné avec un cours
                        programmé établi ad hoc. Utilisation individuelle.

7 - TRAINING ORGANIZATIONS / ORGANISMES ASSURANT UNE FORMATION

ASSOCIATION NATIONALE POUR LE PERFECTIONNEMENT DES ADULTES (A.F.P.A.)
13, place de Villiers, 93 Montreuil
Nature de l'organisme: Para-public
Public intéressé: Formateurs d'adultes. Enseignants.

ASSOCIATION INTERENTREPRISES POUR LE DEVELOPPEMENT DE L'ENSEIGNEMENT
PROGRAMME (A.I.D.E.P.)
20, rue d'Arcueil, 75 Paris 14°. Tél: 589.10.02
Nature de l'organisme: Société privée
Public intéressé: Formateurs des ingénieurs. Cadres.

CEGOS
91, rue Jean Jaurès, 92 Puteaux
Nature de l'organisme: Société privée
Public intéressé: Toute personne désirant acquérir une formation
                    dans le cadre de son travail professionnel (y
                    compris une formation à l'enseignement programmé)

France

ECOLE PRATIQUE DES HAUTES ETUDES (Maison des Sciences de l'Homme)
54, Boulevard Raspail, 75 Paris 6°.   Tél: 544.03.49
Public intéressé: Etudiants.   Formateurs.

EUREQUIP,
177, avenue du Roule, 92 Neuilly
Nature de l'organisme: Société privée
Public intéressé: Toutes catégories

INFA (INSTITUT NATIONAL POUR LA FORMATION DES ADULTES)
Rue de Saurupt, 54 Nancy, et 51 Boulevard de Montmorency, 75 Paris 16°
Nature de l'organisme: Gouvernemental
Public intéressé: Formateurs d'adultes. Enseignants.

INSTITUT DE PSYCHOLOGIE DE LA FACULTE DES LETTRES ET SCIENCES
HUMAINES DE PARIS
28, rue Serpente, 75 Paris 6°.   Tél: 033.24.13

- Laboratoire d'informatique
  Faculté des sciences, 118 route de Narbonne, 31 Toulouse.   Tél: 52.12.12

- UER de Didactique des disciplines scientifiques (D.D.S.)
  2 Place Jussieu, 75 Paris 5°. Tél: 336.25.25

- UER des sciences de l'éducation
  17, rue de la Sorbonne, 75 Paris 5°.   Tél: 325.24.13

- UER des sciences de l'éducation
  Route de la Tourelle, 75 Paris (Vincennes) 12°

INSTITUT DE MATHEMATIQUES APPLIQUEES DE GRENOBLE (IMAG)
Université scientifique et médicale de Grenoble
B.P.53.   38041 Grenoble-Cedex

SEMA (Département enseignement programmé)
9, rue Georges Pitard, 75 Paris 15°. Tél: 842.68.00
Nature de l'organisme: Société privée
Public intéressé: Formateurs d'adultes

SINTRA (Machines MITSI, Département formation)
2, rue Malakoff, 92 Asnières.   Tél: 783.69.80
Nature de l'organisme: Société privée
Public intéressé: Futurs utilisateurs de la machine MITSI

S.P.C.I.
31, rue des Francs-Bourgeois, 75 Paris 4°
Nature de l'organisme: Société privée
Public intéressé: Formateurs. Relais de formation.   Spécialistes
         de l'audio-visuel.

8 - DOCUMENTATION CENTRES / CENTRES DE DOCUMENTATION

INSTITUT NATIONAL POUR LA FORMATION DES ADULTES (Centre de
documentation sur l'enseignement programmé)
29, rue d'Ulm, 75 Paris 5°
Nature de l'organisme: Gouvernemental
Nature des services: Diffusion de l'information. Documentation.
             Bibliothèque

Centres de documentation à vocation partielle sur l'enseignement programmé:

ASSOCIATION FRANÇAISE POUR LA CYBERNETIQUE ECONOMIQUE ET TECHNIQUE (A.F.C.E.T.)
Immeuble du Centre Dauphine, Place du Maréchal de Lattre de Tassigny,
75 Paris 16°
Nature de l'organisme: Société savante

CENTRE NATIONAL DE LA RECHERCHE SCIENTIFIQUE (C.N.R.S.)
15, Quai Anatole France, 75 Paris 7°. Tél: 555.26.70, 555.0360
Nature de l'organisme: Gouvernemental

ECOLE NORMALE SUPERIEURE DE SAINT CLOUD (C.R.E.F.E.D.)
2, avenue du Palais, 92 Saint Cloud. Tél: 603.18.00
Nature de l'organisme: Gouvernemental

INSTITUT NATIONAL DE RECHERCHE ET DE DOCUMENTATION PEDAGOGIQUES
29, rue d'Ulm, 75 Paris 5°
Nature de l'organisme: Gouvernemental

II - PUBLICATIONS

1 - BOOKS/LIVRES

ANTOINE, P.; DESBROUSSES, H. *L'enseignement programmé.* Nancy, I.N.F.A. 1969. Points forts, points faibles, développement, formation.

FREICHE, J.; HIGELE, P. *Utilisation de l'enseignement programmé dans un enseignement par correspondance.* Nancy, I.N.F.A. - C.U.C.E.S., novembre 1969.

GAVINI, G.P. *Manuel de formation aux techniques de l'enseignement programmé.* Puteaux, Hommes et Techniques, 1969 (nouvelle édition)

LAMERAND, R. *Théories d'enseignement programmé et laboratoires de langues.* Paris, Labor/Fernand Nathan, 1969,

MONTMOLLIN, M. de *L'enseignement programmé.* Paris, P.U.F., 3ème édition, 1971, 128 p.

OTAN *La recherche en enseignement programmé. Tendances actuelles.* (Actes du symposium OTAN, Nice, mai 1968). Paris, Dunod, 360 p.

OTAN *La simulation du comportement humain.* (Actes d'un Symposium OTAN). Paris, Dunod, 1967, 1969, 475 p.

POCZTAR, J. *Théories et pratique de l'enseignement programmé.* Paris, Unesco, 1971, 186 p. (Monographies sur l'éducation No.VII)

———— *Les algorithmes.* (Textes traduits sous la direction de P. Vermeesch). Laboratoire de psychologie du travail, EPHE, 200 p.

SCHESTAKOW, et al. *L'enseignement programmé et les machines à enseigner en URSS.* Paris, Dunod, 1968, 210 p.

France

TALYZINA, F. Principes théoriques de l'enseignement programmé. (Traduction réalisée sous la direction de J. Pocztar. ENS de St. Cloud (CREFED). Document de travail. Paris, Unesco, 1970, 110 p.

2 - ARTICLES

BONVALOT, G. "L'enseignement programmé dans les entreprises: la détermination des objectifs", in Enseignement programmé, No.5, mars 1969, 8 p.

BOUTIN, Am. "Enseignement programmé et formation professionnelle dans les entreprises", in Enseignement programmé, No.5, mars 1969, 32 p. Enquête

Collectif "Une expérience d'enseignement de biologie assisté par ordinateur à la Faculté des Sciences de Paris", in Enseignement programmé, No.8, décembre 1969, p.21-47

DELACOUDRE, N. "Recensement et analyse des ouvrages d'enseignement programmé en langue française sur l'informatique", in Enseignement programmé, Nos.9-10, mars-juin 1970, p.63-74. Etude documentaire

D'HAINAUT, L. "Un modèle pour la détermination et la sélection des objectifs pédagogiques du domaine cognitif", in Enseignement programmé, No.11, septembre 1970, p.21-38.

DEMARNE, P.J. "Programme en dents de scie et spatialisation des concepts d'enseignement", in Enseignement programmé, No.6, juin 1969, 10 p.

———————. "Quelques caractéristiques de l'ordinateur d'enseignement" in IBM Informatique, No.43, 1969, 17 p.

DUBOST, Pierre-Julien. "Enseignement et traitement de l'information", in Science et vie. Hors série No.82 sur l'informatique (1968)

———————————. "Vers une pédagogie industrielle, pourquoi?" in Promotion Sociale Tribune, No.35, juin 1969

FARGETTE, H.P. "L'ordinateur, auxiliaire de l'enseignement", in Automatisme, No.9, tome XIV, septembre 1969, 7 p.

GAVINI, G.P.; BARRAUD, D. "Une expérimentation d'enseignement programmé en mathématiques". No.1, BINOP 1969, p.27-33

LE CORRE, Y. "L'expérience d'enseignement assisté par ordinateur" réalisé à la Faculté des Sciences de Paris", in Revue générale de l'Electricité, No.11, novembre 1971, t.80

PERRIAULT, J. "Domaines actuels d'utilisation des calculateurs dans l'enseignement", in Enseignement programmé, No.1, mars 1968, 12 p. Panorama

———————. "Les machines à enseigner", in Enseignement programmé, No.7, septembre 1969, 10 p.

POCZTAR, J.   "En enseignement programmé quoi de nouveau?" in *Revue française de pédagogie*, No.2, 1971, p.5-14

RICHE, N.   "Les principes de l'enseignement programmé" in *Bulletin de l'Union des Physiciens*, No.531, janvier 1971

III - RESEARCH AND APPLICATIONS / REALISATIONS

1 - RESEARCH / RECHERCHES

Thème: PROGRAMMATION PAR FILTRAGE DU SIGNAL ACOUSTIQUE
Organisme: Préfecture de Paris, Direction de l'enseignement, Hotel des Examens, 3 bis rue Mabillon, 75 Paris 6°

Thème: REALISATION DE DOCUMENTS MAGNETOSCOPES
Organisme: Société UNITEL, 62 rue St. Lazare, 75 Paris 9°

/ La Délégation générale à la Recherche scientifique et technique (D.G.R.S.T.) a financé tout ou partie des recherches indiquées ci-dessous /

Thème: ETUDE CRITIQUE, A PARTIR DE PROGRAMMES EXPERIMENTAUX, DES POSSIBILITES ET LIMITES DES METHODES CLASSIQUES DE L'ENSEIGNEMENT PROGRAMME
Organisme: Ecole normale supérieure de Saint-Cloud, Groupe d'étude et de recherche pour l'enseignement programmé
Public intéressé: Elèves des écoles secondaires

Thème: ETUDE DE LA PROGRESSION DE L'ELEVE A PARTIR D'UNE PROGRAMMATION RAMIFIEE
Organisme: SINTRA, 26 rue Malakoff, 92 Asnières.   Tél: 793.69.80

Thème: ENSEIGNEMENT PROGRAMME DE GRAMMAIRE ALLEMANDE EN MILIEU ETUDIANTS
Organisme: Faculté des lettres et sciences humaines, Paris, Chaire de Philologie germanique.
Public intéressé: Etudiants

Thème: INFLUENCE DE L'APPRENTISSAGE DANS LA DECOUVERTE D'UNE LOI D'ALTERNANCE
Organisme: Laboratoire de Psychologie, Faculté des lettres et sciences humaines, Nantes.
Public intéressé: Enfants de 5 à 7 ans

Thème: LOGIQUE D'UNE ELABORATION DES PROGRAMMES ET RECHERCHES DE CRITERES EN ENSEIGNEMENT PROGRAMME
   1) Enseignement programmé des procédures aéronautiques de communications radio-téléphoniques en langue anglaise
   2) Expérience d'enseignement à distance par calculateur (exercices de mathématiques sur les exposants et puissances)

France

Organisme: Centre d'études et de recherches psychologiques de l'Air (CERPAIR) St. Cyr l'Ecole.

Thème: MISE AU POINT D'UN SYSTEME INTEGRE UTILISANT DES SUPPORTS AUDIOVISUELS POUR ENSEIGNEMENT, INTERROGATION ET DOCUMENTATION
Organisme: Service technique d'étude des moyens modernes d'enseignement 46, rue Barrault, 75 Paris 13°

Thème: MISE AU POINT ET EXPERIMENTATION D'UN ENSEIGNEMENT PROGRAMME DE LA GRAMMAIRE RRANCAISE
Organisme: Centre régional de recherche et de documentation pédagogiques (C.R.D.P.), 75 cours d'Alsace-Lorraine, 33 Bordeaux
Public intéressé: Elèves des écoles primaires

Thème: MISE AU POINT EXPERIMENTALE D'UNE METHODE AUDIO-VISUELLE D'APPRENTISSAGE DE LA LECTURE
Organisme: Faculté des lettres et sciences humaines, 14 Caen
Public intéressé: Elèves des écoles primaires

Thème: ORGANISATION ET TRANSMISSION DES CONNAISSANCES PAR L'ENSEIGNEMENT PROGRAMME
Organisme: Laboratoire de psychologie génétique, 17 rue de la Sorbonne, 75 Paris 5°

Thème: PRODUCTION ET EXPERIMENTATION D'UNE PRESERIE, PUIS PRODUCTION D'UNE SERIE D'EMISSIONS TELEVISEES D'ENSEIGNEMENT PROGRAMME DE TECHNOLOGIE
Organisme: Centre régional de recherche et de documentation pédagogiques (C.R.D.P.), 75 cours d'Alsace-Lorraine, 33 Bordeaux
Public intéressé: Elèves des écoles secondaires (1er et 2° cycles)

Thème: RECHERCHE SUR L'ENSEIGNEMENT ASSISTE PAR ORDINATEUR
Organisme: O.P.E., Université Paris VII

Thème: RECHERCHE SUR L'UTILISATION D'UNE STATION D'INTERROGATION COLLECTIVE POUR LA CONSTITUTION ET LA VALIDATION D'EMISSIONS DE RADIO ET DE TELEVISION EDUCATIVES
Organisme: Institut pédagogique national, Département de la radio-télévision scolaire, 92 Montrouge

Thème: STRUCTURATION DE LA MATIERE A ENSEIGNER
Organisme: S.E.M.A. Laboratoire d'ergonomie et d'enseignement programmé

Thème: SYSTEME CONVERSATIONNEL ET ENSEIGNEMENT PROGRAMME
Organisme: Université de Grenoble. Service de Mathématiques appliquées.

2 - PUBLISHED PROGRAMMED COURSES / COURS PROGRAMMES PUBLIES

AIDEP. Statistiques et probabilités. Cours programmé à l'usage des cadres. Collection "L'enseignement programmé au service de l'entreprise". Paris, Editions Dunod, 1970, 400 p. fig.
Programme linéaire. Adultes.

――――. Introduction à la mathématique moderne, applications à la formulation des problèmes d'entreprise. Collection "L'enseignement programmé au service de l'entreprise". Paris, Editions Dunod, 1971, 373 pp.
Programme linéaire. Adultes.

――――. EDF/GDF. Utilisation pour la simplification des circuits logiques. Collection "L'enseignement programmé au service de l'entreprise". Paris, Editions Dunod, 1970, 430 pp.
Programme linéaire. Adultes.

ALBERTINI, J. M. Premiers pas en économie, initiation économique en méthode semi-programmée. Economie et humanisme, Paris, Les Editions Ouvrières, 1969, 238 p., illust. 959 items.
Programme linéaire. Niveau secondaire et adultes.

BAISSAS; d'HAINAUT. Cahiers programmés. "Arrondir et estimer", 96 pages; "Poids et masse", 64 pages; "Puissances de 10", 128 pages; "La règle à calcul", 192 pages; "Les incertitudes de mesure", 184 pages. Paris, Hachette, 1969.
Programme linéaire. Niveau 2ème cycle de l'enseignement secondaire et adultes.

BLUM; BRISSON. Syntaxe latine et apprentissage de la version (Tomes 1 et 2). Paris, A. Colin, 1965. (2ème édition 1969)
Programme linéaire. Classe de 3ème.

BOLAND, R.G.A.; ARCANGUES, M. d'. Parlons comptes et bilans. Collection "INSEAD Management", Paris, Editions d'Organisation, 1970, 160 p.
Programme linéaire. Adultes.

CEGOS. Statistiques et probabilités. Cours programmé, réalisé pour l'AIDEP.
Programme linéaire. Adultes.

――――. L'intéressement des travailleurs aux bénéfices de l'entreprise. Paris, Editions Hommes et Techniques, 1969, 167 p.
Programme linéaire. Adultes
(La CEGOS a également assuré la réalisation de cours programmés pour diverses entreprises)

CRDP de NANCY. Langue latine de cinquième, initiation programmée. Nancy, CRDP, 1970, 12 fascicules.
Programme linéaire. Niveau secondaire.

DECRETON, J.M.; PORET, B. Mathématique, cours de 2e A.C.T.
1. "Langage des ensembles". 2. "Algèbre. Corps des réels". Paris, Editions Gamma, 1970, 168 p.; 208 p.

DEMARNE, A.　　L'automobile en enseignement programmé. Paris, Editions Gamma, 1970, 220 p. illust. 730 items
Programme linéaire.

Editions d'organisation, SPCI. Initiation aux mécanismes comptables.
4 dossiers programmés (par d'Abouille, Dubost), 1969.

EUREQUIP.　　Initiation à l'ordinateur. Collection "Langages de l'action", Paris, Fayard, 1972, 163 p. illust. 100 items.
Programme à branchement, glossaire. Adultes, classes terminales

————————. La périphérie de l'ordinateur. Collection "Langages de l'action", Paris, Fayard, 1972. 197 p. illust. 94 items.
Programme à branchement, glossaire. Adultes, classes terminales.

————————. Logique de la décision Tome 1 - Initiation (ordinogrammes, tables de décision). Collection "Langages de l'action", Paris, Fayard, 1972. 171 pages illust. 86 items.
Programme à branchement, index. Adultes, classes terminales.

————————. Treize critères pour tester votre jugement. Collection "Langages de l'action", Paris, Fayard, 1971, 132 p.
Programme à branchement. Classes terminales. Adultes.

FERRAND, L.　　Les mathématiques nouvelles au cycle d'observation.
Paris, Editions Gamma, 1970, 260 p.

FRANCOIS, L.　　Premières leçons de la théorie des ensembles. Paris, Editions Gamma, 1969, 144 p. 175 items.
Programme linéaire. Niveau secondaire.

————————. Initiation à la mathématique moderne. Trois volumes. Paris, Editions Gamma, 1970.
Programme linéaire. Niveau secondaire.

————————. Initiation à l'algèbre. Paris, CNTE, Ministère de l'éducation nationale, 1969
Programme linéaire. Niveau secondaire

————————. Géométrie. Paris, CNTE, Ministère de l'éducation nationale, 1969
Programme linéaire. Niveau secondaire

GOUREVITCH, G.　　Algèbre (5 volumes). Collection ORT, Paris, Editions Gamma, 1969, 106 items.
Programme linéaire. Niveau secondaire.

————————. Logarithmes décimaux, théorie et applications.
Collection O.R.T. Paris, Editions Gamma, 1970, 178 p.
Trigonométrie. Programme linéaire. Niveau secondaire

HELLE, D.　　Les techniques de prévision au service de l'entreprise.
Collection "INSEAD Management". Paris, Editions d'Organisation, 1970, 128 p. Statistiques.
Programme linéaire. Adultes.

IBM Informatique. "Initiation aux ordinateurs". "Initiation au 360" "Fortran IV". "Gobol 360". G A P 360". "Assembleur de base 360/370". Paris, IBM, France, 1967 à 1970.
Programme linéaire. Formation professionnelle des adultes

LABIN, Ed. Mathématiques en "programme" (11 volumes). Collection "Quantos", Paris, Editions Bordas, 1970.
Programme linéaire. Niveau secondaire. Adultes.

LAVIGNE-PRIGENT. Comptabilité générale. C.N.T.E., Ministère de l'éducation nationale, 1970, 10 fascicules.

MALZAC, J.; BIANCHERI, A.; COSTE, P. Grammaire nouvelle (Tomes 1 et 2) Paris, Editions Gamma 1969.
Programme linéaire. Niveau 1er cycle de l'enseignement secondaire.

O.I.P. Cours de vocabulaire médical par l'étymologie. Paris, O.I.P., 1969. 2 volumes, 480 pages.
Programme linéaire. Niveaux secondaire et supérieur.

PIERSON, R. Initiation à la lecture des courbes de performances d'un tracteur agricole. Paris, A.C.T.A. 1970, 120 p. 104 items.
Programme linéaire. Adultes.

PLOQUIN, F.; LANDOWSKI, E. Français, montée en seconde, Collection "Revoir et Préparer". Paris, Editions pédagogie moderne, 1969. (Critique de textes, méthode programmée de recherche).
Programme linéaire. Niveau secondaire

POSTES ET TELECOMMUNICATIONS (Service de Formation). Formation professionnelle des préposés du service de la distribution postale. Paris, Ministère des postes et télécommunications, 1970, 3 fascicules de 60 p. Illustrations.
Programme linéaire

———————————. Formation professionnelle des guichetiers. Paris, Ministère des postes et télécommunications, 6 fascicules de 140 p. Illustrations.
Programme linéaire.

RAMEAU, C. Les mathématiques, un outil du management. Tomes 1 et 2. Collection "INSEAD MANAGEMENT", Paris, Editions d'Organisation, 1969, 127 et 117 p. Statistiques.
Programme linéaire. Adultes

SCHANDELONG, L. Calcul pour le chauffage (10 fascicules). Paris, Comité scientifique et technique des industries du chauffage (COSTIC).
Programme linéaire. Professionnels du chauffage

SEJOURNANT, Guihard. Initiation à la géographie générale. C.N.T.E., Ministère de l'éducation nationale. Second cycle. 6 carnets et tests d'entrée. 1971.
Programme linéaire Adultes

France

SEMA.　　　　　La carte perforée. Paris, Dunod, 1969, 176 p. illust.
　　　　　　　136 items.
　　　　　　　Programme à branchement. Adultes.

―――――― .　　Utilisation du chronomètre. Paris, Dunod, 1969, 104 items.
　　　　　　　Programme linéaire. Adultes.

―――――― .　　Initiation à la pratique des statistiques. Paris, Dunod,
　　　　　　　2ème édition, 1969, 237 p. 268 items. fig.
　　　　　　　Programme mixte. Adultes. Niveau élémentaire

SIMMONET (Mme); FOUET (Chef d'escadron); MOUKHWAS, V. (Lieutenant).
　　　　　　　La route est à vous. Paris, Organisme nationale de
　　　　　　　sécurité routière (ONSER) et Gendarmerie nationale.
　　　　　　　6 fascicules (L'agglomération, La route, L'autoroute,
　　　　　　　Les intersections, Nuit et intempéries, Avant le permis).
　　　　　　　Illustration couleur. Formation des candidats au permis
　　　　　　　de conduire.
　　　　　　　Programmes mixtes, linéaires et à branchements

SPCI.　　　　　Formation des agents de maîtrise. (Méthodologie des
　　　　　　　Communications. Simplification du Travail. Art d'instruire).
　　　　　　　3 séries de 6 fascicules. SPCI, 1970.

―――――― .　　Formation générale élémentaire (20 livrets). SPCI, 1971.

3 - COMPUTER ASSISTED INSTRUCTION / ENSEIGNEMENT ASSISTE PAR ORDINATEUR

CHAIRE DE CLINIQUE DES MALADIES DU SANG

Organisme:　　　　Faculté de médecine, Paris. Tél: 202.88.11
Destinataires:　　Etudiants (certificats de spécialité)
Type de l'ordinateur: CII 9080
Type des terminaux:　SPERAC
Langage utilisé:　　Coursewriter
Objet:　　　　　　Contrôle des connaissances

CONTRIBUTION A L'ETUDE DE L'ENSEIGNEMENT PROGRAMME A L'AIDE D'UN
CALCULATEUR - (PROPORTIONNALITE). EN PROJET, COMPARAISON DE
L'ENSEIGNEMENT PAR ORDINATEUR, LIVRE BROUILLE ET MAGISTRAL

Organismes:　　　Faculté des Sciences de Toulouse. Tél: 52.12.12
　　　　　　　　 C.R.D.P. (Centre régional de Recherche et de Documentation
　　　　　　　　 pédagogiques), 3, rue Roquelaine, 31 Toulouse. Tél: 62.54.54
Destinataires:　 Elèves de dernière année du cycle élémentaire (Cm 2), et
　　　　　　　　 de première année du cycle secondaire (sixièmes).
Type de l'ordinateur: C.A.E. 510 dévalué (un 10070 à 7 pupitres va être
　　　　　　　　 utilisé)
Type des terminaux: Télétypes.

ENSEIGNEMENT DU VOCABULAIRE

Organisme:　　　　Centre national d'études des télécommunications, 22 Lannion
Destinataires:　　Elèves de l'Institut universitaire de technologie
Type de l'ordinateur: IL Ramsès
Type des terminaux: Télétypes ASR 33
Langage utilisé:　 Langage CNET-SIGMA

France

ENSEIGNEMENT ET DIAGNOSTIC DES ERREURS

Destinataires: Elèves du niveau élémentaire
Type de l'ordinateur: I.B.M. 360/40
Type des terminaux: I.B.M. 2250 écran cathodique et clavier alphanumérique
Langage utilisé: Assembleur 360 F.

ENSEIGNEMENT DE LA LOI DE LA PROPORTIONNALITE

Organisme: Faculté des sciences de Toulouse. Tél: 52.12.12
                   CRDP de Toulouse et ENS de St. Cloud (CREFED)
Destinataires: Elèves des écoles primaires
Type de l'ordinateur: CAE 51 0
Type des terminaux: Télétypes

ENSEIGNEMENT DE LA PHYSIQUE

Organisme: Université Paris VII, Ordinateur pour Etudiants (OPE)
                   2 Place Jussieu, 75 Paris 5e. Tél: 366.25.25
Destinataires: Elèves du secondaire (1er et 2° cycles)
Type de l'ordinateur: IBM 360/30
Type des terminaux: Télétypes
Objets: Contrôle des connaissances. Enseignement.

ENSEIGNEMENT PROGRAMME D'ALGOL

Organisme: Faculté des sciences, Laboratoire d'informatique, Toulouse.
Destinataires: Etudiants
Type de l'ordinateur: CAE 51 0
Type des terminaux: Télétypes

JEU DU DIAGNOSTIC

Organisme: IBM France. Tél: 637.30.60: 637.35.60
Destinataires: Etudiants en médécine
Type de l'ordinateur: I.B.M. 360/3
Type des terminaux: Console 2260
Objet: Simulation du diagnostic

LA MEIOSE DANS LE REGNE ANIMAL

Organisme: Université Paris VII, Ordinateur pour étudiants (OPE),
                   2 Place Jussieu, 75 Paris 5°. Tél: 366.25.25
Destinataires: Etudiants PCEM
Type de l'ordinateur: IBM 360/0
Type des terminaux: Télétypes
Objets: Enseignement. Contrôle des connaissances.

LINGUISTIQUE ANGLAISE, REGLES, OPERATIONS, METALANGUE

Organisme: Université Paris VII, Ordinateur pour Etudiants   (OPE)
                   2 Place Jussieu, 75 Paris 5°. Tél: 366.25.25.
Destinataires: Elèves des écoles primaires
Type de l'ordinateur: 360/30
Type des terminaux: Télétypes
Objet: Enseignement

NOUVEL ENSEIGNEMENT FONCTIONNEL (NEF)

Organisme: SPCI. Tél: 277.43.20
Objets: Contrôle des connaissances. Enseignement

TRAVAUX PRATIQUES DE PROGRAMMATION

Organisme: Université Paris VII, Ordinateur pour Etudiants (OPE)
                   2 Place Jussieu, 75 Paris 5°. Tél: 366.25.25.
Types des terminaux: Télétypes
Langage utilisé: Minitran 2

GERMANY, FEDERAL REPUBLIC OF / ALLEMAGNE, REPUBLIQUE FEDERALE D'

I - ORGANIZATIONS AND ACTIVITIES / STRUCTURES ET ACTIVITES

1 - CENTRES

BILDUNGSTECHNOLOGISCHES ZENTRUM GmbH. (BTZ)
(CENTRE FOR EDUCATIONAL TECHNOLOGY)
Bodenstedstrasse 7, 62 Wiesbaden
Nature of organization: Private

FORSCHUNGS- UND ENTWICKLUNGSZENTRUM FÜR OBJEKTIVIERTE LEHR- UND LERNVERFAHREN GmbH. (FEoLL)
(CENTRE FOR RESEARCH AND DEVELOPMENT OF TEACHING AND LEARNING METHODS)
Rathenaustrasse 69-71, 479 Paderborn
Nature of organization: Private

INSTITUT FÜR ERZIEHUNGSWISSENSCHAFT, UNIVERSITÄT AACHEN
(INSTITUTE FOR THE SCIENCE OF EDUCATION)
Eilfschornsteinstrasse 16, 51 Aachen
Nature of organization: University

INSTITUT FÜR PROGRAMMIERTES LERNEN, UNIVERSITÄT GIESSEN
(Institute for Programmed Learning)
Karl-Gloeckner-Strasse 21, 63 Giessen
Nature of organization: University

KOMMISSION FÜR PROGRAMMIERTEN UNTERRICHT UND UNTERRICHTSTECHNOLOGIE IN DER GEW BERLIN
(COMMITTEE FOR PROGRAMMED INSTRUCTION AND EDUCATIONAL TECHNOLOGY OF THE GEW BERLIN)
Achenseeweg 9, 1 Berlin 45

ZENTRALSTELLE FÜR PROGRAMMIERTEN UNTERRICHT AN GYMNASIEN
89 Augsburg, Schertlinstrasse 7

ZENTRALSTELLE FÜR PROGRAMMIERTEN UNTERRICHT AN VOLKSSCHULEN
89 Augsburg, Jacoberstrasse 14

2 - ACTIVITIES/MANIFESTATIONS

CONFERENCE (National, international, annual)
Organized by: Kommission für Programmierten Unterricht und Unterrichts-
                 technologie in der GEW Berlin (Committee for Programmed
                 Instruction and Educational Technology of the GEW Berlin)

Place and dates: Berlin (Autumn 1968, Autumn 1971)
Participants: Research workers. School, university and vocational teachers. Adult educators. Publishers, producers of hardware and software.
Proceedings: Reports and papers of the Berlin Conferences on Programmed Instruction are published in the following numbers of the journal "Berliner Lehrerzeitung" of the Berlin Teachers' Association (Gewerkschaft Erziehung und Wissenschaft, Landesverband, Berlin) No.1, 1968, No.1, 1969, (Ahornstrasse 5, I Berlin 30).

G.P.I. CONFERENCE (National, international, annual)
Organized by: Gesellschaft für Programmierte Instruktion (G.P.I.) (Association for Programmed instruction)
Place and dates: Munich (Spring 1968); Wien (Spring 1969); Basel (1970); Köln (Spring 1971); Berlin (Spring 1972)
Participants: Research workers. School, university and vocational teachers. Adult educators. Publishers, producers of hardware and software.
Proceedings: Fortschritte und Ergebnisse der Unterrichtstechnologie (Progress and results of educational technology). München, Brigitte Rollett and Klaus Weltner, eds. Ehrenwirth-Verlag, 1971, 312 p.
Perspektiven des Programmierten Unterrichts. (Perspectives of programmed instruction). Wien/München, Brigitte Rollett and Klaus Weltner, eds. Oesterreichischer Bundesverlag, 1970, 304 p.
Theorie und Praxis des Programmierten Unterrichts. (Theory and practice of programmed instruction). Stuttgart, Brigitte Rollett, ed. E. Klett-Verlag, 1970, 136 p.

3 - PUBLISHERS/MAISONS D'EDITION

BAYERISCHER SCHULBUCH-VERLAG
8 München 19, Hubertusstrasse 4
Nature of organization: Commercial publisher

DEUTSCHE VERLAGS-ANSTALT (DVA)
7 Stuttgart-O, Neckarstrasse 121-125
Nature of organization: Commercial publisher

EHRENWIRTH-VERLAG
8 München 80, Vilshofener Strasse 8
Nature of organization: Commercial publisher

FRANZ CORNELSEN-VERLAG
1 BERLIN 33, Bingerstrasse 62
Nature of organization: Commercial publisher

GEORG-WESTERMANN-VERLAG
33 Braunschweig, Georg Westermann-Allee 66
Nature of organization: Commercial publisher

W. GIRARDET VERLAG
43 Essen, Girardetstrasse 2-36
Nature of organization: Commercial publisher

HERMANN SCHROEDEL-VERLAG
3 Hannover-Doehren, Zeiss-Strasse 10
Nature of organization: Commercial publisher

JULIUS BELTZ-VERLAG
694 Weinheim, Hauptbahnof 10
Nature of organization: , Commercial publisher

JULIUS KLINKHARDT-VERLAG
8173 Bad Heilbrunn/Obb.
Nature of organization: Commercial publisher

E. KLETT-VERLAG
7 Stuttgart-W., Rotebuehlstrasse 77
Nature of organization: Commercial publisher

MORITZ DIESTERWEG-VERLAG
6 Frankfurt/Main, Hochstrasse 31
Nature of organization: Commercial publisher

R. OLDENBOURG-VERLAG
8 München 80, Rosenheimer Strasse 145
Nature of organization: Commercial publisher

PÄDAGOGISCHE BETREUUNG UND ORGANISATION (PBO)
Gerd Stuckert
8031 Puchheim, Bäumlstrasse 12

RUDOLF-MÜLLER-VERLAG
5 Köln Braunsfeld, Stolberger Strasse 84
Nature of organization: Commercial publisher

SCHNELLE-VERLAG
2085 Quickborn, Heinrich-Lohse Strasse 69
Nature of organization: Commercial publisher

4 - PERIODICALS / PERIODIQUES

AULA. FACHZEITSCHRIFT FÜR ARBEITSMITTEL, UNTERRICHTSHILFEN, LEHRMITTEL
AUSSTATTUNGEN FÜR ALLE BILDUNGS-UND ERZIEHUNGSSTATTEN
Publisher: Verlag K. Ihl & Co.
Address: 8630 Koburg/Bayern, P.O.B. 683
Periodicity: Bi-monthly

AV-PRAXIS. ZEITSCHRIFT FÜR AUDIOVISUELLE KOMMUNIKATION IN DER PÄDAGOGIK
Publisher: Heering-Verlag
Address: 8 München 25, Ortlerstrasse 8
Periodicity: Monthly

GRUNDLAGENSTUDIEN AUS KYBERNETIK UND GEISTEWISSENSCHAFT
Publisher: Hermann Schroedel Verlag KG
Address: Zeiss-strasse 10, 3000 Hannover
Periodicity: Quarterly

NEUE UNTERRICHTSPRAXIS
Publisher: Verlagsgesellschaft Rudolf Müller
Address: 5 Koln-Braunsfeld, Stolberger Strasse 84 P.O.B. H410949
Periodicity: Bi-monthly

PROGRAMMIERTES LERNEN, UNTERRICHTSTECHNOLOGIE UND UNTERRICHTSFORSCHUNG
Publisher: F. Cornelsen Verlag
Address: I Berlin 33, Bingerstrasse 62
Periodicity: Quarterly

SCHULMANAGEMENT
Publisher: Georg Westermann Verlag
Address: 33 Braunschweig, Westermann-Allee 66
Periodicity: Quarterly

ZENTRALBLATT DER GESELLSCHAFT FÜR PROGRAMMIERTE INSTRUKTION
Publisher: Verlagsgesellschaft Rudolf Müller
Address: 5 Köln-Braunsfeld, Stolberger Strasse 84 P.O.B. H410949
Periodicity: Half-yearly

5 – PROFESSIONAL ORGANIZATIONS/ORGANISATIONS PROFESSIONNELLES

ARBEITSGRUPPE INFORMATION
5 Köln 1, Herwarthstrasse 17
Activities: Information, research work, in-service training, consultation

GESELLSCHAFT FÜR PROGRAMMIERTE INSTRUKTION E.V. (G.P.I.)
(ASSOCIATION FOR PROGRAMMED INSTRUCTION)
479 Paderborn, Rathenaustrasse 69-71
Activities: Information, research work, in-service training

INSTITUT FUR WISSENSCHAFTLICHE LEHRMETHODEN JENS UWE MARTENS (IWL) UND
LEHRSYSTEM IM MEDIENVERBUND GMBH & CO. (LIM)
8 München 81, Pienzenauerstrasse 89
Activities: Information, research work, in-service training

KOMMISSION FÜR PROGRAMMIERTEN UNTERRICHT UND UNTERRICHTSTECHNOLOGIE IN
DER GEW BERLIN (COMMITTEE FOR PROGRAMMED INSTRUCTION AND EDUCATIONAL
TECHNOLOGY OF THE GEW BERLIN)
1 Berlin 45, Achenseeweg 9
Public
 concerned: Teachers' associations
Activities: Information, in-service training, consultation

6 – MANUFACTURERS OF TEACHING MACHINES/FABRICANTS DE MACHINES A ENSEIGNER

ALLGEMEINE ELEKTRIZITAETS-GESELLSCHAFT, AEG TELEFUNKEN
6 Frankfurt/M., AEG-Hochhaus

BASF
67 Ludwigshafen/Rhein

EDUCOMP KG DELTA LEHRTECHNIK GMBH & CO.
1 Berlin 30, Kurfürstenstrasse 84

I.B.M. DEUTSCHLAND GMBH
7 Stuttgart 80, Pascalstrasse 100

NIXDORF COMPUTER AG. GESCHÄFTSBEREIGH LEHRSYSTEME LEHRPROGRAMME
479 Paderborn, Fürstenweg

PHILIPS ELEKTRONIK INDUSTRIE GMBH
2 Hamburg 70, Ahrensburger Strasse 130

SIEMENS AG.
8 München 25, Baierbrunnerstrasse 28

7 - TRAINING ORGANIZATIONS/ORGANISMES ASSURANT UNE FORMATION

GESELLSCHAFT FÜR LEHRTECHNIK MBH & CO. (GFL KG)
1 Berlin 15, Mommsenstrasse 71,
Nature of organization: Business
Public concerned: Vocational teachers. Adult educators.

ILS INSTITUT FÜR INFORMATIONS-UND LERNSYSTEME (ILS INSTITUTE FOR
INFORMATION AND LEARNING SYSTEMS)
61 Darmstadt, Rheinstrasse 24
Nature of organization: Business
Public concerned: Vocational teachers. Adult educators. Industrial
                           trainers, in-service training

LEHRSYSTEME IM MEDIENVERBUND GMBH & CO. (LIM)
8 München 71, Pienzenauerstrasse 89
Nature of organization: Business
Public concerned: Vocational teachers. Adult educators. Industrial
                           trainers, in-service training

8 - DOCUMENTATION CENTRES/CENTRES DE DOCUMENTATION

PÄDAGOGISCHES ZENTRUM
1 Berlin 31, Berliner Strasse 40-41
Nature of organization: Governmental
Type of services: Documentation, bibliographies

II - PUBLICATIONS

1 - BOOKS/LIVRES

ANKERSTEIN, HILMAR S. (ed.) Lernprogramme und ihre Verwendung im Unterricht
(Teaching programmes and their application in instruction). Köln, Verlagsgesellschaft R. Müller, 1971, 122 p.

CORRELL, WERNER. Zur Theorie und praxis des programmierten lernens (Theory
and practice of programmed learning). Darmstadt, Wissenschaftliche
Buchgesellschaft, 1969, 345 p.

──────────── . Programmiertes Lernen und schöpferisches Denken (Programmed
learning and creative thinking). München, E. Reinhardt-Verlag, 5th ed., 1970,
103 p.

──────────── ; SKINNER, B.F. Denken und Lernen. Braunschweig, Georg
Westermann Verlag 1970, 2nd ed.

──────────── ; SCHWARZE, H. Lernpsychologie programmiert. Donauwörth,
Verlag Ludwig Auer, 1971. 2nd ed.

_____; _____. Pädagogische Psychologie programmiert. Donauwörth, Verlag Ludwig Auer, 1971.

_____; _____. Lernstörungen programmiert. Donauwörth, Verlag Ludwig Auer, 1971, 2nd ed.

CUBE, FELIX VON. Kybernetische Grundlagen des Lernens und Lehrens (Elements of cybernetics for learning and teaching). Stuttgart, E. Klett-Verlag, 2nd ed 1969, 237 p.

Empfehlungen für die Prüfung von Unterrichtsprogrammen. (Recommendations for the evaluation of programmes). Berlin, F. Cornelsen-Verlag, 1969, 24 p.

FLECHSIG, KARL-HEINZ. Die Technologische Wendung in der Didaktik. (The technological change in the field of "Didaktik" (Education)). Konstanz, Universitätsverlag Konstanz, 1969, 41 p.

FRANK, HELMAR. Kybernetische Grundlagen in der Pädagogik (Elements in the field of pedagogy). Baden-Baden, Agis-Verlag, 2nd ed. 1969, Vol.I, 409 p., Vol 2, 290 p.

KLOTZ, GUENTER. Programmierter Unterricht. Ein Verfahren für morgen. (Programmed Instruction: A method for tomorrow). München, Kösel-Verlag, 1969, 195 p.

KUSCH, LOTHAR. Mathematik für Schule und Beruf. Arithmetik: Addieren und Subtrahieren. Rechenarten und Algebra.
Programmierte Ausgabe 63 p. Übungen und Lösungen 228 p.

_____. JAKOBS, LUDWIG. Bruchrechnen, Zusammenzahlen, Abziehen, Malnehmen, Teilen, Rechnen mit Hochzahlen und Wurzeln.
Programmierter Text 41 p.
Übungen und Lösungen 130 p.

_____. Mathematik für Hauptschulen. Arithmetik: Einführung in das Rechnen mit Variablen und Gleichungen, Teil 1.
Programmierte Ausgabe und Lösungen 122 p.

LEHNERT, UWE (ed.) Elektronische Datenverarbeitung in Schule und Ausbildung (Data processing in school and training). München, Verlag R. Oldenbourg, 1970, 224 p.

Lernen und Verhalten, Frankfurt, Fischer Taschenbuch, 1971

Lernpsychologie. Donauwörth, Verlag Ludwig Auer, 1971, 11th ed. (auch in italienischer, tschechischer, spanischer, portugiesischer, französischer und polnischer Übersetzung)

Leseleiter. Leselernprogramm für kleine Kinder, Bad Homburg, Kretschmer Verlag 1972

MÜLLER, DAGULF, D. "Zur gegenwärtigen Situation des Programmierten Unterrichts in der Bundesrepublik Deutschland unter besonderer Berücksichtigung der vorliegenden Programme" (The present situation of programmed instruction in the Federal Republic of Germany with special consideration of existing programmes), in Kybernetik, Automation, Programmierter Unterricht und Grenzgebiete, 1968, p. 1-XVII

_____. "Auswahl, Beurteilungs- und Anwendungskriterien von Lehr- und Unterrichtsprogrammen." (Criteria for the selection, evaluation and application of programmes), in Kybernetik, Automation, Programmierter Unterricht und Grenzgebiete, 1969, p. VI-XXVII

_____; RAUNER, FELIX (eds.) Bildungstechnologie zwischen Wunsch und Wirklichkeit. (Educational technology between Desire and Reality). Döffingen bei Stuttgart, Lexika-Verlag, 1972, 280 p.

NICKLIS, WERNER S. Programmiertes Lernen (Programmed learning). Bad Heilbrunn/Obb. J. Klinkhardt-Verlag, 1969, 196 p.

Pädagogische Verhaltenpsychologie. München/Basel, Ernst Reinhardt Verlag, 1970, 4th ed. (auch in spanischer Übersetzung)

RAUNER, FELIX; TROTIER, JÜRGEN. Computergesteuerter Unterricht. Das ALCU-Projekt. (Computer-assisted instruction. The ALCU-project). Stuttgart, Kohlhammer-Verlag, 1971, 228 p.

RECUM, HASSO VON. Aspects of educational technology, in Educational Reform in the Federal Republic of Germany. Unesco Institute for Education, Hamburg, 1970, p.145-162

ROLLETT, BRIGITTE (ed.) Theorie und Praxis des Programmierten Unterrichts. (Theory and practice of programmed instruction). Stuttgart, E. Klett-Verlag, 1970, 136 p.

_____; WELTNER, KLAUS (eds.) Perspektiven des Programmierten Unterrichts. (Perspectives of programmed instruction) Wien and München, Österreichischer Bundesverlag, 1970, 304 p.

_____; _____. Fortschritte und Ergebnisse der Unterrichtstechnologie. (Progress and Results of Educational Technology) München, Ehrenwirth Verlag, 1971, 312 p.

"Tipsi", Schreibmaschinenprogramm für kleine Kinder, München, Intertip AG, Josephspitalstrasse 15, 1969

Vorläufige Auswertung der Erhebungsbögen über programmierten Unterricht (Analysis of a survey on programmed instruction). Unpublished study of the Deutsche Städtetag, 1970, 73 p. Mimeographed.

ZIELKE, WOLFGANG. Programmierte Instruktion in der Wirtschaft (Programmed instruction in economy, industry). München, Verlag Moderne Industrie, 1970, 253 p.

ZIFREUND, WALTHER. Schulmodelle. Programmierte Instruktion und Technische Medien. (School models, programmed instruction and technical media). München, Ehrenwirth-Verlag, 1968, 488 p.

2 - ARTICLES

EINSIEDEL, HILDEBRAND VON. "Erhebung über die Verbreitung der Programmierten Instruktion in den west deutschen allgemeinbildenden Schulen". (Survey concerning the distribution of programmed instruction in schools of West Germany), in Grundlagenstudien aus Kybernetik und Geisteswissenschaft, No.2, vol. 10, June 1969, p.57-66.

3 - BIBLIOGRAPHIES

BASSEN, HEIDEMARIE; DELFS, DORA. Deutschsprachige Lehrprogramme (German programmes). Berlin, Pädagogisches Zentrum, 1972, 106 p.

MÜLLER, DAGULF. Jahreskatalog: Kybernetik, Automation, Programmierter Unterricht und Grenzgebiete. Berlin, Elwert und Meurer, 1968, XXIV, 200 p.; 1969, XI, 212 p.; 1970, XIV, 149 p.; 1971, XXVI, 214 p.; 1972, approx., 200 p.

_____ . Lehr- und Unterrichtsprogramme. Programm-Katalog (Programme Catalogue). Berlin, Elwert und Meurer, 1968, 46 p.; 1972, approx., 100 p.

SCHMIDT, HEINER; LUTZENKIRCHEN, F.J. Bibliographie zum Programmierten Lernen und zum Einsatz schulbezogener Arbeitsmittel (Bibliography on programmed learning and the application of teaching aids in schools). Weinheim, Beltz-Verlag, 1969, 388 p.

4 - AUDIO-VISUAL PRODUCTIONS/PRODUCTIONS AUDIO-VISUELLES

INSTITUT FÜR FILM UND BILD IN WISSENSCHAFT UND UNTERRICHT (FWN).
8022 München-Grünwald, Bavaria-Film-Platz 3.
Official centre for the production of audio-visual materials.

III - RESEARCH AND APPLICATIONS / REALISATIONS

1 - RESEARCH / RECHERCHES

See section I - 2: ORGANIZATION AND PERSONNEL - ACTIVITIES

Voir section I - 2: STRUCTURES ET PERSONNALITES - MANIFESTATIONS

2 - PUBLISHED PROGRAMMED COURSES/COURS PROGRAMMES PUBLIES

ARBEITSGRUPPE INFORMATION.
1. Führungspraxis. Erfolg, Kritik, Autorität. Deutsche Verlags-Anstalt, 1969, 238 p.
2. Informieren - Delegieren. Der verantwortliche Mitarbeiter. Deutsche Verlags-Anstalt, 1970, 200 p.
3. Entscheidungen vorbereiten. Technik der Problemanalyse. Deutsche Verlags-Anstalt, 1971, 204 p.
4. Verantwortung abgrenzen. Kybernetisches Führungsmodell. Deutsche Verlags-Anstalt, 1971, 204 p.
Vocational education.

BILSHAUSEN, HANS; THIESEMANN, FRIEDEL H.H.; WEPPNER, HARALD. Grundbegriffe und Grundkonstruktionen der Geometrie. 5 Teile, insgesamt 671 Lerneinheiten. Hermann Schroedel Verlag KG, 1969
Secondary education

CAPPEL, WALTER; STRITTMATTER, PETER. Schwerelosigkeit beim Raumflug. Ein Lernprogramm zur Einführung in die Mechanik. 2nd ed., 1969, 300 items.
Secondary, technical and vocational education.

CORRELL, WERNER; SCHWARZE, HUGO. Lernpsychologie - programmiert (Psychology of learning). Auer-Verlag, 1969, 324 p.
University level.

DAUENHAUER, E. Einführung in die Buchführung. G. Westermann-Verlag, 2nd ed., 1968, 208 p.
Vocational education

HARDE, OTTO; ANKE, ANNEMARIE. Programmierter Mathematikunterricht.
"Punktmengen und Geraden - Die lineare Funktion", 252 Lerneinheiten, Klasse 8-9; "Die quadratische Funktion und ihr Graph", 270 Lerneinheiten, Klasse 9-10; "Einführung in die Verknüpfungsstrukturen - Potenzrechnung", 235 Lerneinheiten, Klasse 9-10; "Zentrische Streckung", 238 Lerneinheiten, Klasse 9-10; "Trigonometrie", 279 Lerneinheiten, Klasse 10-11; "Kongruenzabbildungen - Geraden und Kreise", 232 Lerneinheiten, Klasse 10-12. Herman Schroedel Verlag KG, 1970, 1971.
Secondary education.

HEINEMANN, HORST. Wie lesen wir das Neue Testament? 494 Lerneinheiten, in 1 Band und in 3 Bänden erhältlich. Hermann Schroedel Verlag KG, 1970.
Upper primary education.

INSTITUT FÜR WISSENSCHAFTLICHE LEHRMETHODEN J. U. MARTENS (IWL). Konferenztechnik. Arbeitsweise und Aufgabenverteilung. Eine programmierte Unterweisung der Ford-Werke AG. Deutsche Verlags-Anstalt, 1972, 244 p.
Vocational education.

KEIL, KARL-AUGUST. Einführung in die Raumgeometrie. Bayerischer Schulbuch-Verlag, 3rd ed., 1968, 137 items, 144 p.
Secondary education.

KRACHT, RUDOLF H. Technische Begriffe aus der Werkstatt. Sprachprogramm für ausländische Arbeitnehmer und Auszubildende. Deutsche Verlags-Anstalt, 1972, 200 p.
Vocational education.

NENTWIG, JOACHIM; KREUDER, MANFRED; MORGENSTERN, KARL. Lehrprogramme Chemie, Band I. Verlag Chemie, 1969, 672 p.
Secondary education.

OTT, ERNST. Optimales Lesen, Schneller lesen - mehr behalten. Deutsche Verlags-Anstalt, 1970, 240 p.
Adult education. Vocational education.

PETERSEN, C; FEDDERSEN, E. Trigonometrie. Kernprogramm. H Schroedel Verlag, 1969, 333 items.
Secondary education.

_____; _____. Logarithmenrechnen. 2nd revised ed., 1972 500 Lerneinheiten. Hermann Schroedel Verlag KG.
Secondary education.

SCHIEFELE, HANS; HUBER, GUNTER L. Programmierte Unterweisung programmiert. Ehrenwirth-Verlag, 1969, 120 p.
University level. Adult education.

SCHIRM, ROLF W.; Programmiertes Lernen. Eine Einführung in die Praxis moderner Lerntechnologie. Deutsche Verlags-Anstalt 1971, 77 p.
Adult education. Vocational education.

SCHROETER, GERHARD. Lesen-Verstehen-Vorstellen. Eine programmierte Einführung in das technische Zeichnen (Technical drawing). Verlag W. Girardet, 3rd ed., 1971, 256 p.
Adult educators. Secondary, technical and vocational education.

_____; SCHROETER, CHARLOTTE. Umformen von Gleichungen. Eine programmierte Einführung in die Algebra. G. Westermann-Verlag, 3rd ed., 1970, 128 p.
Adult educators. Secondary, technical and vocational education.

_____; _____; SCHEICK, HANS. Element und Menge. Eine programmierte Einführung in die Mengenlehre. (Mathematics). Verlag W. Girardet 3rd ed., 1971, 167 p.
Adult education. Secondary, technical and vocational education.

STEMPELL, DIETER. Programmierte Einführung in FORTRAN. Westdeutscher Verlag, 1970, 108 items, 127 p.
Adult education. Technical education.

_____. Programmierte Einführung in die Wahrscheinlichkeitsrechung. Vieweg Verlag, 1968, 146 items, 175 p.
University level.

WELTNER, KLAUS; ZORN, ROLF. Gewicht und Masse. Klett-Verlag, 1969, 197 items.
Secondary education.

_____; KUNZE, WOLFGANG. Viertaktmotor. Klett-Verlag, 1969, 268 items.
Secondary education.

WOLFF, LORENZ. Netzplantechnik. R. Müller-Verlag, 2nd ed., 1969, 147 p.
University. Technical education.

3 - COMPUTER ASSISTED INSTRUCTION/ENSEIGNEMENT ASSISTE PAR ORDINATEUR

SYSTEM "BAKKALAUREUS"

Organization: Institut für Kybernetik, am FEOLL (Institute for Cybernetics)
Type of
  computer: Nixdorf
Types of
  language: ALZUDI. COGENDI. ALSKINDI (Formal didaktiten)
Purpose: Research and teaching.

HUNGARY/HONGRIE

I - ORGANIZATIONS AND ACTIVITIES / STRUCTURES ET ACTIVITES

  1 - CENTRES

  EÖTVÖS LÓRÁND TUDOMÁNYEGYETEM
  Pesti Barnabás u., Budapest
  Nature of organization: University

FELSÖOKTATÁSI PEDAGÓGIAI KUTATÓ KÖZPONT
Rigó u.16, Budapest VIII
Nature of organization: Research centre of pedagogical higher educational aids

JOZSEF ATTILA TUDOMÁNYEGYETEM
Táncsics Mihály u.2, Szeged
Nature of organization: University

KOSSUTH LAJOS TUDOMÁNYEGYETEM
Debrecen 10
Nature of organization: University

MÜM MÓDSZERTANI INTÉZETE (Institute of the Ministry of Labour)
Könyves Kálmán Körut 48, 52, Budapest VIII
Nature of organization: Governmental

OMFB AUDIO VIZUÁLIS ÁLLANDÓ BIZOTTSÁGA (Committee of Audio-Visual)
Martinelli tér 8, Budapest V
Nature of organization: Governmental

ORSZÁGOS PEDAGÓGIAI INTÉZET (National Institute for Education)
Gorkij Fasor 17-21, Budapest VII
Nature of organization: Governmental

2 - ACTIVITIES/MANIFESTATIONS

IN SERVICE CONTINUATION COURSE (Information)
Regional Annual Conference
Place and date: University of Szeged, 1968
Participants: School teachers

INTERNATIONAL AUDIOVISUAL CONFERENCE
Organized by: Department of the Council of County Heves
Place and date: Eger, June 1970
Participants: Research workers, pedagogues of the universities,
               middle and primary schools, workers of institutions
               of audio-visual school equipments

SEMINAR (Mutual information, coordination)
National Annual Conference
Organized by: Országos Pedagógiai Intézet
Place and date: Budapest, 28-30 December
Participants: Research workers, school and university teachers,
                 adult educators
Proceedings: Báthory-Gyaraki, Programmed Instruction:
                 results and tasks, Budapest OPI, 1969

THE METHODICAL QUESTIONS OF THE EMPLOY OF THE TELEVISION
AND FILM
International Conference
Place and date: Eger, June 1968
Organized by: Department of Education of Eger

3 - PUBLISHERS / MAISONS D'EDITION

ORSZÁGOS MŰSZAKI KÖNYVTÁR ÉS DOKUMENTÁCIÓS KÖZPONT
(Hungarian Central Technical Library and Documentation Centre)
Reviczky u.6, Budapest VIII
Nature of organization: Governmental

TANKÖNYVKIADÓ VÁLLALAT
Szalay u.10-14, Budapest V
Nature of organization: Governmental. Publisher of textbooks

4 - PERIODICALS / PERIODIQUES

AUDIOVIZUÁLIS TECHNIKAI ES MÓDSZERTANI KÖZLEMÉNYEK
Publisher: Országos Műszaki Könyvtár és Dokumentációs Központ
(Hungarian Central Technical Library and Documentation Centre)
Address: Reviczky u.6, Budapest VIII
Periodicity: Bi-monthly
Fields of interest: Application, topical events. Contents also in English, German and Russian.

MAGYAR PEDAGÓGIA
Publisher: Akadémiai Kiadó
(Publishing House of the Hungarian Academy of Sciences)
Address: Alkotmány u.21, Budapest V
Periodicity: Quarterly
Fields of interest: Research, application.

PEDAGÓGIAI SZEMLE (Journal of Education)
Publisher: Országos Pedagógiai Intézet
(National Institute for Education)
Address: Gorkij fasor 17-21 Budapest VII
Periodicity: Monthly
Fields of interest: Research, application, topical events.

6 - MANUFACTURERS OF TEACHING MACHINES/FABRICANTS DE MACHINES A ENSEIGNER

ELEKTRO-AKUSZTIKAI GYÁR
Fogarasi ut 5, Budapest XIV
Type of machine: BC 02
Characteristics: Linear and branching programme with adaptability, depending on the selected response
Purpose: Evaluation; teaching

ELEKTRO-AKUSZTIKAI GYÁR
Fogarasi ut 5, Budapest XIV
Type of machine: MAGISTER, ACP 101
Characteristics: Multiple-choice response (for 40 students)
Purpose: Evaluation; deed-back

ELEKTRO-AKUSZTIKAI GYÁR
Fogarasi ut 5, Budapest XIV
Type of machine: DIACORR, BYO 01
Characteristics: Linear programme; selected response
Purpose: Evaluation; teaching; individual use

ELEKTRO-AKUSZTIKAI GYÁR
Fogarasi ut 5, Budapest XIV
Type of machine: DIACORR, BYO 02
Characteristics: Branching programme
Purpose: Individual teaching

ELEKTRO-AKUSZTIKAI GYÁR
Fogarasi ut 5, Budapest XIV
Type of machine: UNISYNCHRO, AMP 202
Characteristics: Separated head for the pilot signals; forward
                      rewind; synchronization of slides
Purpose: Synchronized presentation of A-V programme

ELEKTRO-AKUSZTIKAI GYÁR
Fogarasi ut 5, Budapest XIV
Type of machine: SYNCHRO, AMP 206
Characteristics: Selective pilot signals
Purpose: Slide projector synchronizer for 4-track tape recorders

TANÉRT
Szentkirályi utca 12, Budapest VIII
Type of machine: Co-repetitor
Characteristics: Linear programme; storage of replies;
                      individual use
Purpose: Teaching. Application exercises

TANÉRT
Szentkirályi utca 12, Budapest VIII
Type of machine: DIDACTOMAT
Characteristics: Branching programme; storage of replies;
                      collective use
Purpose: Evaluation

TANÉRT
Szentkirályi utca 12, Budapest VIII
Type of machine: AUDIAVOX
Characteristics: Linear programme; storage of replies;
                      integrated audio-visual device; individual
                      and collective use
Purpose: Teaching; application exercises

7 - TRAINING ORGANIZATIONS / ORGANISMES ASSURANT UNE FORMATION

ORSZÁGOS PEDAGÓGIAI INTÉZET (National Institute for Education)
Gorkij Fasor 17-21, Budapest VII
Nature of organization: Governmental
Public concerned: School teachers. Adult educators

8 - DOCUMENTATION CENTRES / CENTRES DE DOCUMENTATION

BUDAPESTI MÜSZAKI EGYETEM KÖZPONTI KÖNYVTARA
(Central Library of the Technical university of Budapest)
Budafoki ut 4-6, Budapest XI
Nature of organization: University
Type of services: Library; documentation; information;
                   research aid

ORSZÁGOS MÜSZAKI KÖNYVTÁR ÉS DOKUMENTÁCIÓS KÖZPONT
(Hungarian Central technical library and documentation centre)
Reviczky u.6, Budapest VIII
Nature of organization: Governmental
Type of services: Information; documentation; library; methodology

ORSZÁGOS PEDAGÓGIAI KÖNYVTÁR ÉS MUZEUM
(Central library of education and Museum)
Honvéd u. 19, Budapest V
Nature of organization: Governmental
Type of service: Information; documentation

II - PUBLICATIONS

I - BOOKS/LIVRES

DUZS, János; FÜRJES, József. Audio-vizuális technika - Müszaki információ. I-II. (Audio-visual techniques - technical information), Budapes OMKDK. Módszertani kiadványok 28-29 sz. 1968, 339 p.

FÜRJES, József; BISZTERSZKY, Elemére. Tanitógépek és programok (Teaching machines and programmes). Budapest, OMKDK, 1972, 260 p.

Selected Readings: A programozott tanitás: Eredmények és feladatok (Programmed instruction: results and tasks). Budapest, Országos Pedagógiai Intézet, 1969, 328 p. Papers read at the O.P.I. Seminar 1968.

Selected readings of Hungarian and Czechoslovakian authors.
Tanulmányok a Neveléstudomány Köréböl 1969-1970. (Theoretical studies: types of programmes experimented). Budapest, Akadémiai Kiadó, 1970, 500 p.

2 - ARTICLES

DUZS, János; FÜRJES, József. "A 15 éves a-v technikai és módszertani fejlödés elözetes prognózisa" 1971. (Preliminary prediction of the 15-year technical and methodological development in the field of audio-visual teaching), in Audio-Vizuális Technikai és Módsz. Közl., No.6, 1971, p.703-734 - No.1, 1972. p.1-24

FÜRJES, József. "Az oktatástechnikai eszközrendszer szerepe és jelentösége a tanitás és tanulás hatékonyságának növelésében". (Role and importance of the educational technical aids for increasing the effectiveness of teaching and learning), in Audio-Vizuális Technikai és Módsz. Közl., No.1, 1971, p.55-74.

GYARAKI, F. Frigyes. "Programozott anyagok helye és szerepe a kereskedelmi szakképzésben". (Place and role of programmed curricula in commercial training) in, Audio Vizuális Közlemények, No.4, 1971. 20 p.

KISS, Árpád.; GYARAKI, F. Frigyes. "A számitógépek pedagógiai alkalmazása" (Computer assisted instruction), in Pedagógiai Szemle, No.6, 1968, 15 p.

3 - BIBLIOGRAPHIES

VALER, Pál (Mrs.) A korszerü oktatási eszközök és eljárások magyar nyelvü irodalmának bibliografiája (Bibliography of new techniques and methods), in Tanulmányok a neveléstudomány köréböl 1969-1970. Budapest, Akadémiaikiadó

III - RESEARCH AND APPLICATIONS / REALISATIONS

1 - RESEARCH / RECHERCHES

Theme: ADAPTATION OF PROGRAMMED MATERIALS TO ADULT EDUCATION
Organized by: Országos Pedagógiai Intézet Közgazdasági Egyetem
Public concerned: Adults

Theme: EVALUATION AND CORRECTION OF PROGRAMMES (GRAMMAR, MATHEMATICS, SCIENCES)
Organized by: Országos Pedagógiai Intézet
Public concerned: Pupils of the general schools, 11-14 years old.

Theme: FACTORS IN LEARNING EFFICIENCY (METHODS OF PROGRAMMING)
Organized by: Országos Pedagógiai Intézet
Public concerned: Pupils of different types of schools

2 - PUBLISHED PROGRAMMED COURSES / COURS PROGRAMMES PUBLIES

ÁBRAHÁM, Károlyné; KOLTAI, Gézáné. Verb, noun, adjective (in Russian) (Teaching). Tankönyvkiadó Vállalat,1971, 211 p., 156 items

GYARAKI, F.F.; KUTTNER, Alfrédné; SZEKELY, György. Milk and dairy products (Teaching). Belker. Min. Tempó Nyomda V. 1971. 120 p., 100 items

GYARAKI, F.F.; KUTTNER, Alfrédné; RIEMER, László. Conservation of foodstuffs. (Teaching). Belker. Min. Tempó Nyomda V. 1971. Technical education

LÁNG, Robert. Fundamental conception of geography (map-reading). (Experimental). Tankönyvkiadó Vállalat, 54 p., 42 items

MICHALOVSZKY, Csabáné. Programmed in chemistry (neutralization and termochemistry). (Experimental). Tankönyvkiadó Vállalat, 83 p., 75 items

SZENDE, Aladár. Grammar (Experimental). Tankönyvkiadó Vállalat, 311 p., 200 items

_____. Grammar (syntax) (Teaching). Tankönyvkiadó Vállalat, 1968, 180 p., 600 items

SZTANO, Tamásné. Mathematics (simultaneous equations) (Teaching). Tankönyvkiadó Vállalat, 1971. 229 p., 100 items

TEAM OF TEACHERS. Mathematics (direct and inverse proportionality) (Teaching). Tankönyvkiadó Vállalat, 1969-1970, 150 p., 600 items

_____. Mathematics (fractions) (Experimental teaching). Tankönyvkiadó Vállalat, 1969-1970, 120 p., 600 items. Primary and vocational education

_____. Mathematics (calculation of percentages) (Experimental teaching). Tankönyvkiadó Vállalat, 1969-1970, 100 p., 400 items

TEAM WORK - CO-OPERATIVE OF TEACHERS. Grammar (parts of speech) (Experimental). Tankönyvkiadó Vállalat, 1969-1970, 250 p., 1000 items. Primary education

ZÁTONYI, Sándor, et al. Physics (Teaching). Tankönyvkiadó Vállalat, 1969-1970, 240 p., 800 items. Primary and secondary education

INDIA/INDE

I - ORGANIZATIONS AND ACTIVITIES / STRUCTURES ET ACTIVITES

  1 - CENTRES

  ARMY CADET COLLEGE
  Poona 1
  Nature of organization: Governmental

  BOMBAY CHAPTER OF THE INDIAN ASSOCIATION OF PROGRAMMED LEARNING
  National Institute of Bank Management
  85 Nepean Sea Road, Bombay 6
  Nature of organization: Voluntary

  CENTRE FOR ADVANCED STUDIES IN EDUCATION, UNIVERSITY OF BARODA
  Baroda, Gujarat State
  Nature of organization: University

  DEPARTMENT OF EDUCATIONAL PSYCHOLOGY AND FOUNDATIONS OF EDUCATION, NATIONAL INSTITUTE OF EDUCATION
  Aurbindo Marg, New Delhi 16
  Nature of organization: Government-sponsored research and training organization

  DEPARTMENT OF PSYCHOLOGY, DELHI UNIVERSITY
  Delhi 7
  Nature of organization: University

  INDIAN ASSOCIATION OF PROGRAMMED LEARNING
  c/o Centre for Advanced Studies in Education, University of Baroda
  Baroda, Gujarat State
  Nature of organization: Voluntary

  NATIONAL INSTITUTE OF BANK MANAGEMENT
  85 Nepean Sea Road, Bombay 6
  Nature of organization: Governmental

2 - ACTIVITIES / MANIFESTATIONS

ANNUAL CONFERENCE OF THE ASSOCIATION OF PROGRAMMED LEARNING
(National conference)
Organized by: Indian Association of Programmed Learning, co-sponsored by the National Council of Educational Research and Training and universities in India
Places and dates: Delhi University, February 1968
Baroda University, October 1969
Bombay, November 1970
Participants: Research workers. School and university teachers. Vocational teachers. Adult educators

SEQUENTIAL COURSE ON PROGRAMMED LEARNING
Organized by: Army Cadet College, Poona-1
Place and date: Poona, June 1969
Participants: Officers of Army Cadet College
Purpose: Train instructors

SEQUENTIAL COURSE ON PROGRAMMED LEARNING (Annual Workshop cum-regional conference, in 2 phases)
Organized by: Department of Educational Psychology and Foundations of Education of National Institute of Education
Places and dates: 1st phase, May-June, in different states of India
2nd phase, October-November, New Delhi
Participants: Research workers. School and university teachers. Adult educators
Purpose: Train programmers

3 - PUBLISHERS / MAISONS D'EDITION

INDIAN ASSOCIATION OF PROGRAMMED LEARNING
c/o Centre for Advanced Studies in Education, University of Baroda
Baroda, Gujarat State
Nature of organization: Voluntary

NATIONAL INSTITUTE OF BANK MANAGEMENT
85, Nepean Sea Road, Bombay 6
Nature of organization: Government-sponsored research and training organization

NATIONAL INSTITUTE OF EDUCATION
Aurbindo Marg, New Delhi 16
Nature of organization: Autonomous research organization

4 - PERIODICALS / PERIODIQUES

INDIAN ASSOCIATION OF PROGRAMMED LEARNING - NEWSLETTER
Publisher: Faculty of Education, University of Baroda, Baroda, Gujarat State
Periodicity: Quarterly
Fields of interest: Research. Application. Topical events

5 - PROFESSIONAL ORGANIZATIONS / ORGANISATIONS PROFESSIONNELLES

BOMBAY MUNICIPAL CORPORATION, EDUCATION DIVISION
Opp. Victoria Terminus, Mahapalika Marg, Bombay 1
Activities: Development of Primary Education

CENTRAL INSTITUTE OF INDIAN LANGUAGES
Manasagangotri, Mysore 6
Nature of organization: Government-sponsored research and training
organization
Activities: Research and training in Indian languages

DEPARTMENT OF EDUCATIONAL PSYCHOLOGY AND FOUNDATIONS OF EDUCATION,
NATIONAL INSTITUTE OF EDUCATION
Aurbindo Marg, New Delhi 16
Nature of organization: Governmental
Activities: Improvement of school education

NATIONAL INSTITUTE OF BANK MANAGEMENT
85, Nepean Sea Road, Bombay 6
Nature of organization: Government-sponsored
Activities: To provide training facilities for bank employees

STATE INSTITUTE OF EDUCATION
Raikhad, Ahmedabad 1, Gujarat State
Nature of organization: Government-sponsored research and training
organization
Activities: Improvement of primary education in the State. Training and
research courses in Programmed Learning for secondary and
primary school teachers

7 - TRAINING ORGANIZATIONS / ORGANISMES ASSURANT UNE FORMATION

CENTRE FOR ADVANCED STUDIES IN EDUCATION, UNIVERSITY OF BARODA
Baroda, Gujarat State
Nature of organization: University
Public concerned: School teachers. University teachers. Adult teachers

DEPARTMENT OF PSYCHOLOGY, DELHI UNIVERSITY
Delhi 7
Nature of organization: University
Public concerned: M.A. and Ph.D. students in psychology. College and
university teachers

NATIONAL INSTITUTE OF EDUCATION
Aurbindo Marg, New Delhi 16
Nature of organization: Government-sponsored research and training
organization
Public concerned: School teachers. University teachers. Adult teachers.
Adult educators

II - PUBLICATIONS

1 - BOOKS / LIVRES

BASU, C.K. et al. A Handbook of Programmed Learning. Baroda, IAPL and
CASE, University of Baroda, 1971, 200 p.
Comprehensive book on theory, research and application
of programmed learning in Indian context

_____, et al. Programmed Instruction in Industries, Defence, Health and Education. New Delhi, Indian Association of Programmed Learning, 1969, 72 p.
Programmed learning and summaries of research studies conducted in India

BHOSALE, N.B.; SHETE, S.S. Kramanvita Adhyana. Poona, Shri Vidya Pnakashan, 1968, 135 p. (In Marathi.)
Introductory theory and description of programmed learning and some specimen programmed learning material

DEWAL, O.S.; SHAH, G.B. Technology knocks at the door of education, Baroda, CASE, University of Baroda, 1970, 45 p.
An introduction to educational technology in India

SHAH, G.B. Abhikramit Adhyana, Baroda, 1969 (In Gujarati.)

SHAH, M.S. Programmed algebra, Ahmedabad, Balgovinda Kuberdas & Co., 1970, 122 p. (In Gujarati.)

_____. What is programmed learning. Ahmedabad, State Institute of Education, n.d.

III - RESEARCH AND APPLICATIONS / REALISATIONS

2 - PROGRAMMED COURSES PUBLISHED / COURS PROGRAMMES PUBLIES

BASU, C.K.; MURARKA, I. Descriptive statistics. Delhi, Delhi University, n.d.
University level, first and second year

BHAGIRATH, S.S.; KULKARNI, S.S. Seeds (Botany). New Delhi, National Institute of Education, 1969, 20 p.
Secondary level

DATAR, V.D. Introduction to lenses. Poona, Army Cadet College, 1968, 15 p.
Secondary level

_____; PATHAK, N.D. Ohm's law. Poona, Army Cadet College, 1969, 54 p.
Secondary level

_____; _____. Specific heat. Poona, Army Cadet College, 1969, 15 p.
Secondary level

GHOSH, A.S. Bengali script self-taught (for Hindi-knowing adults). New Delhi, National Institute of Education, 1970, 127 p.

GUPTA, H.N.; KULKARNI, S.S. How to use slide rule (Mathematics). New Delhi, National Institute of Education, 1969, 33 p.
University and secondary levels

MULLICK, S.P.; KULKARNI, S.S. Rank correlation (A programmed book on statistics). New Delhi, National Institute of Education, 35 p., n.d.
University level

NAGABHUSHAN, R.M.; KRISHNAMURTY, G.B.; THAIGARAJAN, S. Accurate Arithmetic. Baroda, Indian Association of Programmed Learning, 1969, 32 p.
Adult education, secondary level

——————————; KULKARNI, S.S. Flowers (Botany). New Delhi, National Institute of Education, 1968, 24 p.
Secondary level

PARMAR, O.P. Use of articles. Poona, Army Cadet College, 1969, 28 p.
Secondary level

SHAH, G.B. A programme on addition and subtraction of directed numbers (Arithmetic). New Delhi, National Institute of Education, 1969, 31 p.
University and secondary levels

SHAH, M.S.; GHODADRA, R.L. Help yourself (Indirect narration). Ahmedabad, State Institute of Education, n.d.

——————————; MODI, A.R. Percentages. Ahmedabad, State Institute of Education, n.d.

——————————; PATEL, R.S. Profit and loss. Ahmedabad, State Institute of Education, n.d.

ISRAEL/ISRAEL

I - ORGANIZATIONS AND ACTIVITIES / STRUCTURES ET ACTIVITES

1 - CENTRES

HENRIETTA SZOLD INSTITUTE
National Institute for Research in the Behavioural Sciences
Department of Programmed Instruction
Colombia Street, Kiryat Menachem, Jerusalem
Nature of organization: Independent Research Institute

INSTITUTE FOR PREPARATION OF TEACHING AIDS
Ministry of Labour, Ministry of Education and Culture
Eylat Street N° 59, Tel-Aviv
Nature of organization: Governmental

JOINT COMMITTEE FOR PROGRAMMED INSTRUCTION
Ministry of Education and Culture, and Organization
for Rehabilitation through Training (ORT) - Israel
39, S'derot David Ha-Melekh, Tel-Aviv
Nature of organization: Governmental. International

MINISTRY OF EDUCATION AND CULTURE
Shivtey Israel Street, Jerusalem
Nature of organization: Governmental

2 - ACTIVITIES / MANIFESTATIONS

IN-SERVICE TRAINING (Annual national conference)
Organized by: Ministry of Education and Culture and Teacher's Union
Place and date: Haifa, July 1969
Participants: School teachers

ONE DAY WORKSHOP. DISCUSSIONS ON PRINCIPLES OF PROGRAMMED INSTRUCTION
AND ITS INTEGRATION IN INSTRUCTION (Monthly, national conference)
Organized by: Ministry of Education and Culture
Place and date: Kiryat Gat, Nahariya, Tel-Aviv, 1969
Participants: School teachers

3 - PUBLISHERS / MAISONS D'EDITION

HENRIETTA SZOLD INSTITUTE
National Institute for Research in the Behavioural Sciences
Colombia Street, Kiryat Menachem, Jerusalem
Nature of organization: Independent Research Institute

INSTITUTE FOR PREPARATION OF TEACHING AIDS
Ministry of Labour, Ministry of Education and Culture
Eylat Street N° 59, Tel-Aviv
Nature of organization: Governmental

JOINT COMMITTEE FOR PROGRAMMED INSTRUCTION
Ministry of Education and Culture and Organization for
Rehabilitation through Training   (ORT) - **Israel**
39 S'derot David Ha-Melekh, Tel-Aviv
Nature of organization: Governmental

"LE DORI" PUBLISHING COMPANY
Bezalel Yaffe Street, No.4, Tel-Aviv
Nature of organization: Commercial publisher

MINISTRY OF EDUCATION AND CULTURE
Shivtey Israël Street, Jerusalem
Two Departments: The Curriculum Centre
                 The Pedagogic Secretariat for Primary Education
Nature of organization: Governmental

6 - MANUFACTURERS OF TEACHING MACHINES/FABRICANTS DE MACHINES A ENSEIGNER

TECHNION-ISRAEL INSTITUTE OF TECHNOLOGY
Mount Carmel, Haifa
Type of machine: Experiment in production of low-priced machines
                   for branched programmed instruction
Characteristics: Branching programme. Storage of replies. Individual use
Purpose: Teaching

7 - TRAINING ORGANIZATIONS/ORGANISMES ASSURANT UNE FORMATION

BAR-ILAN UNIVERSITY
Ramat-Gan
Nature of organization: University
Public concerned: Undergraduate and graduate students

HEBREW UNIVERSITY
Jerusalem
Nature of organization: University
Public concerned: Graduate students

ORT - ISRAEL
39 S'derot David Ha-Melekh, Tel-Aviv
Nature of organization: International organization (network of vocational schools)
Public concerned: Vocational teachers

TECHNION-ISRAEL INSTITUTE OF TECHNOLOGY
Haifa
Nature of organization: University
Public concerned: Undergraduate and graduate students

TEL-AVIV UNIVERSITY
Ramat-Aviv, Tel-Aviv
Nature of organization: University
Public concerned: Graduate students

II - PUBLICATIONS

2 - ARTICLES

GOTTHOLD, Y.   Hora'a Metukhnetet Ke-Emza'i Bi-Y'dey Ha-Moreh (Programmed instruction as a tool for teachers). 1970.
Teacher's Guide

ISRAEL. MINISTRY OF EDUCATION AND CULTURE. "Programmed instruction", in English Teachers' Journal, No. 2, April 1968.

___. ___, PEDAGOGIC CENTRE. "Advancement of exceptional pupils through study aid apparatus", in Journal for Technology in Education, May 1971

LEVI, A.; SILVERMAN, R.E. ; FLIEDEL, J. Hora'a Metukhnetet (Programmed instruction). 1st ed. 1968-69 ; 2nd ed. 1969-70.
Survey. Report of experience.

_____ ; _____ ; _____ . Nissu'y Be-Hora'at Algebra Be-Khitot Tet Be-Shitat Ha-Hora'a Ha-Metukhnetet (Experiment in teaching algebra to 9th graders with programmed material). 1968-69.
Report of experience

III - RESEARCH AND APPLICATIONS/REALISATIONS

1 - RESEARCH/RECHERCHES

Theme: ADVANCEMENT OF CHILDREN THROUGH PROGRAMMED INSTRUCTION
Organized by: Dr. Y. Gotthold (private research)
Public concerned: Children from culturally disadvantaged surroundings

Themes: a) IS MATERIAL INCLUDED IN PROGRAMMED INSTRUCTION COURSE ABSORBED BY PUPILS ?

b) DOES PROGRAMMED INSTRUCTION HELP PUPILS TO BETTER ACHIEVEMENTS IN MATHEMATICS ?

c) WHAT ARE THE FACTORS WHICH AID THE SUCCESS OF INSTRUCTION WITH PROGRAMMED MATERIAL ?

Organized by: Joint Committee for Programmed Instruction, Organization for Rehabilitation through training (ORT), Tel-Aviv
Public concerned: 9th grade pupils

Theme: USE OF SIMPLE MACHINES
Organized by: Ministry of Education and Culture, Jerusalem
Public concerned: Pupils in different frameworks of special education network

2 - PUBLISHED PROGRAMMED COURSES/COURS PROGRAMMES PUBLIES

AMOTZ, Ben. Quadratic Equations. (Edited by Mr. Krupnik). Israel, Joint Committee for Programmed Instruction, ORT, 1967 to 1969, 1359 items, 276 p.
Secondary, technical and vocational education.

. Logarithms. (Edited by Mr. Krupnik). Israel, Joint Committee for Programmed Instruction, ORT, 1969-1970, 700 items, 127 p.
Secondary, technical and vocational education.

FLIEDEL, J. Algebra A. (Edited by U. Melamed). Israel, Joint Committee for Programmed Instruction, ORT, 1967-1970, 1333 items, 191 p.
Vocational education.

. Algebra B. (Edited by U. Melamed). Israel, Joint Committee for Programmed Instruction, ORT, 1633 items, 285 p.
Vocational education.

GAMZU, U. Function and Graphical Representation (A+B). Israel, Joint Committee for Programmed Instruction, O.R.T., 1967-1969. A: 1001 items (417 p.); B: 661 items (314 p.)
Secondary and technical education.

HALEVI, A. Elements in Arithmetic and Algebra. Israel, Joint Committee for Programmed Instruction, ORT, 1968-1970, 217 items, 50 p.
Post primary pupils in schools for children from culturally disadvantaged surroundings.

LAMDAN, P. Simple English (Books, A, B, C, D, + primer to Book A and teachers' guide for each book). Jerusalem, Henrietta Szold Institute - National Institute for Research in the Behavioural Sciences, 1968-1969. Primer: 73 items (15 p.); Book A: 233 items (92 p.); Book B: 433 items (133 p.); Book C: 308 items (95 p.); Book D: 494 items (90 p.).
Primary education.

MELAMED, U. Algebra C. Israel, Joint Committee for Programmed Instruction, ORT, 1967-1969, 876 items, 302 p.
Vocational education.

. Algebra D. Israel, Joint Committee for Programmed Instruction, ORT, 1967-1969, 1622 items, 260 p.
Vocational education

MORRIS, L. A) Basic Principals in Vulgar Fractions. B) <u>Addition and substraction in Fractions</u>. C) <u>Multiplication and Division</u>. Tel-Aviv, "Le-Dori" Publishing Company, 1968-1969. A: 761 items (86 p.); B: 852 items (50 p.); C: 861 items (79 p.). Supplementary material: Guide for Teachers (published by the Ministry of Education and Culture).
Primary education.

ROSENFARB, D. <u>Physics, Elementary Hydraulics</u>. Israel, Joint Committee for Programmed Instruction, ORT, 1969-1970, 1027 items, 259 p.
Post-primary schools for children from culturally disadvantaged surroundings

ITALY/ITALIE

I - ORGANIZATIONS AND ACTIVITIES / STRUCTURES ET ACTIVITES

1 - CENTRES

ASSOCIAZIONE NAZIONALE CENTRI I.R.I. PER LA FORMAZIONE E L'ADDESTRAMENTO PROFESSIONALE (QNCIFAP)
Piazza della Repubblica 59, Rome
Nature de l'organisme: Association bénéficiant d'une participation de l'Etat

CENTRO DI CALCOLO INTERFACOLTÀ, UNIVERSITÀ DI ROMA
Città Universitaria, Rome
Nature de l'organisme: Universitaire

CENTRO DI CALCOLO NUMERICO, ISTITUTO DI MATEMATICA, UNIVERSITÀ DI MILANO
Via Saldini 50, Milan
Nature de l'organisme: Universitaire

CENTRO DIDATTICO NAZIONALE PER LA SCUOLA MEDIA
Via della Civiltà del Lavoro, EUR, Rome
Nature de l'organisme: Gouvernemental

CENTRO EUROPEO COORDINAMENTO ISTRUZIONE LAVORO (CECIL)
Piazza Liberty 4, Milan
Via di Villa Patrizi 4, Rome
Nature de l'organisme: Association à but non lucratif

CENTRO EUROPEO DELL'EDUCAZIONE
Villa Falconieri, Frascati
Nature de l'organisme: Gouvernemental

CENTRO NAZIONALE ITALIANO DELLE TECNOLOGIE EDUCATIVE (CNITE)
Via Marche 84, Rome
Nature de l'organisme: Fondation indépendante

CONSIGLIO NAZIONALE DELLE RICHERCHE, ISTITUTO DI PSICOLOGIA, ISTITUTO APPLICAZIONI CALCOLO
Via de Lollis 12, Rome
Nature de l'organisme: Gouvernemental

FONDAZIONE DELLE ASSOCIAZIONI SCIENTIFICHE E TECNICHE (FAST)
Piazzale R. Morandi 2, Milan
Nature de l'organisme: Fondation indépendante

ISTITUTO PER LA FORMAZIONE E L'ADDESTRAMENTO PROFESSIONALE-CENTRO I.R.I.
PER LO STUDIO DELLE FUNZIONI DIRETTIVE (IFAP)
Piazza della Repubblica 59, Rome
Nature de l'organisme: Association à but non lucratif

ISTITUTO DI PEDAGOGIA, FACOLTÀ DI MAGISTERO, UNIVERSITÀ DI ROMA
Piazza della Repubblica, Rome
Nature de l'organisme: Universitaire

ISTITUTO DI PEDAGOGIA, UNIVERSITA DI MILANO
Via Festa del Perdono 7, Milan
Nature de l'organisme: Universitaire

ISTITUTO PER LE APPLICAZIONI DEL CALCOLO (CNR)
Piazzale delle Science 7, Rome
Nature de l'organisme: Gouvernemental

OLIVETTI
Ivrea, Milan, Florence
Nature de l'organisme: Entreprise

ORGANIZZAZIONI SPECIALI
Via R. Franchi 5, Florence
Nature de l'organisme: Société de services

2 - ACTIVITIES / MANIFESTATIONS

AUDIO-VIDEO-REGISTRAZIONE E LABORATORI LINGUISTICI
(Enregistrement audio-visuel et laboratoires de langues; table ronde; démonstrations)
Organisateur: Centro Nazionale Italiano Tecnologie Educative
Lieu et date: Bologne, 10 avril 1972
Participants: Spécialistes des techniques de l'information et de l'éducation

AUTOMAZIONE E STRUMENTAZIONE NELL'EDUCAZIONE (Automatisation et enseignement)
(Exposition et congrès internationaux annuels)
Organisateurs: Fondazione delle Associazioni Scientifiche et Technice (FAST),
Lieu et date: Milan, 25-26 novembre 1968   Olivetti
Participants: Chercheurs. Enseignants scolaires. Universitaires. Adultes.
               Spécialistes
Objet: Examen de la situation générale et des problèmes spécifiques
               de l'enseignement programmé dans divers pays; échange
               d'expériences; information sur les matériels
Actes publiés par: Il saggiatore, Milan

GIORNATA TECNOLOGICA (Journée de la technologie; manifestation nationale)
Organisateur: Centro Europeo dell'Educazione
Lieu et date: Villa Falconieri, Frascati, 20 janvier 1972
Participants: Spécialistes des techniques pédagogiques, producteurs (hardware,
              software), représentants de la RAI-TV
Objet: Echanges de vues et de données d'expérience sur le rôle des
              techniques pédagogiques en Italie

MACCHINE PER INSEGNARE E ISTRUZIONE MEDIANTE ELABORATORE ELETTRONICO
(Les machines à enseigner - Table ronde)
Organisateur: Centro Nazionale Italiano Tecnologie Educative
Lieu et date: Bologne, 11 avril 1972
Participants: Universitaires; représentants de l'IBM - Italia

MEZZI AUDIOVISI AVANZATI PER L'ISTRUZIONE PROGRAMMATA (Moyens audio-visuels perfectionnés pour l'enseignement programmé - manifestation nationale)
Organisateur: Centre commercial américain de Milan
Lieu et date: Milan, 21-25 octobre 1969

NET-ROUND-TAVOLA ROTONDA SULLE NUOVE TECNOLOGIE EDUCATIVE (Table ronde sur les nouvelles techniques pédagogiques - manifestation internationale annuelle)
Organisateur: Centro Europeo dell'Educazione
Lieu et date: Villa Falconieri, Frascati, 12-14 juin 1969
Participants: Chercheurs, enseignants scolaires, universitaires, spécialistes
Objet: Rencontre d'exposants (enseignement, industrie, armée) et d'experts Faire le point de la situation en Italie: problèmes et perspectives
Actes publiés par: Centro Europeo dell'Educazione

NUOVE TECNICHE DI COMMUNICAZIONE NELLA SCUOLA DELL'OBBLIGO (Nouvelles techniques de communication dans l'enseignement obligatoire - manifestation nationale annuelle)
Organisateur: Istituto di Pedagogia, Université de Rome
Lieu et date: Roseto degli Abruzzi, 1-4 mai 1969
Participants: Chercheurs, enseignants scolaires, universitaires
Objet: Diffusion de l'enseignement programmé à l'école obligatoire
Actes publiés par: Istituto di Pedagogia, Université de Rome

NUOVE TECNOLOGIE DELLA COMMUNICAZIONE NELL'APPRENDIMENTO (Les nouvelles techniques d'information dans l'apprentissage)
Organisateurs: Ente Autonomo per le Fiere di Bologna. Università Studi di Bologna. Fondazione Guglielmo Marconi
Lieu et date: Bologne, 4-6 avril 1971
Participants: Universitaires, représentants de la RAI-TV, spécialistes de la formation professionnelle, enseignants
Objet: Echanges de vues; problèmes et perspectives de la diffusion des nouvelles techniques
Actes publiés par: les organisateurs

SEMINARI INFORMATIVI (Séminaires d'information - manifestation nationale bi-annuelle)
Organisateur: Centro Europeo Coordinamento Istruzione Lavoro (CECIL)
Lieu et date: Milan, mai 1968 et 1969; Rome, octobre 1968 et 1969
Participants: Chercheurs, enseignants scolaires et universitaires, maîtres de l'enseignement professionnel, formateurs d'adultes

SEMINARIO NAZIONALE DI AGGIORNAMENTO E DI STUDIO SULLE NUOVE TECNOLOGIE EDUCATIVE (Séminaire national de recyclage et d'étude des nouvelles techniques pédagogiques)
Organisateur: Ministerio della Pubblica Istruzione
Lieu et date: Bologne, 5-10 avril 1972
Participants: Enseignants
Objet: Examen des perspectives culturelles et des problèmes politiques et administratifs liés à l'application des nouvelles techniques pédagogiques à l'école

TECNOLOGIE EDUCATIVE IN UN SISTEMA INTEGRATO DI APPRENDIMENTO (Les techniques pédagogiques dans un système intégré d'apprentissage)
Organisateur: Centro Nazionale Italiano Tecnologie Educative, Université de Bologne
Lieu et date: Bologne, 3 avril 1971
Participants: Universitaires
Objet: Possibilité d'emploi des techniques pédagogiques à l'école

TENDENZE ATTUALI DELLE TECNOLOGIE EDUCATIVE (Tendances actuelles des techniques pédagogiques - Table ronde)
Organisateur: Centro Nazionale Italiano Tecnologie Educative
Lieu et date: Bologne, 9 avril 1972
Participants: Universitaires
Objet: Echanges de vues

3 - PUBLISHERS / MAISONS D'EDITION

ABETE
Corso Vittorio Emanuele II 39, Rome
Nature: Editions scolaires

ARMANDO-ARMANDO
Via della Gensola 60, 61, Rome
Nature: Maison d'édition privée

CENTRO EUROPEO COORDINAMENTO ISTRUZIONE LAVORO (CECIL)
Via di Villa Patrizi 4, Rome
Nature: Association à but non lucratif

ETAS KOMPASS
Largo V° Alpini 5, Milan
Nature: Maison d'édition privée

FRANCO ANGELI SPA
Viale Monza 106, Milan
Nature: Maison d'édition privée

LOESCHER SPA
Via V. Amedeo II, 18, Turin
Nature: Editions scolaires

LA NUOVA ITALIA EDITRICE
Pza. Indipendenza 29, 50129 Florence
Nature: Editions scolaires

ORGANIZZAZIONE SPECIALI
Via R. Franchi 5, Florence 50137
Nature: Société de services

SAGGIATORE-MONDADORI
Via Bianca di Savoia, 20, Milan
Nature: Maison d'édition privée

LA SCUOLA
Via Cadorna II, Brescia
Nature: Editions scolaires

SOCIETA EDITRICE INTERNAZIONALE (SEI)
Corso Regina Margherita 176, Turin
Nature: Editions scolaires

VALLECHI EDITORE
Via dei Mille 90, Florence; Via Principe Eugenio 5, Milan
Nature: Editions scolaires

4 - PERIODICALS / PERIODIQUES

CIVILTA DELLE MACCHINE
Editeur: Gruppo IRI
Adresse: Via Torino, 95, Rome
Périodicité: Bi-mensuel
Centre d'intérêt: Actualité

FORMAZIONE E LAVORO
Editeur: ENAIP
Adresse: Via Pascarella 31, Rome
Périodicité: Mensuel
Centre d'intérêt: Recherches, réalisations, actualité

I PROBLEMI DELLA PEDAGOGIA
Editeur: Istituto di Pedagogia, Università di Roma
Adresse: Via Corsini 12, Rome
Périodicité: Bi-mensuel
Centre d'intérêt: Recherches, réalisations

NOTIZIE OLIVETTI
Editeur: Ufficio Stampa della Soc. Olivetti
Centre d'intérêt: Réalisations en matière d'enseignement programmé

LA RICERCA
Editeur: Loescher
Adresse: Via Principe Amedeo 18, Turin
Centre d'intérêt: Recherches, réalisations

RIFORMA DELLA SCUOLA
Editeur: S.G.R.A.
Adresse: Via dei Frentani 4E, Rome
Périodicité: Mensuel
Centre d'intérêt: Recherches, réalisations

SCUOLA E CITTA
Editeur: La Nuova Italia
Adresse: Pza. Indipendenza 29, 50129 Florence
Périodicité: Mensuel
Centre d'intérêt: Recherches, réalisations

SERVIZIO INFORMAZIONI AVIO
Editeur: Armando-Armando
Adresse: Lungotevere degli Anguillara 12, 00153 Rome
Périodicité: Mensuel
Centre d'intérêt: Politique et administration scolaires, recherche pédagogique

TECNOLOGIE EDUCATIVE
Editeur: Centro Nazionale Italiano delle Tecnologie Educative (CNITE)
Adresse: Via Marche 84, Rome
Périodicité: Quatre numéros par an
Centre d'intérêt: Recherches, réalisations, actualité

5 - PROFESSIONAL ORGANIZATIONS / ORGANISATIONS PROFESSIONNELLES

ASSOCIAZIONE NAZIONALE CENTRI IRI PER LA FORMAZIONE E L'ADDESTRAMENTO PROFESSIONALE (ANCIFAP)
Nature de l'organisation: Association bénéficiant d'une participation de l'Etat

Activité:	Formation et perfectionnement de la maîtrise et des cadres moyens du Groupe IRI

CENTRO FORMAZIONE E STUDI PER IL MEZZOGIORNO (FORMEZ)
Via Salaria 229, Rome
Nature de l'organisation: Semi-officiel
Activité: Co-ordination et promotion des centres de formation pour l'Italie méridionale

ENTE NAZIONALE ACCI PER L'ISTRUZIONE PROFESSIONALE (ENAIP)
Via C. Pascarella 31, Rome
Nature de l'organisation: Organisation agréée par l'Etat
Activité: Formation et perfectionnement des apprentis

IBM
Milan
Nature de l'organisation: Patronale
Activité: Formation du personnel

ISTITUTO PER LA FORMAZIONE E L'ADDESTRAMENTO PROFESSIONALE - CENTRO IRI PER LO STUDIO DELLE FUNZIONI DIRETTIVE (IFAP)
Piazza della Repubblica 59, Rome
Nature de l'organisation: Association à but non lucratif
Activité: Formation professionnelle

ISTITUTO PER LE RICERCHE DI PSICOSOCIOLOGIA INDUSTRIALE (IRPI)
Via R. Franchi 5, Florence
Nature de l'organisation: Société de services
Activité: Recherches en matière de psychosociologie industrielle

ISTITUTO PERELLI
Via Sarca 223, Milan
Nature de l'organisation: Patronale
Activité: Perfectionnement et formation du personnel

OLIVETTI
Via G. Jervis 77, Ivrea
Nature de l'organisation: Patronale
Activité: Perfectionnement et formation du personnel

7 - TRAINING ORGANIZATIONS / ORGANISMES ASSURANT UNE FORMATION

ASSOCIAZIONE NAZIONALE CENTRI IRI PER LA FORMAZIONE E L'ADDESTRAMENTO PROFESSIONALE (ANCIFAP)
Piazza della Repubblica 59, Rome
Nature de l'organisme: Association bénéficiant d'une participation de l'Etat
Public intéressé: Enseignants scolaires et universitaires, maîtres de l'enseignement professionnel, formateurs d'adultes

CENTRO EUROPEO COORDINAMENTO ISTRUZIONE LAVORO (CECIL)
Via di Villa Patrizi 4, Rome
Piazza Liberty 4, Milan
Nature de l'organisme: Association à but non lucratif
Public intéressé: Enseignants scolaires et universitaires, adultes, spécialistes, formateurs d'adultes, forces armées

CENTRO EUROPEO DELL'EDUCAZIONE
Villa Falconieri, Frascati, Rome

Nature de l'organisme: Gouvernemental
Public intéressé: Enseignants scolaires et universitaires, adultes, spécialistes, formateurs d'adultes

CENTRO NAZIONALE ITALIANO DELLE TECNOLOGIE EDUCATIVE (CNITE)
Via Marche 84, Rome
Nature de l'organisme: Fondation indépendante
Public intéressé: Enseignants scolaires et universitaires, adultes, spécialistes, formateurs d'adultes

ISTITUTO PER LA FORMAZIONE E L'ADDESTRAMENTO PROFESSIONALE - CENTRO IRI PER LO STUDIO DELLE FUNZIONI DIRETTIVE (IFAP)
Piazza della Repubblica 59, Rome
Nature de l'organisme: Association à but non lucratif
Public intéressé: Adultes, professionnels, formateurs d'adultes, cadres des entreprises du Groupe IRI

ISTITUTO PER LE RICERCHE DI PSICOSOCIOLOGIA INDUSTRIALE (IRPI)
Via R. Franchi 5, Firenze
Nature de l'organisme: Société de services
Public intéressé: Futurs cadres de gestion

MAGISTERO DI ROMA
Piazza della Repubblica, Rome
Nature de l'organisme: Universitaire
Public intéressé: Enseignants scolaires et universitaires, adultes, spécialistes, formateurs d'adultes

8 - DOCUMENTATION CENTRES / CENTRES DE DOCUMENTATION

CENTRO NAZIONALE ITALIANO DELLE TECNOLOGIE EDUCATIVE (CNITE)
Via Marche 84, Rome
Nature de l'organisme: Fondation indépendante
Nature des services: Rassemblement et publication d'études, de résultats de recherches, etc.

ENTE NAZIONALE PREVENZIONE INFORTUNI (ENPI)
Centro Ricerche, Monte Porzio, Catone, Rome
Nature de l'organisme: Gouvernemental
Nature des services: Etudes et recherches sur l'application de l'enseignement programmé

IRI - FORMAZIONE ADDESTRAMENTO PROFESSIONALE (IFAP)
Via Torino 107, Rome
Nature de l'organisme: Association à but non lucratif
Nature des services: Rassemblement et publication d'études, de résultats de recherches, d'informations; service de bibliothèque, etc.

ISTITUTO PER LA FORMAZIONE E L'ADDESTRAMENTO PROFESSIONALE - CENTRO IRI PER LO STUDIO DELLE FUNZIONI DIRETTIVE (IFAP)
Piazza della Repubblica 59, Rome
Nature de l'organisme: Association à but non lucratif
Nature des services: Rassemblement et publication d'études, de résultats de recherche, de bulletins d'information; service de bibliothèque, etc.

MAGISTERO DI ROMA
Via E. Orlando 10, Rome
Nature de l'organisme: Universitaire
Nature des services: Bibliothèque; publication de revues et de notices

II - PUBLICATIONS

1 - BOOKS / LIVRES

BERTIN, G.M.	Educazione alla ragione. Lezioni di pedagogia generale, 1971, 368 p.
BEST, F. et al.	Trattato delle scienze pedagogiche, 1971, 210 p.
BOSCOLO, P.	Cibernetica e didattica, Florence, La Nuova Italia, 1969
BRUNER, J.S.	Dopo Dewey. Il processo di apprendimento nelle due culture, 1970
─────── et al.	La sfida pedagogica americana, 1970, 244 p.
C.E.E.	L'alternativa tecnologica. Il Rapporto Perkins-McMurrin, Frascati, 1971
DETERLINE, W.	Introduzione all'istruzione programmata. Bologne, Zanichelli, 1970
DOTTRENS, R. et al.	Nuove lezioni di didattica. 1970, 376 p.
FONTANA TOMASSUCCI, L.	Istruzione programmata e macchine per insegnare. Rome, A. Armando, janvier 1969, 200 p.
FRY, E.B.	Macchine per insegnare e istruzione programmata. Turin, Loescher, 1969
GAVINI, G.P.	Tecniche dell'istruzione programmata. Rome, A. Armando, 1971
─────── .	Tecniche dell'istruzione programmata. La formazione dei programmatori. 1971, 344 p.
LAENG, M.	L'educazione nella civiltà tecnologica. Rome. A. Armando, 1969, 316 p.
─────── .	Educazione in prospettiva '70. 1971, 140 p.
MONTMOLLIN, M. de	L'istruzione programmata (traduit du français: L'enseignement programmé). Turin, Società Editrice Internazionale, mars 1968, 138 p.
RICHMOND, K.W.	La rivoluzione nell'insegnamento. Rome, A. Armando, 1969, 281 p.
─────── .	L'industria dell'educazione. Rome, A. Armando, 1971, 362 p.

SKINNER, B.F.	La tecnologia dell'insegnamento. Brescia, La Scuola, 1970
VARI	Automazione nell'educazione. Milan, Il Saggiatore-Mondadori, 1969, 296 p. Actes du Congrès. FAST, Milan 1968
———.	Nuove tecnologie della communicazione nell'apprendimento. Bologne, Ente per le Fiere, 1971 Actes du Congrès (Bologne, 4-6 avril 1971)
———.	Programmazione tecnologica e processi di comunicazione. Bologne, Ente per le Fiere - CNITE, 1972
VOGT, H.H.	L'imbuto di Morimberga: Macchine per insegnare. (traduction de M. Tagliaferri), Brescia, La Scuola, 1969, 88 p.

2 - ARTICLES

BIANCHI VALENTINI, B.	"Tecnologie dell'apprendimento: un programma di autoistruzione sul 'Codice della vita'," in La Ricerca 15 janvier 1971 (Serie scuole secondarie superiori.)
BROCCOLINI, G.	"L'istruzione programmata", in Servizio Informazioni Avio, No.11-12, novembre-décembre 1970, p.478-480
———.	"La pedagogica cibernetica", in Servizio Informazioni Avio, No.7-8, juillet-août 1971, p.293-299
FONTANA TOMASSUCI, L.	"L'individualizzione nell'insegnamento: dalla scheda al calcolatore", in I Problemi della Pedagogia, No.4, 1969
———.	"Mezzi e strumenti della comunicazione, nuovi sussidi didattico-tecnologici e loro effetto sull'innovazione dei sistemi formativi", in Formazione e Lavoro, No.39, septembre-octobre 1969
———.	"Rassegna di studi e iniziative sull'istruzione programata in Italia", in I Problemi della Pedagogia, No.1, 1969
———.	"Un esempio di tecnologia dell'insegnamento", in Scuola e Città, No.4, avril 1971
GROPPO, M.	"Ricerca sperimentale sull'istruzione programmata", in Orientamenti Pedagogici, vol. 91, No.1 Rapport d'expérience
LAENG, M.	"L'istruzione programmata mediante monitori automatici in I Problemi della Pedagogia, vol.XV, No.1, 1969 Panorama
———.	"Istruzione programmata in Italia", in Sapere, No.704, 1968
———.	"I nuovi linguaggi tecnologici e la realtà educativa", in Formazione e Lavoro, No.39, septembre-octobre 1969

MENDUNI, E.	"La dinamica del corso programmato nelle sue fasi", in Bolletino di psicologia applicata, Nos.85-87, 1968 Rapport d'expérience
MOLTEDO, L.	"Linguaggi CAI: una classificazione", in Tecnologie educative, No.2, 1971
_____.; PANI, P.	"Un esperimento di insegnamento programmato", in Giornale di Ivrea, vol. XI, No.2, 1970
TITONE, R.	"Tecnologie educative e docenti", in Servizio Informazioni Avio, No.12, décembre 1971, p.434-437
TRISCIUZZI, L.	"Un modelo cibernetico nella metodologia dell' apprendere-insegnare", in Scuola e Città, No.4, avril 1971
VERTECCHI, B.	"Analisi didattica: 1° Questioni di metodo; II° Le caratteristiche degli allievi; III° La struttura dei contenuti", in La Ricerca, 1971, octobre-novembre-décembre
_____.	"Che cos'è la Computer Assisted Instruction", in La Ricerca, 1971
VISALBERGHI, A.	"Dimensioni sociali delle tecnologie educative", in Programmazione tecnologica e processi di comunicazione, Ente Fiere di Bologna - CNITE, 1972
_____.	"Funzione delle tecnologie educative in una società in transformazione", in Tecnologie educative, No.10, 1970
_____.	"Istruzione programmata e individualizzazione dell' insegnamento", in La Ricerca, No.1, 1968 Panorama

3 - BIBLIOGRAPHIES

FONTANA TOMASSUCCI, Luciana. Bibliografia, in Prospettive didattiche dell'istruzione programmata (monographie de la série "I problemi della pedagogia"). No.1, 1969, Rome, Istituto di pedagogia dell'Università di Roma, 1969, 27 p.

4 - AUDIO-VISUAL PRODUCTIONS / PRODUCTIONS AUDIO-VISUELLES

L'ISTRUZIONE PROGRAMMATA.   45 mn (janvier 1970)
Réalisateur: M. Mainetti, Président du Centro Europeo Coordinamento Istruzione Lavoro (CECIL), Via di Villa Patrizi 4, Rome

III - RESEARCH AND APPLICATIONS / REALISATIONS

1 - RESEARCH / RECHERCHES

COMPARAISON DE L'ENSEIGNEMENT PROGRAMME ET DE L'ENSEIGNEMENT TRADITIONNEL DANS LA FORMATION PROFESSIONNELLE
Organisme: Ufficio Personale, Soc. Montecatini Edison, Ferrara
Public intéressé: Ouvriers de l'industrie pétrochimique

COMPARAISON DE L'ENSEIGNEMENT PROGRAMME ET DE L'ENSEIGNEMENT TRADITIONNEL
Organisme: Istituto di Psicologia, Università Cattolica "S. Cuore" - Milan
Public intéressé: Etudiants diplômés de l'Istituto Magistrale

CONTROLE DES EFFETS DE RENFORCEMENT SUR LES REPONSES DES ELEVES DANS UN PROGRAMME DE LOGIQUE FORMELLE ELEMENTAIRE
Organismes: Istituto di Psicologia, Consiglio Nazionale Ricerche.
Training Research Laboratory, University of Illinois
Public intéressé: 128 étudiants de 3° de lycées classiques

EMPLOI DE PROGRAMMES A CHOIX MULTIPLES AVEC DES MACHINES "CANTERBURY" POUR L'ENSEIGNEMENT DES MATHEMATIQUES
Organisme: Scuola media "D'Alessandro"

FORMATION A LA SECURITE
Organisme: Divisione di Psicologia, ENPI
Public intéressé: Etudiants-géomètres de l'Istituto Tecnico

MESURE DE L'EFFICACITE DE PROGRAMMES LINEAIRES POUR L'ENSEIGNEMENT DES MATHEMATIQUES
Organismes: Centro Didattico Nazionale Scuola Media.
Istituto di Pedagogia, Università di Roma, Rome
Public intéressé: Elèves de l'école moyenne

2 - PUBLISHED PROGRAMMED COURSES / COURS PROGRAMMES PUBLIES

CROWDER, N.A.; MARTIN, G.C. Introduzione all'algebra. Florence, Vallecchi, 1968, 353 p. Niveau secondaire

FRIEL, B.K. Decimali e percentuale. Florence, Vallecchi, 1969. 500 items. Niveau secondaire. Enseignement technique. Formation professionnelle

GARDNER, Nelly. Pratica di direzione aziendale. Florence, Vallecchi, 1969, 264 items. Niveau supérieur

GRASSETI, B.; MAINETTI, M. Elementi di statistica. Rome, CECIL, Via di Villa Patrizi, 4, 30 mai 1969, 317 items, 168 p. Universitaires, Adultes. Spécialistes. Enseignement technique

HANCOCK, J.D. Addizione. Florence, Organizzazioni speciali, 1968. 134 items. Niveau primaire

—————. LUCAS, Y.S. Sottrazione. Florence, Organizzazioni speciali, 1968, 80 items. Niveau primaire

HUGHES, R.J.; PIPE, P. Elettronica. Florence, Vallecchi, 1968, 418 items. Formation professionnelle

MARTIN, G.C.; SMALLEY, A. Matematica pratica. Florence, Vallecchi, 1968, 695 items. Formation professionnelle

OWENS; SANBORN. Elettricità. Florence, Vallecchi, septembre 1968. 524 items. Education des adultes. Enseignement technique. Formation professionnelle

SACKHEIM, G. Nomenclatura dei composti inorganici. Florence, Organizzazioni
          speciali, 1968. 405 items. Niveau secondaire. Education des
          adultes

SAFFOLD; SMALLEY, A. Il regolo calcolatore. Florence, Vallecchi, 1969.
          468 items. Enseignement technique. Formation professionnelle

SMITH, M.D. Decimali e percentuale. Florence, Organizzazioni speciali, 1968.
          623 items. Niveau secondaire

Collection "IP" éditée par Organizzazioni speciali, Florence

   ALBERS, H.H.; SCHOER, L. Principi direzionali nell'azienda, 1971. 269 items

   ALLEN, P.   Il calcolatore elettronico, 1972

   ANTHONY, R.N. Elementi di contabilità, 1970

   CARMAN, R.A. Introduzione a i vettori, 1972

   DAUSCH, V.L. et al. Espressioni ed equazioni, 1971

   ──────.   et al. Punti, rette e piani, 1971

   FEDERAL ELECTRIC CORPORATION, Il Pert, 1969. 151 items

   ──────────; Tecnica della comunicazione aziendale, 1971. 335 items

   HANCOCK, F.D.; O'BRIEN, J.J. Jr., Moltiplicazione, 1968. 338 items

   ──────────; SCHNEIDER, P.C., Divisione, 1968. 244 items

   JOSEPH, A.; LEAHY, D.J. Corso programmato di fisica. Parte III: Ottica
          e Onde. 1972

   MAVRINAC et al. Asia Sud-orientale, 1970. 536 items

   MOSKOVITZ, M.M., Testa o croce ? (Introduzione alla teoria della probabilità),
          1970. 102 items

   NICHOLS, E.D.; KALIN, R.; GARLAND, H. Geometria delle coordinate. 1970.

   ──── ; ──── ; ──── ; Introduzione agli insiemi, 1968. 255 items

   ──── ; ──── ; ──── ; Numeri relativi, 1970. 413 items

   ──── ; ──── ; ──── ; Uguaglianze, disuguaglianze e equazioni, 1968. 284 items

   PANARES, R.R. Forza (Materia in movimento)

   ──────.; SCHULTZ, R. Moto (Materia in movimento)

   RAMSEY, N.; KLEPPNER, D. Elementi di analisi matematica, 1971. 402 items

   SACKHEIM, G. Impariamo a dare un nome agli idrocarburi semplici, 1967. 264 items

   SELTZER, M.; ZOLL, E.J. Numeri in varie basi, 1968

Collection "Istruzione Programmata" éditée par Ed. Armando, Rome

    CLARKE, J.   Gli insiemi, 2 vol. 1972

    ———.   Le frazioni, 2 vol. 1972

    ———.   La numerazione, 2 vol. 1972

    FIELDHOUSE, J. Il fagiolo rampicante, 2 vol. 1972

    LEEDHAM, J.; PARKER, D.V. Area e volume, 1972

Collection "Organizzazione Aziendale" éditée par Franco Angeli, Milan

    BOLAND, R.G.; FEATHERS, J.Q. Introduzione alla contabilità dei costi, 1972

    EUREQUIPE.   Introduzione al calcolatore elettronico, 1971

    ILO-ISEO.   Introduzione al marketing, 1971

    KARMIER, L.J. Principi di direzione e organizzazione aziendale, 1971

Collection "Scienze" éditée par Franco Angeli, Milan

    A.A.V.V.   Il comportamento umano, 1971

    CHRISTIENSEN, H.; PALMER, G.A. Cinetica ed enzimatica, 1971

    ELZEY, F.   Introduzione alla statistica, 1971

    I.T.T. - FEDERAL ELECTRIC CORPORATION. L'algebra booleana, 1971

    KIMBLE, D.P. Psicofisiologia, 1970

    MARL, M.   Termodinamica, 1972

    STONES, E.   Apprendimento e insegnamento, 1971

Collection "Tecnica" éditée par Franco Angeli, Milan

    GEORGE, L.; BRUGNOT, J. Come tenere l'amministrazione di un'impresa, 1972

    NEW YORK INSTITUTE OF TECHNOLOGY, Elettricità, 1969

    ———————.   Elettronica, 2 vol. 1969

    ———————.   Transistori, 2 vol. 1970

Collection "Tutor" éditée par Vallecchi-FPCT, Florence

    CHAPMAN, R.E. L'essenziale per lo studio della musica, 3 vol. 1971

    CROWDER, N.A. Aritmetica per i calcolatori elettronici, 2 vol., 1968

    ————.   Introduzione alla genetica, 1970

    ————.; MARTIN, G.C. Trigonometria, 1967

    FRIEL, B.K. Frazioni, 2 vol. 1969

GARDNER, N.D.   Organizzazione aziendale

————.; DAVIS, J.N.   La delega delle responsabilità direttive

LEACH, R.B.; EWING, G.W.   Chimica, 2 vol. 1970

OWENS, J.B.; SANBORN, P.   Tubi elettronici, 2 vol. 1970

SANBORN, P.   I Transistori, 2 vol. 1972

SCOTT, T.G.   Fondamenti di programmazione per i calcolatori, 2 vol. 1970

————.   Tecniche di programmazione per i calcolatori, 3 vol. 1971

Nouvelle collection "Quaderni di istruzione programmata" éditée par Vallechi - FPCT, Florence

   I costi standard di produzione. Una esperienza aziendale. 1972

3 - COMPUTER ASSISTED INSTRUCTION / ENSEIGNEMENT ASSISTE PAR ORDINATEUR

ADDESTRAMENTO PERSONALE NAVIGANTE (Perfectionnement du personnel navigant)
Organisme: ALITALIA
Destinataires: Pilotes et personnel navigant
Type de l'ordinateur: LINK Aviation Inc.
Type des terminaux: LINK Trainers
Objet: Entraînement aux différentes situations de vol

ALGEBRE
Organisme: General Electric, Université de Padoue
Objet: Démonstration publique

ENSEIGNEMENT
Organisme: CNUCE, Centro studi IBM, Pise
Type de l'ordinateur: IBM 1620

ENSEIGNEMENT DE LA PHYSIQUE
Organisme: Université de Bari
Type de l'ordinateur: IBM 360/40

ENSEIGNEMENT, RECHERCHE
Organisme: Centro Studi Sistemi Controllo e Calcolo Automatico del C.N.R., c/o Ist. Automatica-Facoltà Ingegneria, Università di Roma
Type de l'ordinateur: UNIVAC 1108 - IBM 1130

JAPAN/JAPON

I - ORGANIZATIONS AND ACTIVITIES / STRUCTURES ET ACTIVITES

1 - CENTRES

CENTRE FOR ABILITY DEVELOPMENT ENGINEERING
18-2, Igusa 4-Chome, Suginami-ku, Tokyo
Nature of organization: Foundation

CENTRE FOR EDUCATIONAL TECHNOLOGY, AICHI UNIVERSITY OF EDUCATION
1 Hirozawa Igaya, Kariya-City, Aichi
Nature of organization: University

CENTRE FOR EDUCATIONAL TECHNOLOGY, FUKUOKA UNIVERSITY OF EDUCATION
729 Akama, Munakata-machi, Munakata-gun, Fukuoka
Nature of organization: University

CENTRE FOR EDUCATIONAL TECHNOLOGY, HOKKAIDO UNIVERSITY OF EDUCATION
Nishi 13-chome, Minami 24-jo, Sapporo City
Nature of organization: University

CENTRE FOR EDUCATIONAL TECHNOLOGY, TOKYO GAKUGEI UNIVERSITY
I-I, Nukui-Kitamachi 4-chome, Koganei City,
Tokyo
Nature of organization: University

CENTRE FOR THE SCIENCE OF LEARNING, KEIO UNIVERSITY
15-45, Mita 2-Chome, Minato-ku, Tokyo
Nature of organization: University

DEPARTMENT OF PEDAGOGY, FACULTY OF LITERATURE, OSAKA UNIVERSITY
1, Machikaneyama-Machi, Toyonaka, Osaka
Nature of organization: University

DEPARTMENT OF PEDAGOGY, TOKYO INSTITUTE OF TECHNOLOGY
12-I, Ookayama 2-chome, Meguro-ku, Tokyo
Nature of organization: University

JAPAN ASSOCIATION FOR EDUCATIONAL TECHNOLOGY
c/o Tokyo Gakugei University, I-I, Nukui-Kitamachi 4-Chome, Koganei City,
Tokyo
Nature of organization: Professional association

JAPAN SOCIETY FOR THE PROMOTION OF MACHINE INDUSTRY
5-3 Chome No.21, Shiba-Koen, Minato-ku, Tokyo
Nature of organization: Foundation

NATIONAL INSTITUTE FOR EDUCATIONAL RESEARCH
5-22 Shimomeguro 6-Chome, Meguro-ku, Tokyo
Nature of organization: Governmental

2 - ACTIVITIES/MANIFESTATIONS

EVALUATION MEETING OF THE EXPERIMENTAL PROJECT ON PROGRAMMED
INSTRUCTION IN ASIA (International conference)

Organized by: Unesco
Place and date: Tokyo, May 1972
Participants: Administrators. Research workers. School teachers. University teachers
Purpose: To review the Experimental Project and to formulate future action

MEETING OF ORGANIZERS AND PROGRAMMERS OF THE EXPERIMENTAL PROJECT
ON PROGRAMMED INSTRUCTION IN ASIA (International conference)

Organized by: Japanese National Commission for Unesco
Place and date: Tokyo, February 1971
Participants: Administrators. Research workers. School teachers.
                  University teachers

NATIONAL CONFERENCE ON BROADCASTING EDUCATION (National annual conference)

Organized by: National Association for Broadcasting Education
Place and date: Seindai City, October 1969
Participants: Research workers. School teachers. University teachers.
                  Vocational teachers
Purpose: Study and research on broadcasting education

NATIONAL CONVENTION ON AUDIO-VISUAL EDUCATION (National annual conference)

Organized by: Japan Association for Audio-Visual Education at School
Places, dates: Fukuoka City, November 1969; Sapporo City, November 1970;
                  Yamaguchi Prefecture, November 1971; Tokyo, November 1972.
Participants: Research workers. School teachers. University teachers.
                  Vocational teachers
Purpose: Studies on audio-visual education

NATIONAL CONVENTION ON PROGRAMMED LEARNING (National annual conference)

Organized by: Japan Association for Programmed Learning
Places, dates: 6th Convention: Toyama City, August 1968;
                  7th Convention: Tokyo, August 1969
Participants: Research workers. School teachers. University teachers.
                  Vocational teachers
Purpose: Study and exchange of information

NATIONAL CONVENTION ON PROGRAMMED SHEET LEARNING (National annual conference)

Organized by: Japan Association for Programmed Sheet Learning
Places and dates: Tokyo, 1969; Ibaraq Prefecture, 1970;
                  Osaka, 1971; Gunma Prefecture, 1972
Participants: Research workers. School teachers. University
                  teachers. Vocational teachers
Purpose: Study and research on synchrofax

SEMINAR ON EDUCATIONAL TECHNOLOGY

Organized by: Tokyo Association for educational technology
Places and dates: Tokyo, July 1970; Tokyo, July 1971; Tokyo, July-August 1972
Participants: Research workers. School teachers. University teachers.
                  Vocational teachers
Purpose: Programming of subject matter and systematizing of
                  educational processes

WORKSHOP OF THE EXPERIMENTAL PROJECT ON PROGRAMMED INSTRUCTION
IN ASIA (International conference)

Organized by: Unesco
Place and date: Tokyo, Osaka, February and March 1970
Participants: Administrators. Research workers. School teachers.
                  University teachers.
Purpose: To promote programmed instruction in Asian countries

3 - PUBLISHERS / MAISONS D'EDITION

AUDIO-VISUAL CONSULTANT CENTRE
1-17, Koraku 2-chome, Bunkyo-ku, Tokyo
Nature of organization: Commercial publisher

DAINIHON TOSHO CO., LTD.
9-10, Ginza 1-chome, Chuyo-ku, Tokyo
Nature of organization: Commercial publisher

GAKUSHU KENKYUSHA CO., LTD.
40-5, Kamiikedai 4-Chome, Ota-ku, Tokyo
Nature of organization: Commercial publisher

KODANSHA LTD.
2-12-21, Otowa, Bunkyo-ku, Tokyo 112
Nature of organization: Commercial publisher

KYOIKU KOGAKU SHA CO., LTD.
4-3, Fujimi 2-chome, Chiyoda-ku, Tokyo
Nature of organization: Commercial publisher

KYOKEN CO., LTD.
11-3, Iidabashi 2-chome, Chiyoda-ku, Tokyo
Nature of organization: Commercial publisher

MEIJI-TOSHO CO., LTD.
5-39, Minami-Otsuka 2-chome, Toshima-ku, Tokyo
Nature of organization: Commercial publisher

OHM CO., LTD.
3-1, Kanda-Nishiki-cho, Chiyoda-ku, Tokyo
Nature of organization: Commercial publisher

OSAKA SHOSEKI CO., LTD.
2-25, Tsumori-Higashi, Nishinari-ku, Osaka
Nature of organization: Commercial publisher

4 - PERIODICALS/PERIODIQUES

AUDIO-VISUAL EDUCATION
Publisher: Japan Audio-Visual Education Association
Address: 26, Nishikubo Sakuragi-cho, Shiba, Minato-ku, Tokyo
Periodicity: Monthly
Fields of interest: Research. Application. Topical events

AUDIO-VISUAL TECHNICAL METHOD
Publisher: Audio-Visual Consultant Centre
Address: 1-17, Koraku 2-chome, Bunkyo-ku, Tokyo
Periodicity: Monthly
Fields of interest: Research. Application. Topical events

CONTEMPORARY EDUCATIONAL TECHNOLOGY
Publisher: Meiji-Tosho Co., Ltd.
Address: 5-39, Minami-Otsuka 2-chome, Toshima-ku, Tokyo
Periodicity: Monthly
Fields of interest: Research. Application. Topical events

EDUCATIONAL TECHNOLOGY
Publisher: Kyoiku Kogaku Sha Co., Ltd.
Address: 4-3, Fujimi 2-chome, Chiyoda-ku, Tokyo
Periodicity: Monthly
Fields of interest: Research. Application. Topical events

RADIO - T.V. EDUCATION
Publisher: Japan Broadcasting Education Association
Address: 12-3, Nishi-Shinbashi 2-chome, Minato-ku, Tokyo.
Periodicity: Monthly
Fields of interest: Research. Application. Topical events

STUDIES ON EDUCATIONAL SYSTEMS
Publisher: Neiji Tosho Co., Ltd.
Address: 5-39, Minami-Otsuka 2-chome, Toshima-ku, Tokyo
Periodicity: Quarterly
Fields of interest: Research. Application

TEACHING TECHNOLOGY
Publisher: Meiji Tosho Co., Ltd.
Address: 5-39, Minami-Otsuka 2-chome, Toshima-ku, Tokyo
Periodicity: Quarterly
Fields of interest: Research. Application

5 - PROFESSIONAL ORGANIZATIONS/ORGANISATIONS PROFESSIONNELLES

EDUCATIONAL TECHNOLOGY COMMITTEE
c/o The Institute of Electronics and Communication Engineers of Japan,
Kikai Shinko Building, 5-3-21, Shiba-Koen, Minato-ku, Tokyo
Activities: Studies on educational technology

HYOGO-KEN ASSOCIATION FOR EDUCATIONAL TECHNOLOGY
c/o Hyogo Prefectural Hyogo Industrial Upper Secondary School
43, Kawanaka-cho, Hyogo-ku, Kobe
Nature of organization: Teachers' Association
Activities: Studies on educational technology

JAPAN ASSOCIATION FOR AUDIO-VISUAL EDUCATION AT SCHOOLS
c/o Waseda Elementary School, 25, Waseda Minami-cho, Shinjuku-ku, Tokyo
Nature of organization: Teachers' Association
Activities: Studies on audio-visual education

JAPAN ASSOCIATION FOR EDUCATIONAL TECHNOLOGY
c/o Tokyo Gakugei University, 1-1, Nukui-Kitamachi 4-chome, Koganei City,
Tokyo
Nature of organization: Teachers' Association
Activities: Information centre

JAPAN ASSOCIATION FOR PROGRAMMED SHEET LEARNING
c/o Meidai Lower Secondary School, 9-5, Kasuga 2-chome, Bunkyo-ku, Tokyo
Nature of organization: Teachers' Association
Activities: Studies on synchrofax and O.H.T.

KAGAWA ASSOCIATION FOR EDUCATIONAL ENGINEERING
c/o Takamatsu Lower Secondary School, attached to Kagawa University,
1, Miyawaki-cho 1-chome, Takamatsu City, Kagawa Prefecture
Nature of organization: Teachers' Association
Activities: Studies on educational technology

NAGOYA ASSOCIATION FOR EDUCATIONAL TECHNOLOGY
10-7, Oyuki-Machi, Higashi-ku, Nagoya.
Nature of organization: Teachers' Association
Activities: Studies on educational technology

6 - MANUFACTURERS OF TEACHING MACHINES/FABRICANTS DE MACHINES A ENSEIGNER

GAKUSHU KENKYU SHA CO., LTD.
40-5, Kamiikedai 4-chome, Ota-ku, Tokyo
Type of machine: Gakken Auto-trainer
Characteristics: Linear programme. Storage and analysis of replies.
                    Integrated audio-visual device. Collective use
Purposes: Evaluation. Teaching

GAKUSHU KENKYU SHA CO., LTD.
40-5, Kamiikedai 4-chome, Ota-ku, Tokyo
Type of machine: Tutor-Pack teaching machine
Characteristics: Branching-type programme with learning tools
Purposes: Mathematics and Natural Sciences in primary schools

HITACHI SEISAKUSHO CO., LTD.
6-2, Otemachi 2-chome, Chiyoda-ku, Tokyo
Type of machine: Teaching machine system
Characteristics: Linear programme. Storage and analysis of replies.
                    Integrated audio-visual device. Collective use
Purposes: **Evaluation. Teaching**

MATSUSHITA TSUSHIN KOGYO CO., LTD.
880, Tsunashima-cho, Kohoku-ku, Yokohama City
Type of machine: CAI System
Characteristics: Branching programme. Storage and analysis of
                    replies. Integrated audio-visual device. Individual
                    and collective use
Purposes: Teaching. Recording. Score and evaluation

NIPPON ELECTRIC CO., LTD.
7-15, Shiba 5-chome, Minato-ku, Tokyo
Type of machine: CAI System
Characteristics: Branching programme. Storage and analysis of
                    replies. Integrated audio-visual device. Individual
                    use
Purposes: Teaching. Recording. Score and evaluation

Type of machine: Response Analyse
Characteristics: Storage and analysis of replies. Integrated audio-visual device. Individual use.
Purposes: Teaching. Recording. Score and evaluation

RICOH KYOIKUKIKI CO., LTD.
10-2, Fujimi 2-chome, Chiyoda-ku, Tokyo
Type of machine: Syncrofax
Characteristics: Linear programme. Integrated audio-visual device. Individual use
Purpose: Teaching

SHIMADZU SCIENTIFIC INSTRUMENT LTD.
Nijo Kawaramuchi Sagaru, Nakagyo-ku, Kyoto
Type of machine: Response Analyser
Characteristics: Storage and analysis of replies. Adaptable audio-visual device. Collective use
Purposes: Evaluation. Teaching

TOKYO SHIBAURA DENKI CO., LTD.
I, Uchisaiwai-cho, Chiyoda-ku, Tokyo
Type of machine: Toshiba Personal Teaching Machine
Characteristics: Branching programme. Integrated audio-visual device. Individual use
Purpose: Teaching

7 - TRAINING ORGANIZATIONS/ORGANISMES ASSURANT UNE FORMATION

CENTRE FOR ABILITY DEVELOPMENT ENGINEERING
18-2, Igusa 4-chome, Suginami-ku, Tokyo
Public concerned: School teachers. Vocational teachers

JAPAN ASSOCIATION FOR EDUCATIONAL TECHNOLOGY
c/o Tokyo Gakugei University, 1-1, Nukui-kitamachi 4-chome, Koganei City, Tokyo
Public concerned: School teachers. Vocational teachers

JAPAN SOCIETY FOR THE PROMOTION OF MACHINE INDUSTRY
5-3 chome No.21, Shiba-Koen, Minato-ku, Tokyo
Public concerned: Businessmen. Teachers. Students

II - PUBLICATIONS

1 - BOOKS / LIVRES

AZUMA, Hiroshi (ed.). Kyoju Gakushu Shisutemu (Teaching-Learning System). Educational technology series, vol.3. Tokyo, Dainihon Tosho Co.Ltd., November 1971, 268 p.

HORIUCHI, Toshio (ed.). Puroguramu Gakushu to TM (Programmed instruction and TM). Educational technology series, vol.4. Tokyo, Dainihon Tosho Co.Ltd., July 1972, 300 p.

―――. Sangyo ni Okeru Kyoiku Kogaku (Educational technology in industries). Educational technology series, vol.8. Tokyo, Dainihon Tosho Co.Ltd., April 1971, 278 p.

―――, et al. (eds.) Educational Technology. Tokyo, Dainihon Tosho Co. Ltd., 1971

KOBAYASHI, Kazuya. Jissen Kyoiku Kogaku. (Practical educational technology). Tokyo, Reimei Shobo Co.Ltd., April 1970, 277 p.

NISHIMOTO, Yoichi (ed.). Kyoiku Keiei to Kyoiku Kogaku (Educational management and educational technology). Educational technology series, vol.2. Tokyo, Dainihon Tosho Co.Ltd., November 1971, 298 p.

NUMANO, Ichio (ed.). Programme Gakushu no Jissen (Practice on programmed instruction). Tokyo, Yukyu Publishing Co.Ltd., May 1968, 280 p. Programming, practice in school education

OUCHI, Shigeo, et al. (eds.) New trends in education and educational technology. Tokyo, Meiji Tosho Co.Ltd., 1971

SAKAMOTO, Takashi (ed.). Gendai Shakai ni Okeru Kyoiku Kogaku (Educational technology in contemporary society). Educational technology series, vol.1. Tokyo, Dainihon Tosho Co.Ltd., January 1971, 247 p.

―――. Systems approach to education. Principles and practices of educational technology. Tokyo, Meiji Tosho Co.Ltd., 1971

SHUHARA, Masao (ed.). Programme Gakusku Jireishu. (Some examples on programmed instruction). Tokyo, Audio-Visual Consultant Centre, 1969, 431 p.

TAKAHAGI, Ryutaro (ed.). Kiki Riyo no Kyoiku Kogaku. (Educational technology by use of educational equipment). Educational technology series, vol.5. Tokyo, Dainihon Tosho Co.Ltd., January 1971, 269 p.

TANIGUCHI, Hirokuni (ed.). Kyoiku Shisetsu Kankyo no Keikaku (Planning for educational facilities and environment). Educational technology series, vol.7. Tokyo, Dainihon Tosho Co.Ltd., July 1972, 330 p.

WATANABE, Shigeru (ed.). Kyoiku ni Okeru Johokogaku (Information technology in education). Educational technology series, vol.6. Tokyo, Dainihon Tosho Co.Ltd., October 1971, 264 p.

2 - ARTICLES

AKAGI, Aiwa. Programme Gakushu Kenkyu no Keiko (New trends on the studies of programmed instruction). Report of Osaka Sciences Education Centre, No.36, 1968, 5 p. Survey

KOBAYASHI, Shigehiro et al. Kyoiku Kogaku no Kenkyu (Studies on educational engineering). No.1, 1971; No.2, 1972. Annual report

III - RESEARCH AND APPLICATIONS / REALISATIONS

1 - RESEARCH / RECHERCHES

Theme: CAI SYSTEM
Organized by: Centre for Ability Development Engineering
Public concerned: Primary, secondary and vocational schools

Theme: EXPERIMENTAL STUDIES ON OPTIMISATION OF CAI SYSTEM
Organized by: Laboratory of Educational Psychology, Tokyo Gakugei University
Public concerned: Primary and secondary schools

Theme: PROGRAMMED INSTRUCTION AND CREATIVITY
Organized by: Laboratory of Educational Psychology, Osaka University

Theme: STUDY AND RESEARCH ON CAI SYSTEM
Organized by: Department of Educational Psychology, Osaka University
Public concerned: Primary and secondary schools

Theme: SYSTEMS APPROACH TO EDUCATION. STUDIES ON CAI
Organized by: Department of Education, Tokyo Institute of Technology
Public concerned: All levels of learners

2 - PUBLISHED PROGRAMMED COURSES/COURS PROGRAMMES PUBLIES

Kiso Butsuri (Basic Physics), vols. 1-7. Centre for Ability Development Engineering, July 1968, 6178 p.
Vocational schools. Business firms.

Seizu no Kiso (Basic Drawing), vols. I and II. Kantochiku Kikai Kogyo Kyoiku Kenkyukai, April 1969. I - 41 p. II - 51 p.
Industrial upper secondary schools

TANAKA, S.; MIYAWAKI, K. Basic Electricity (1 and 2). (Teaching basic electricity in engineering). Osaka Science and Technology Centre, 1968. 1 - 1000 items, 186 p; 2 - 1174 items, 250 p.
Upper Secondary and Technical Schools

_____ ; _____ . Electronics Circuits I (Science). Osaka Science and Technology Centre, 1969, 1900 items, 1230 p.

_____ ; _____ . Kiso denki riron (Fundamental theory on electricity). Vols. I and II. Osaka Science and Technology Centre. Vol. I, 1968, 30 items, 186 p. Vol. II, 1969, 30 items, 259 p.
Technical education at industrial upper secondary schools and business firms. Secondary and vocational schools

3 - COMPUTER ASSISTED INSTRUCTION / ENSEIGNEMENT ASSISTE PAR ORDINATEUR

CAI FOR LOWER SECONDARY SCHOOLS (MATHEMATICS)

Organization: Kagawa University, Physics Department, Takamatsu
Type of computer: NEAC M4
Type of terminals: Key board, Screen and Voice
Purposes: Evaluation. Teaching

CAI FOR PRIMARY AND SECONDARY EDUCATION

Organization: Osaka University
Type of computer: HITAC
Type of terminals: Key board
Purposes: Evaluation. Teaching

CAI FOR VOCATIONAL EDUCATION

Organization: Japan Society for the Promotion of Machine Industry
Type of computer: K.S.K.
Type of terminals: CRT Graphic display 8. CRT Character display 22
Types of language: Fortran. Cobol
Purposes: Evaluation. Teaching

CAI SYSTEM OF CADE (Centre for Ability Development Engineering)

Organization: Centre For Ability Development Engineering
Type of computer: NEAC 2200-50
Types of terminals: Key board and screen
Purposes: Evaluation. Teaching

STATISTICS

Organization: Laboratory of Educational Psychology, Osaka University
Public concerned: College students
Type of computer: HITAC 10
Types of terminals: Slide projector and typewriter
Purposes: Teaching. Research

KOREA, REPUBLIC OF / COREE, REPUBLIQUE DE

I - ORGANIZATIONS AND ACTIVITIES / STRUCTURES ET ACTIVITES

1 - CENTRES

CENTRAL EDUCATION RESEARCH INSTITUTE
8, Yejang-dong, Choong-ku, Seoul

THE INSTITUTE OF EDUCATIONAL RESEARCH, YONSEI UNIVERSITY
134, Shinchon-dong, Seudaemun-ku, Seoul
Nature of organization: University

KOREAN INSTITUTE FOR RESEARCH IN THE BEHAVIOURAL SCIENCES
163, Ankook-dong, Chongro-ku, Seoul

3 - PUBLISHERS / MAISONS D'EDITION

KYO YOOK JA RYO SA
167, Dangjoo-dong, Chongro-ku, Seoul
Nature of organization: Commercial publisher

KYO YOOK KWA HAK SA
8, Yejang-dong, Choong-ku, Seoul
Nature of organization: Commercial publisher

8 - DOCUMENTATION CENTRES / CENTRES DE DOCUMENTATION

CENTRAL EDUCATION RESEARCH INSTITUTE
8, Yejang-dong, Choong-ku, Seoul
Type of services: Distribution of research reports

KOREAN INSTITUTE FOR RESEARCH IN THE BEHAVIOURAL SCIENCES
163, Ankook-dong, Chongro-ku, Seoul
Type of services: Distribution of research reports

II - PUBLICATIONS

1 - BOOKS/LIVRES

KIM, Hongwon. The principles of mastery learning. Seoul, Bae Young Sa, 1970, 286 p.

LEE, Sung-jin. The principles of behaviour modification. Seoul, Educational Publishing Company, 1972, 350 p.

_____. Behaviour modification in the schools. Seoul, Bae Young Sa, 1972, 270 p.

2 - ARTICLES

BANG, Chung-ai et al. A feasibility-cost study of producing and utilizing programmed texts for primary and middle schools. C.E.R.I., 1970, 46 p. (Research Report).

LEE, Eun-jin. The effect of interaction between the length of learning program and the reading ability on achievement. Graduate School of Education of Seoul National University, 1971 (Unpublished M.Ed., thesis).

3 - BIBLIOGRAPHIES

LEE, Yung-dug. The process of education. Seoul, Bae Young Sa, 1969, 381 p.

III - RESEARCH AND APPLICATION / REALISATIONS

1 - RESEARCH / RECHERCHES

EXPLORE THE FEASIBILITY OF PRODUCING AND USING PROGRAMMED TEXTS IN A SELECTED NUMBER OF SUBJECT MATTER FIELDS OF PRIMARY AND MIDDLE SCHOOL CURRICULA
Organized by: Central Education Research Institute, Seoul
Public concerned: Primary and secondary school pupils

MASTERY LEARNING IN THE MIDDLE SCHOOL
Organized by: Korean Institute for Research in the
                  Behavioural Sciences, Seoul
Public concerned: Secondary school pupils

MASTERY LEARNING PROJECT FOR THE QUALITATIVE IMPROVEMENT OF SCHOOL LEARNING IN MIDDLE SCHOOL LEVEL
Organized by: Korean Institute for Research in the
                  Behavioural Sciences, Seoul
Public concerned: Secondary school pupils

PILOT STUDY FOR MASTERY LEARNING
Organized by: Korean Institute for Research in
                  Behavioural Sciences, Seoul
Public concerned: Secondary school pupils

2 - PUBLISHED PROGRAMMED COURSES / COURS PROGRAMMES PUBLIES

KOREAN INSTITUTE FOR RESEARCH IN THE BEHAVIOURAL SCIENCES. **A collection of programmed courses in Korean** (Mathematics, Sciences and English). Korean Ability Development Publishing Company

MEXICO/MEXIQUE

I - ORGANIZATIONS AND ACTIVITIES / STRUCTURES ET ACTIVITES

   1 - CENTRES

BANCO DE COMERCIO, S.A.
Venustiano Carranza 44, México 1, D.F.
Nature de l'organisme: Privé

BANCO NACIONAL DE MÉXICO, S.A., Departamento de Desarrollo del Personal, Sección de Desarrollo de los Empleados
Fray Servando Teresa de Mier 174, México 1, D.F.
Nature de l'organisme: Privé

COMISIÓN DE OPERACIÓN Y FOMENTO DE ACTIVIDADES ACADÉMICAS DEL INSTITUTO POLITÉCNICO NACIONAL
Tolsá y Tres Guerras, México 1, D.F.
Nature de l'organisme : Gouvernemental

INSTITUTO NACIONAL DE INVESTIGACIÓN EDUCATIVA
Avenida Presidente Masarik 526, México 5, D.F.
Nature de l'organisme: Gouvernemental

INSTRUCCIÓN PROGRAMADA DE MÉXICO, S.A.
Bolívar 202 - A, México 1, D.F.
Nature de l'organisme: Société privée d'édition et de formation professionnelle industrielle

OFICINA DE CAPACITACIÓN Y ADIESTRAMIENTO DE LA COMISIÓN FEDERAL DE ELECTRICID
Río Elba 22, México 5, D.F.
Nature de l'organisme: Privé

UNIVERSIDAD NACIONAL AUTÓNOMA DE MÉXICO (UNAM)
    Comisión de Nuevos Métodos de Enseñanza
    Centro de Didáctica, Dirección General del Profesorado
    Instituto de Ingeniería, División de Investigaciones, Facultad
        de Ingeniería
Ciudad Universitaria, México, D.F.
Nature des organismes: Universitaires

2 - ACTIVITIES / MANIFESTATIONS

CONFERENCES (Manifestations nationales, à périodicité variable)
Organisateurs: Instituto de Ingniería, UNAM
Comisión de Nuevos Métodos de Enseñanza, UNAM
Lieu: Cité Universitaire de Mexico
Participants: Chercheurs. Universitaires. Public intéressé par l'enseignement programmé
Objet: Faire connaître l'enseignement programmé et ses applications

COURS ANNUEL D'ENSEIGNEMENT PROGRAMME
Organisateur: Oficina de Capacitación y Adiestramiento de la Comisión Federal de Electricidad
Lieu: Mexico
Participants: Responsables de la promotion ouvrière
Objet: Information sur l'enseignement programmé. Conseils pour l'utilisation de cette méthode

CYCLE DE CONFERENCES SUR L'ENSEIGNEMENT PROGRAMME (Manifestation nationale)
Organisateur: Comisión de Operación y Fomento de Actividades Académicas del Instituto Politécnico Nacional
Lieu et date: Mexico, juin 1968
Participants: Directeurs d'établissements d'enseignement moyen et supérieur
Objet: Information sur l'enseignement programmé et son utilité dans l'enseignement; formation.

SEMINAIRE INTERNATIONAL SUR LES NOUVELLES METHODES ET TECHNIQUES PEDAGOGIQUES (Manifestation internationale)
Organisateur: Comisión de Operación y Fomento de Actividades Académicas del Instituto Politécnico Nacional
Lieu et date: Mexico, août 1970
Participants: Chercheurs. Professeurs de l'enseignement général, professionnel et supérieur. Directeurs d'établissements d'enseignement moyen et supérieur
Objet: Vulgarisation de la technologie de l'enseignement en général et de l'enseignement programmé en particulier

SERIE DE CONFERENCES SUR LES AUXILIAIRES PEDAGOGIQUES ET PLUS PARTICULIEREMENT SUR L'ENSEIGNEMENT PROGRAMME (Manifestation nationale
Organisateur: Centro de Didáctica, Dirección General del Profesorado, UNAM
Lieu et date: Cité Universitaire de Mexico, août 1969
Participants: Chercheurs. Universitaires
Objet: Perfectionnement des enseignants universitaires

7 - TRAINING ORGANIZATIONS / ORGANISMES ASSURANT UNE FORMATION

BANCO NACIONAL DE MÉXICO, S.A.
Fray Servando Teresa de Mier, 174, México 1, D.F.
Nature de l'organisme: Privé

INSTRUCCIÓN PROGRAMADA DE MÉXICO, S.A.
Bolívar 202-A, México 1, D.F.
Nature de l'organisme: Société privée d'édition et de formation professionnelle
Public intéressé: Professeurs de l'enseignement général, professionnel et supérieur. Responsables de l'éducation des adultes. Membres de la société, et autres personnes sur demande

OFICINA DE CAPACITACIÓN Y ADIESTRAMIENTO DE LA COMISIÓN FEDERAL DE ELECTRICIDAD
Río Elba 22, México 5, D.F.
Nature de l'organisme: Privé
Public intéressé: Personnel de l'entreprise ayant reçu une instruction
                  limitée

II - PUBLICATIONS

2 - ARTICLES

BALABANIAN, N.   La enseñanza programada. Juin 1970, 60 p.
                 Vulgarisation

COMISIÓN DE NUEVOS MÉTODOS DE LA ENSEÑANZA.   Instrucción programada.
                 Mai 1969, 20 p.
                 Rapport d'expérience

ENRIQUEZ CHAVEZ, X.   "La instrucción programada. Nueva dimensión
                 de la enseñanza", in Nuestro Sistema Bancomer, vol.24,
                 No.229, 3 p.
                 Vulgarisation

FUENTES GONZALEZ, B.   "Posibilidades de aplicación de la enseñanza
                 programada en la capacitación para el trabajo industrial",
                 in El Maestro, (Secretaría de Educación Pública). Octobre
                 1969, No.6, 13 p.
                 Vulgarisation

3 - BIBLIOGRAPHIES

CENTRO NACIONAL DE DOCUMENTACIÓN E INFORMACIÓN EDUCATIVA (Instituto
Nacional de Investigación Educativa). Bibliografía sobre enseñanza
programada y máquinas de enseñar. México, juillet 1970 (ronéotypé,
non diffusé).

COMISIÓN DE NUEVOS MÉTODOS DE ENSEÑANZA, UNAM. "Instrucción programada
teórica e instrucción programada aplicada". (A paraître in Boletín de
la Comisión.)

GARCÍA GONZALEZ, E.   Bibliografía sobre instrucción programada proporcionada
al centro de didáctica de la dirección general del profesorado (UNAM).

4 - AUDIO-VISUAL PRODUCTIONS / PRODUCTIONS AUDIO-VISUELLES

¿QUÉ ES LA ENSEÑANZA PROGRAMADA?   20 minutes, couleur.
Banco Nacional de México, S.A.

III - RESEARCH AND APPLICATIONS / REALISATIONS

1 - RESEARCH / RECHERCHES

Thème: ADAPTATION DE LA MACHINE GRUNDY TUTOR (détermination des temps
                 de réponse des élèves mexicains, établissement des
                 bases d'estimation des réponses correctes et apport
                 des modifications nécessaires pour l'emploi de
                 programmes linéaires et ramifiés)
Organisme: Instituto de Ingeniería, Facultad de Ingeniería, UNAM
Public intéressé: Etudiants

2 - PUBLISHED PROGRAMMED COURSES / COURS PROGRAMMES PUBLIES

ALCOCER CUARON, C. Introducción a la fisiología. México, Dirección
General de Publicaciones, UNAM, 1971. 10 chapitres,
971 items, 299 p.
Enseignement supérieur

CARDENAS, H.E. et al. Algebra. El anillo de los números enteros. Vol.1,
México, Dirección General de Publicaciones, UNAM, 1971.
12 chapitres, 150 items, 55 p.
Enseignement supérieur

—————; et al. Algebra. El campo de los números racionales. Vol.2,
México, Dirección General de Publicaciones, UNAM, 1971.
9 chapitres, 129 items, 62 p.
Enseignement supérieur

—————; et al. Algebra. El campo de los números reales. Vol.3,
México, Dirección General de Publicaciones, UNAM, 1971.
9 chapitres, 118 items, 61 p.
Enseignement supérieur

CASTANEIRA; URYGUEN, S. La unidad de cheques. México, Banco Nacional de
México, S.A., juillet 1970, 7 items, 443 p.
Grand public

COMISIÓN FEDERAL DE ELECTRICIDAD. Curso programado de aritmética elemental.
México, Comisión Federal de Electricidad (Oficialía Mayor),
juin 1970, 9 items.
Niveau primaire

ENRIQUEZ CHÁVEZ, J.; ZELAYORAN, F. Crédito. México, Banco de Comercio, S.A.,
juillet 1969. 14 fascicules, 50 items par fascicule, 490 p.
Personnel de la banque

FERNANDEZ ARENA, J.A. Introducción a la administración de empresas. México
Dirección General de Publicaciones, UNAM, avril 1970, 280 p.
10 chapitres, 1005 items
Niveau universitaire et pré-universitaire

GRAJALES PEREIRA, S.; SHAND, N.O. Nuestro contabilidad. México, Banco
Nacional de México, S.A., novembre 1970
Personnel de la banque et grand public

GUZMÁN TOVAR, C. El pago del cheque. México, Banco Nacional de México, S.A.,
septembre 1970, 5 items, 300 p.
Personnel de la banque

—————; LOS RÍOS PLANNEL, G. de. El ahorro México, Banco Nacional de
México, S.A., avril 1970, 331 p., 4 items
Grand public

INSTITUTO NACIONAL DE INVESTIGACIÓN EDUCATIVA. Mi cuaderno de actividades.
Enseñanza programada para el resfuerzo del aprendizaje de la
lectura y escritura. México, Secretaría de Educación Pública,
1969, 229 p.
Niveau primaire

LOS RÍOS PLANNEL, G. de. La unidad de ahorros. México, Banco Nacional de
México, S.A., août 1970, 6 items, 340 p.
Personnel de la banque

MATEOS, J.L. Química orgánica. México, Dirección General de Publicaciones,
UNAM, avril 1970, 15 items
Niveau universitaire et pré-universitaire

NÁJERA MAGAÑA, R.; GODINEZ BARRERA, G. Curso dinámico de ortografía.
México, Instrucción programada de México, S.A., 1968.
235 items, 95 p.
Niveau de la 4ème année d'enseignement primaire

OCTAVIO, A.; RASCÓN, Ch. Introducción a la estadística descriptiva.
México, Dirección General de Publicaciones, UNAM, avril 1970,
vol.10, 241 p. 6 items
Niveau universitaire et pré-universitaire

RASCÓN, Ch.; OCTAVIO, A. Introducción a la teoría de probabilidades. México
Dirección General de Publicaciones, UNAM, 1971. 9 chapitres,
940 items, 433 p.
Enseignement supérieur

SALAZAR RESINES, J. Introducción a la lógica deductiva y teoría de los
conjuntos. Vol.1, México, Dirección General de Publicaciones,
UNAM, 1970. 6 chapitres, 1027 items, 376 p.
Enseignement supérieur

——————. Introducción a la lógica deductiva y teoría de los conjuntos.
Vol.2, México, Dirección General de Publicaciones, UNAM, 1970.
3 chapitres, 662 items, 239 p.
Enseignement supérieur

SHAND, O.N. El cheque. México, Banco Nacional de México, avril, 1968,
286 p. 5 items
Niveau universitaire. Grand public

——————. El pagaré. México, Banco Nacional de México, S.A., novembre
1970. 7 items, 250 p.
Grand public

VIRAMONTES PAREDES, F.; SHAND, O.N. Contabilidad I. México, Banco Nacional
de México, S.A., septembre 1970, 502 p. 12 items.
Niveau universitaire. Grand public

NETHERLANDS/PAYS-BAS

I - ORGANIZATIONS AND ACTIVITIES / STRUCTURES ET ACTIVITES

1 - CENTRES *

DIDACTISCH INSTITUUT
Universiteits Centrum De Uithof, Budapestlaan, Utrecht
Nature of organization: University

* - Every university now has its own Centre for research of tertiary
education, usually called "Centre for Research of University Teaching".

INSTITUTE OF EDUCATION
Westerhaven 16, Groningen
Nature of organization: University

INSTITUTE OF EDUCATION
Prinsengracht 225, Amsterdam
Nature of organization: University

INSTITUTE OF EDUCATION, DEPARTMENT OF EDUCATIONAL TECHNOLOGY
Kern-fysisch Versneller Instituut Bleekerstraat 5A, Groningen
Nature of organization: University

NEDERLANDS INSTITUUT VOOR COGNITIE ONDERZOEK
8 Weesperplein, Amsterdam
Nature of organization: University

2 - ACTIVITIES / MANIFESTATIONS

RESEARCH AND SIGNIFICANCE OF PROGRAMMED INSTRUCTION
Organized by: Werkgemeenschap voor Vernieuwing van Opvoeding en Onderwijs (New Education Fellowship)
Place and date: Amersfoort, June 1968
Participants: Research workers. School and university teachers. Adult educators
Proceedings: Muusses, Purmerend

TEACHERS' COURSE (Regional annual conference)
Organized by: Institute of Education
Place and date: Groningen University
Participants: School teachers
Purpose: To learn programming

3 - PUBLISHERS / MAISONS D'EDITION

MUUSSES N.V.
Purmerend
Nature of organization: Commercial publisher

N.V. ICU, INFORMATIE EN COMMUNICATIE UNIE (SAMSON LEERSYSTEMEN N.V., SAMSON UITGEVERIJ, N.V., subsidiary houses)
Nature of organization: Commercial publisher

UNIVERSITAIRE PERS
Rotterdam
Nature of organization: Associated with a university

WOLTERS-NOORDHOFF N.V.
Oude Boteringestraat 22, Groningen
Nature of organization: Commercial publisher

4 - PERIODICALS / PERIODIQUES

ONDERWIJS EN MEDIA
Publisher: Muusses / Samsom
Address: Purmerend
Periodicity: Bi-monthly
Fields of interest: Research. Application. Topical events

6 - MANUFACTURERS OF TEACHING MACHINES / FABRICANTS DE MACHINES A ENSEIGNER

N.V. PHILIPS GLOEILAMPENFABRIEKEN and HIG-ELA
Eindhoven
Types of machines: Educational products and systems
Characteristics: Language laboratories, etc. Closed-circuit television systems; electronics trainer systems; practical electronics learning system; educational films and slide sets; programmed individual presentation system (PIP)

7 - TRAINING ORGANIZATIONS / ORGANISMES ASSURANT UNE FORMATION

LERAARSOPLEIDING (Teacher training institute, University of Amsterdam)
(Section: Educational technology and applied educational sciences)
Prinsengracht 225, Amsterdam
Nature of organization: University
Public concerned: University teachers and future educational technologists

II - PUBLICATIONS

1 - BOOKS/LIVRES

DE BLOCK, A.   Geprogrameerde Instructie. Antwerpen, Standaard Wetenschappelijk Uitgeverij, 1968, 203 p.
History. Principles. Programmes. Educational evaluation. Applications.

BUNG, K.   Towards a theory of programmed language instruction. Mouton, The Hague, n.d.

BUTER, E.M.   Didactiek van de biologie (1971). (ISBN 90 231 7027 5). Concerning special methods for teaching biology

———.   Onderwijstechnologie 1, 2 en 3. Part 1 (ISBN 90 14 01534 8), Alphen aan den Rijn, Samsom, 1971, 110 p. Part 2, 1972. Theory and practice of structuring and managing teaching situations.

——— et al.   Overmethodes en technische middelen in het onderwijs (On methods and technical means in teaching). University of Amsterdam, 1970.

2 - ARTICLES

BUTER, E.M.   "Een sandwichmodel als basis voor de opbouw van onderwijzende systemen" (a sandwich model as a base for building teaching systems), in Paedagogische Studiën, 1969

3 - BIBLIOGRAPHIES

Bibliografie, samengesteld ter gelegenheid van het Nationaal Symposium Geprogrameerde Instructie 1968, Werkgemeenschap voor Vernieuwing van Opvoeding en Onderwijs en de Vereniging voor Geprogrameerde Instructie

III - RESEARCH AND APPLICATIONS / REALISATIONS

  2 - PUBLISHED PROGRAMMED COURSES / COURS PROGRAMMES PUBLIES

   BOLAND, R.G.A.; HALL, D.; BLOM, F.W.C. <u>Stap voor stap door de jaarrekening.</u>
              Alphen aan den Rijn, Samsom, 1972.
              Financial company reports. Secondary level

   HUIJSMANS, F.J.M. <u>Verkenning in planning voor de gemeentelijke overheid. 1.</u>
              Alphen aan den Rijn, Samsom, 1970.
              An introduction to planning techniques for local
              officials. Secondary level

   VROLIJK, A.; DIJKEMA, M.F.; TIMMERMAN, G. <u>Gespreksmodellen.</u> Alphen aan
              den Rijn, Samsom, 1971.
              Programmes on seven types of interview. University level

NORWAY/NORVEGE

I - ORGANIZATIONS AND ACTIVITIES / STRUCTURES ET ACTIVITES

  1 - CENTRES

   EUROPEAN HOME STUDY COUNCIL
   NKI-skolen, Prof. Dahls gt 18, Oslo

   INSTITUTE FOR EDUCATIONAL RESEARCH, UNIVERSITY OF OSLO
   P.O.Box 1092, Blindern, Oslo 3
   Nature of organization: University

   INSTITUTE FOR PROGRAMMED LEARNING
   Industrigt 41, Oslo 3
   Nature of organization: Business

   THE NATIONAL COUNCIL FOR INNOVATION IN EDUCATION
   Sandakerveien 56, Oslo-Dep., Oslo 1
   Nature of organization: Governmental

  4 - PERIODICALS / PERIODIQUES

   EPISTOLODIDAKTIKA
   Publisher: European Home Study Council
   Address: NKI-skolen, Prof. Dahls gt 18, Oslo
   Periodicity: Bi-annual
   Field of interest: Education by correspondence

  6 - MANUFACTURERS OF TEACHING MACHINES/FABRICANTS DE MACHINES A ENSEIGNER

   ARNFINN JOHANSEN
   Forsöksrådet for Skoleverket, Oslo - Dep., Oslo 1
   Type of machine: For linear programmes
   Characteristics: Linear programme. Integrated audio-visual device.
                       Individual use.
   Purpose: Teaching

7 - TRAINING ORGANIZATIONS/ORGANISMES ASSURANT UNE FORMATION

INSTITUTE FOR EDUCATIONAL RESEARCH, UNIVERSITY OF OSLO
P.O. Box 1092, Blindern, Oslo 3
Nature of organization: University
Public concerned: School teachers. Research workers.

III - RESEARCH AND APPLICATIONS / REALISATIONS

1 - RESEARCH / RECHERCHES

Themes: (a) To test material for self instruction in mathematics
(b) To develop suitable methods to use with this material
Organized by: The National Council for Innovation in Education,
Sandakerveien 56, Oslo-Dep., Oslo 1

2 - PUBLISHED PROGRAMMED COURSES / COURS PROGRAMMES PUBLIES

ENGELAND, Øystein. Area Calculations. Oslo, National Council for Innovation in Education, n.d.
Secondary education.

GJERMSTAD, Sudun. Commercial Arithmetic. Oslo, National Council for Innovation in Education, n.d.
Secondary education.

HYLEN, Brage. Power. Oslo, National Council for Innovation in Education, 1969.
Secondary education.

KRISTOFFERSEN, Helge W. Equations. Oslo, National Council for Innovation in Education, 1969.

ØREBERG, Curt; HASTAD, Matts.; SVENSSON, Leif. Individual Mathematics' Instruction. Oslo, National Council for Innovation in Education, in co-operation with the National Board of Education in Sweden, 1968.
Primary education.

SUNDE, Rolf. Percent Calculations. Oslo, National Council for Innovation in Education, 1969.
Secondary education.

THORNES, Jan. Mathematics. Oslo, National Council for Innovation in Education 1969.

WESTBYE, Øivind. Power. Oslo, National Council for Innovation in Education, 1969.
Secondary education.

PERU/PEROU

I - ORGANIZATIONS AND ACTIVITIES / STRUCTURES ET ACTIVITES

1 - CENTRES

PONTIFICIA UNIVERSIDAD CATÓLICA DEL PERÚ, Programa Académico de Educación, Centro Peruano de Pedagogía Cibernética
Lima
Nature de l'organisme: Université

SENATI
Apartado 3638, Lima
Nature de l'organisme: Fondation indépendante

UNIVERSIDAD NACIONAL DE TRUJILLO, Departamento de Ciencias de
la Educación, Sección de Instrucción Programada
Trujillo
Nature de l'organisme: Université

2 - ACTIVITIES / MANIFESTATIONS

CONFERENCE ANNUELLE A L'ECHELON NATIONAL
Organisateur: Universidad Nacional de Trujillo, Departamento de
Ciencias de la Educación, Sección de Instrucción
Programada
Lieu et date: Trujillo, novembre 1968
Participants: Chercheurs. Enseignants scolaires. Adultes. Maîtres
de l'enseignement professionnel
Objet: Information du public
Actes publiés par: Revista Peruana de Instrucción Programada, No.2, UNT,
Sección de Instrucción Programada, Trujillo

CONFERENCE INTERNATIONALE ANNUELLE
Organisateur: Universidad Nacional de Trujillo
Lieu et date: Trujillo, février 1970
Participants: Chercheurs. Enseignants scolaires. Adultes. Spécialistes
Objet: Information du public

4 - PERIODICALS / PERIODIQUES

REVISTA DE PEDAGOGÍA CIBERNÉTICA E INSTRUCCIÓN PROGRAMADA
Editeur: Universidad Nacional de Trujillo, Departamento de
Ciencias de la Educación, Sección de Instrucción Programada
Adresse: Trujillo
Périodicité: Semestriel
Centres d'intérêt: Recherche et réalisations dans le domaine de l'enseignement
programmé

5 - PROFESSIONAL ORGANIZATIONS / ORGANISATIONS PROFESSIONNELLES

ASOCIACIÓN LATINOAMERICANA DE PEDAGOGÍA CIBERNÉTICA E INSTRUCCIÓN PROGRAMADA
Sección de Instrucción Programada, Universidad Nacional de Trujillo
Activité: Susciter l'intérêt du public à l'égard de
l'enseignement programmé

7 - TRAINING ORGANIZATIONS / ORGANISMES ASSURANT UNE FORMATION

PONTIFICIA UNIVERSIDAD CATÓLICA DEL PERÚ, Programa Académico de
Educación, Centro Peruano de Pedagogía Cibernética
Lima
Nature de l'organisme: Université
Public intéressé: Enseignants universitaires. Spécialistes

UNIVERSIDAD NACIONAL DE TRUJILLO, Departamento de Ciencias de la
Educación, Sección de Instrucción Programada
Trujillo
Nature de l'organisme: Université
Public intéressé: Enseignants universitaires. Spécialistes

8 - DOCUMENTATION CENTRES /CENTRES DE DOCUMENTATION

UNIVERSIDAD NACIONAL DE TRUJILLO, Programa de Ciencias de la
Educación, Sección de Instrucción Programada
Trujillo
Nature de l'organisme: Université
Nature des services: Informations bibliographiques

II - PUBLICATIONS

1 - BOOKS/LIVRES

SACO DE CUETO, R.M. La Enseñanza Programada. Lima, Pontificia
Universidad Católica del Perú, septembre 1969, 95 p.

ZIERER, E.   Elementos de pedagogía cibernética para la didáctica
de los idiomas extranjeros. Trujillo, Universidad Nacional de Trujillo,
octobre 1970, 157 p.

3 - BIBLIOGRAPHIES

ZIERER, E. Bibliografía selecta (in Elementos de pedagogía cibernética
para la didáctica de los idiomas extranjeros). Trujillo, Universidad
Nacional de Trujillo, octobre 1970

III - RESEARCH AND APPLICATIONS / REALISATIONS

2 - PUBLISHED PROGRAMMED COURSES / COURS PROGRAMMES PUBLIES

ALIPIO, Francisco Vereau. Bonificaciones que otorga la Ley 15215 a
los docentes. Trujillo, Universidad Nacional de Trujillo, novembre 1968,
38 items.
Formation professionnelle

CRIBILLEROS, Domingo A. Benites. Auto-aprendizaje simultáneo de la
lectura y la escritura, I y II. Trujillo, Universidad Nacional de
Trujillo, février 1970. I - 204 items, II - 50 items.
Education des adultes

POLAND/POLOGNE

I - ORGANIZATIONS AND ACTIVITIES / STRUCTURES ET ACTIVITES

1 - CENTRES

CENTRE INTERUNIVERSITAIRE DE RECHERCHES SUR L'ENSEIGNEMENT SUPERIEUR
rue Nowy Świat 69, Varsovie

ECOLE NORMALE SUPERIEURE
rue Smoluchowskiego 10, Cracovie
Nature de l'organisme: Universitaire

INSTITUT NATIONAL DE RECHERCHES PEDAGOGIQUES
ul. Górczewska 8, Varsovie

UNIVERSITE DE VARSOVIE
rue Krakowskie - Przedmieście 26/28, Varsovie
Nature de l'organisme: Universitaire

2 - ACTIVITIES/MANIFESTATIONS

COLLOQUE SUR LA BASE PSYCHOLOGIQUE DE L'ENSEIGNEMENT PROGRAMME
(Manifestation nationale, annuelle)
Organisateurs: Ministère de l'éducation et de l'enseignement supérieur.
                       Ecole normale supérieure de Cracovie.
Lieu et date: Cracovie, décember 1969
Participants: Chercheurs. Enseignants scolaires
Actes publiés par: Revue Dydaktyka Szkoły Wyższej, No.3(11), 1970

COLLOQUE SUR LES METHODES POUR PROGRAMMER DES TEXTES DIDACTIQUES (Manifestation nationale, annuelle)
Organisateurs: Ministère de l'éducation et de l'enseignement supérieur.
                       Ecole supérieure polytechnique.
Lieu et date: Płock, juin 1968
Participants: Chercheurs. Enseignants scolaires
Actes publiés par: Życie Szkoły Wyższej, 1968-1969 et par Dydaktyka Szkoły
                       Wyższej 1969. Compte rendu de Januszkiewicz

SEMINAIRE (Etudes sanctionnées par un diplôme) (Manifestation régionale
                                                                hebdomadaire)
Organisateur: Université de Varsovie
Lieu et date: Institut national de recherches pédagogiques, Université
                       de Varsovie (une fois par semaine)
Participants: Chercheurs
Objet: Efficacité de divers types de l'enseignement programmé.
                       Les méthodes de programmation.

SEMINAIRE SUR L'ENSEIGNEMENT PROGRAMME
Organisateur: Université de Varsovie
Lieu et date: Institut national de recherches pédagogiques, Université
                       de Varsovie (une fois par mois)
Participants: Chercheurs. Enseignants scolaires
Objet: Analyse des manuels utilisés dans les écoles. L'efficacité
                       de l'enseignement programmé dans les divers degrés de
                       l'enseignement.

3 - PUBLISHERS / MAISONS D'EDITION

PAŃSTWOWE WYDAWNICTWA SZKOLNICTWA ZAWODOWEGO
rue Pankiezicza 3, Varsovie
Nature: Editions scolaires (écoles professionnelles)

PAŃSTWOWE WYDAWNICTWO NAUKOWE
Miodowa 10, Varsovie
Nature: Editions scientifiques

PAŃSTWOWE ZAKŁADY WYDAWNICTW SZKOLNYCH
Place Dabrowskiego 8, Varsovie
Nature: Editions scolaires

4 - PERIODICALS/PERIODIQUES

DYDAKTYKA SZKOŁY WYŻSZEJ (DIDACTIQUE DE L'ECOLE SUPERIEURE)
Editeurs: Ministère de l'éducation et de l'enseignement supérieur.
                     Centre interuniversitaire de recherches sur l'enseignement supér
Adresse: Rue Nowy Świat 69, Varsovie
Périodicité: Trimestriel
Centres
  d'intérêt: Recherche. Applications. Actualités.

KWARTALNIK PEDAGOGICZNY (REVUE TRIMESTRIELLE PEDAGOGIQUE)
Editeur: Państowe Wydawnictwo Naukowe (PWN) - Editions Scientifiques
                     de Pologne
Adresse: ul. Krak. Przedmieście 26/28, Varsovie
Périodicité: Trimestriel
Centres
  d'intérêt: Recherche. Applications. Actualités.

NOWA SZKOŁA (ECOLE NOUVELLE)
Editeur: Państowe Zakłady Wydawnictw Szkolnych
Adresse: Rue Chocimska 28, Varsovie
Périodicité: Mensuel
Centres
  d'intérêt: Recherche. Applications. Actualités.

PRZEGLĄD PEDAGOGICZNY (REVUE PEDAGOGIQUE)
Editeur: Institut national de recherches pédagogiques
Adresse: Rue Górczewska 8, Varsovie
Périodicité: Trimestriel
Centres
  d'intérêt: Recherche. Applications. Actualités.

ŻYCIE SZKOŁY WYŻSZEJ (LA VIE DE L'ECOLE SUPERIEURE)
Adresse: ul. Nowy Świat 69, Varsovie
Périodicité: Mensuel

7 - TRAINING ORGANIZATIONS/ORGANISMES ASSURANT UNE FORMATION

COMITE DU CONSEIL GENERAL POUR LE DEVELOPPEMENT DE LA DIDACTIQUE DES
ECOLES SUPERIEURES
Ministère de l'éducation et de l'enseignement supérieur,
Al. I Armii Wojska Polskiego 25, Varsovie
Nature de l'organisme: Gouvernemental et universitaire

INSTITUT NATIONAL DE RECHERCHES PEDAGOGIQUES
Rue Górczewska 8, Varsovie

8 - DOCUMENTATION CENTRES/CENTRES DE DOCUMENTATION

CENTRE INTERUNIVERSITAIRE DE RECHERCHES SUR L'ENSEIGNEMENT SUPERIEUR
Rue Nowy Świat 69, Varsovie
Nature des services: Publications portant sur l'enseignement programmé,
                       le contrôle des connaissances acquises par cette
                       méthode et l'utilisation des textes programmés dans
                       l'enseignement des travailleurs.

Poland/Pologne

INSTITUT NATIONAL DE RECHERCHES PEDAGOGIQUES
Rue Górczewska 8, Varsovie
Nature des services: Elaboration de textes programmés en diverses matières, et recherches sur l'efficacité de l'enseignement programmé.

II - PUBLICATIONS

1 - BOOKS/LIVRES

BEREZOWSKI, E. Maszyny dydaktyczne (Machines à enseigner). Varsovie, Państwowe Zakłady Wydawnictw Szkolnych, 1969, 247 p.

_____. DŁUGOSZOWA, J. Techniczne środki nauczania/Wzrokowe i słuchowe. Varsovie, Państwowe Zakłady Wydawnictw Szkolnych, 1972, 320 p.

BUDOHOSKA, W.; WŁODARSKI, Z. Psychologia uczenia się. Przegląd badań eksperymentalnych i teorii (Psychologie de l'apprentissage). Varsovie, PWN, 1970, 388 p.

DENEK, K. Efektywność nauczania programowanego w szkole wyższej (Efficacité de l'enseignement programmé dans l'enseignement supérieur). Poznań, Wydawnictwa Uniwersytetu im. A. Mickiewicza, 1971, 163 p.

FLEMMING, E. Programowanie w procesie nauczania (La programmation dans le processus de l'enseignement). Varsovie, Nasza Księgarnia, 1967, 181 p.

_____. JACOBY, J. Środki audiowizualne w dydaktyce szkoły wyższej (Les auxiliaires pédagogiques audio-visuels dans l'enseignement supérieur). Varsovie, PWN, 1969, 269 p.

JANUSZKIEWICZ, F.(ed.) Telewizja dydaktyczna - Telewizja w obwodzie zamkniętym w dydaktyce szkoły wyższej (La télévision pédagogique. La télévision en circuit fermé dans l'enseignement supérieur). Varsovie, 1970, PWN, 267p.

KRUSZEWSKI, K. Nauczanie programowane w systemie dydaktycznym (Enseignement programmé et pédagogique). Varsovie, Państwowe Wydawnictwo Naukowe, 1972.

KUPISIEWICZ, Cz. Nauczanie programowane (L'enseignement programmé). 2e éd. Varsovie, Państwowe Zakłady Wydawnictw Szkolnych, 1970, 250 p.
Etude générale.

_____. Niepowodzenia dydaktyczne (Les insuccès scolaires). Varsovie, Państwowe Wydawnictwo Naukowe, 1969, 424 p.

_____. et al. Metody i przykłady programowania dydaktycznego (L'enseignement programmé: méthodes et exemples). Varsovie, Państwowe Wydawnictwo Naukowe, 1970, 510 p.

_____. et al. Nauczanie programowane w praktyce szkoły podstawowej (L'enseignement programmé à l'école primaire). Varsovie, Państwowe Zakłady Wydawnictw Szkolnych, 1971, 280 p.

LEI, L. (ed.) Film skuteczną pomocą dydaktyczną (Utilité du film en tant que moyen pédagogique). Varsovie, PWN, 1970, 242 p.

OKOŃ, W. Elementy dydaktyki szkoły wyższej (Eléments de pédagogie dans l'enseignement supérieur). Varsovie, PWN, 1971, 359 p.

Planowanie i prognozowanie szkolnictwa wyższego w NRD i PRL, Wyd. Międzyuczelniane Zakładu Badań nad Szkolnictwem Wyższym (La planification et les pronostics dans l'enseignement supérieur en République démocratique allemande et en République populaire de Pologne). Varsovie, PWN, 1970.

SADAJ, B. Problemy kształcenia zawodowego młodzieży w toku studiów wyższych (Problèmes de la formation professionnelle de la jeunesse au cours des études supérieures). Varsovie, PWN, 1970, 144 p.

2 - ARTICLES

BEREZOWSKI, E. "Adaptacyjny system kontroli programowanej" (Système d'adaptation du contrôle programmé), in Dydaktyka Szkoły Wyższej, No.3, 1970

————. "Bezmaszynowy system kontroli programowanej - BSK" (Le système de contrôle programmé BSK sans machines), in Dydaktyka Szkoły Wyższej, No.1-2, 197

————. "Z zagadnień teorii maszyn egzaminacyjnych" (Problèmes liés à la théorie des machines à examiner), in Dydaktyka Szkoły Wyższej, No.1, 1970

DENEK, K. "Efektywność dydaktyczna nauczania programowanego w ksztalceniu dorosłych" (Efficacité pédagogique de l'enseignement programmé dans l'enseignement des adultes), in Kwartalnik Pedagogiczny, No.2, 1971

————. "Ustalenie efektywności nauczania programowanego w drodze eksperymentu (Evaluation expérimentale de l'efficacité de l'enseignement programmé), in Dydaktyka Szkoły Wyższej, No.3, 1971

———— ; KUŹNIAK, I. "Przydatność metod statystycznych w eksperymencie pedagogicznym i w określaniu efektywności kształcenia" (Utilité pratique des méthodes statistiques pour l'expérimentation pédagogique et l'évaluation de l'efficacité de l'enseignement), in Dydaktyka Szkoły Wyższej, No.1-2 (9-10), 1970

GÓRSKA, J. "O metodzie tworzenia tekstów programowanych z matematyki" (Méthode de rédaction des textes programmés de mathématiques), in Biuletyn Pedagogiczny, No.4 (37), 1968, p.47-60

———— ; KUPISIEZICZ, Cz. "Wprowadzenie de programowanego nauczania matematyki (Introduction à l'enseignement programmé des mathématiques), in Wybrane Zagadnień z Metodyki Nauczania Matematyki. Varsovie, PZWS, 1971, p.159-189

HAMAN, J. "Modernizacja dydaktyki a ranga metodyki" (Modernisation de la pédagogie et rôle de la méthodologie), in Dydaktyka Szkoły Wyższej, No.3 (11), 1970

HOJCZAK, Z. "Programowanie nauczania początków języka angielskiego" (Programmation de l'enseignement de l'anglais pour les débutants), in Dydaktyka Szkoły Wyższej, No.4 (16), 1971

KIETLINSKA, Z. "Kształcenie pedagogiczne kadry naukowodydaktycznej" (Formation pédagogique des chercheurs et des enseignants de l'enseignement supérieur), in Dydaktyka Szkoły Wyższej, No.1 (13), 1971

KOSZEWSKA, B. "Dotychczasowe prace nad programowanymi tekstami z zakresu biologii" (Travaux sur la programmation des textes de biologie), in Biuletyn Pedagogiczny, No.4, 1968, p.3-47

————. "Próba programowanego nauczania biologii" (Essai de programmation de l'enseignement de la biologie), in Nowa Szkoła, No.3, 1969, p.32-34

————— ; KUPISIEWICZ, Cz. "Programowane nauczanie biologii" (Programmation de l'enseignement de la biologie), in Biologia w Szkole, No.5, 1968, p.11-19

KOWALIK, J. "Programowany podręcznik ortografii" (Le manuel programmé d'orthographe), in Przegląd Pedagogiczny (Biuletyn Instytutu Pedagogiki), No.4, 1971, p.72-83

KRAJEWSKI, T. "Modernizacja metod nauczania w szkole wyższej i rola środków audiowizualnych" (Modernisation des méthodes pédagogiques et rôle des moyens audio-visuels dans l'enseignement supérieur), in Dydaktyka Szkoły Wyższej, No.3 (11),1970

KRUSZEWSKI, K. "Definicja i wtórne problemy nauczania programowanego" (L'enseignement programmé: définition et problèmes), in Dydaktyka Szkoły Wyższej, No.1, 1971

—————. "Nauczanie programowane w zespole metod nauczania" (Enseignement programmé et méthodes pédagogiques), in Kwartalnik Pedagogiczny, No.3, 1971

KUPISIEWICZ, Cz. "Aktualne problemy nauczania programowanego" (Problèmes actuels de l'enseignement programmé), in Dydaktyka Szkoły Wyższej, No.3, 1970

—————. "Metody programowania" (Les méthodes de programmation), in Dydaktyka Szkoły Wyższej, No.1, 1968

—————. "Nowe tendencje i kierunki badań w nauczaniu programowanym" (Nouvelles tendances des recherches sur l'enseignement programmé), in Nowa Szkoła, 1968. Synthèse
—————. "Zasady programowania" (Principes de programmation), in Kwartalnik Pedagogiczny, No.1, 1968

————— ; TUKALSKI, A. "Recherche de nouvelles conceptions de l'enseignement programmé", in Revue internationale de pédagogie, vol.XV, No.4, 1969

LANDA, Lew N. "Niektóre zagadnienia teoretyczne nauczania programowanego" (Quelques problèmes théoriques de l'enseignement programmé), in Dydaktyka Szkoły Wyższej, No.3 (11), 1970

LUBOWICZ, A. "Próba laczenia nauczania programowanego i konwencjonalnego" (Essai d'association de l'enseignement programmé et de l'enseignement conventionnel), in Dydaktyka Szkoły Wyższej, No.3 (11), 1970

MATULKA, Z. "Próba analizy treści podręczników (Essai d'analyse du contenu des manuels), in Nowa Szkoła, No.5, 1969, p.31-35

—————. "Tekst programowany blokowy ze składni języka polskiego" (Texte du programme global de syntaxe polonaise), in Przegląd Pedagogiczny (Biuletyn Instytutu Pedagogiki), No.4, 1971, p.84-98

NOWACKI, T. "Przydatność nauczania programowanego w nauczaniu działania (Utilité pratique de l'enseignement programmé pour apprendre à agir), in Dydaktyka Szkoły Wyższej, No.3, 1970

OKON, W. "Młodzież akademicka a pracownicy naukowodydaktyczni" (Les étudiants, les chercheurs et les enseignants), in Dydaktyka Szkoły Wyższej, No.1-2 (9-10), 1970

———. "Perspektywy kształcenia pedagogicznego pracowników naukowo-dydaktycznych" (Perspectives de la formation pédagogique des chercheurs et des enseignants), in Dydaktyka Szkoły Wyższej, No.1 (13), 1971

STYPUŁKOWSKA-CHOJECKA, M. "Nauczanie gramatyki języka polskiego za pomocą tekstów programowanych w klasie V szkoły podstawowej" (Enseignement de la grammaire polonaise par les textes programmés en classe V de l'école primaire, in Przegląd Pedagogiczny (Biuletyn Instytutu Pedagogiki), No.4, 1971, p.108-9

TOMASZEWSKI, T. "Psychologiczne aspekty nauczania programowanego" (Aspects psychologiques de l'enseignement programmé), in Dydaktyka Szkoły Wyższej, No. (11), 1970

TUKALSKI, A. "Program blokowy matematyki w samodzielnej pracy uczniów czwartyc klas licealnych" (Le programme global de mathématiques dans le travail individue des élèves des classes terminales), in Przegląd Pedagogiczny, No.4, 1971, p.109-114

———. "Programowane nauczanie algebry" (Programmation de l'enseignement de l'algèbre), in Nowa Szkoła, No.3, 1969

———. "Znaczenie tekstów programowanych z matematyki w samodzielnej pracy uczniów (Le rôle des textes programmés de mathématiques dans le travail individuel des élèves), in Kwartalnik Pedagogiczny, R.XVI, No.3, 1971, p.133-146

WISZNIEWICZ, M. "Programowane nauczanie geografii" (Programmation de l'enseignement de la géographie), Geografia w Szkole, No.2, 1968

———. "Z dóświadczeń programowanego nauczania geografii (Expériences d'enseignement programmé de la géographie), in Nowa Szkoła, No.3, 1969

WOYTOWICZ-NEYMANN, M. "Samokształcenie kierowane. Wstępny etap nauczania programowanego języków obcych na studiach dla pracujących" (Autodidaxie dirigé Etape préliminaire de l'enseignement programmé dans les études des travailleur in Dydaktyka Szkoły Wyższej, No.4 (16), 1971

4 - AUDIO-VISUAL PRODUCTIONS/PRODUCTIONS AUDIO-VISUELLES PROGRAMMEES

L'ENSEIGNEMENT PROGRAMME. 16 mm. et 35 mm. noir et blanc.
Réalisateur: A. Szczygieł

III - RESEARCH AND APPLICATIONS/REALISATIONS

1 - RESEARCH/RECHERCHES

Les recherches ci-après, organisées par l'Université de Varsovie, ont porté sur l'efficacité de la transmission de connaissances scientifiques passives aux élèves, l'approfondissement de ces éléments et leur contrôle et leur classification par les élèves.

Thème: APPLICATION DES TEXTES PROGRAMMES A L'ENSEIGNEMENT INDIVIDUEL DE L'ORTHOGRAPHE

Thème: COMPREHENSION DE LA STRUCTURE DES PHRASES DANS LES TEXTES PROGRAMMES
Public intéressé: 415 élèves en 1re année d'études des lycées (adultes)

Thème:	MANUEL DE ZOOLOGIE ET PRINCIPES ET METHODES DE LA PROGRAMMATION PEDAGOGIQUE
Organisme:	Institut national de recherches pédagogiques, Varsovie
Public intéressé:	380 élèves en 7e année d'études primaires

Thème:	PROGRAMMATION DE L'ENSEIGNEMENT DES MATHEMATIQUES A L'UNIVERSITE DE VARSOVIE
Public intéressé:	600 étudiants

Thème:	PROGRAMMATION DES ACTIVITES COGNITIVES DES ELEVES DANS L'ENSEIGNEMENT DES MATHEMATIQUES: CHOIX ET PROGRESSION DES LEÇONS
Organisme:	Institut national de recherches pédagogiques, Varsovie
Public intéressé:	600 élèves en 8e et 10e années d'études

Thème:	PROGRAMME GLOBAL D'ENSEIGNEMENT DES MATHEMATIQUES
Organisme:	Institut national de recherches pédagogiques, Varsovie
Public intéressé:	243 élèves en 5e année d'études, 255 élèves en 7e année d'études, et 76 élèves des classes terminales

Thème:	PROGRAMME GLOBAL D'ENSEIGNEMENT PROPEDEUTIQUE
Public intéressé:	1200 élèves des petites classes de l'école primaire

Thème:	TEXTES PROGRAMMES DE CHIMIE
Public intéressé:	100 élèves en 9e année d'études des lycées

Thème:	TEXTES PROGRAMMES DE GRAMMAIRE ET D'ORTHOGRAPHE DANS LA LANGUE MATERNELLE
Public intéressé:	163 élèves en 5 et 6e années d'études primaires

Thème:	TEXTES PROGRAMMES DE MATHEMATIQUES
Organisme:	Institut national de recherches pédagogiques, Varsovie
Public intéressé:	712 élèves de lycée et étudiants

Thème:	TEXTES PROGRAMMES DE PHARMACOLOGIE GENERALE
Public intéressé:	40 élèves de l'Ecole d'obstétrique

Thème:	TEXTES PROGRAMMES DE PHYSIQUE ET D'ELECTROTECHNIQUE
Public intéressé:	545 élèves des écoles techniques et professionnelles de Varsovie

2 - PUBLISHED PROGRAMMED COURSES / COURS PROGRAMMES PUBLIES

KOSZEWSKA, B. <u>Programowane nauczanie biologii</u> (Enseignement programmé de la biologie).
Niveau secondaire

KUPISIEWICZ, Cz. <u>Ogólna charakterystyka nauczania programowanego</u> (Caractéristiques générales de l'enseignement programmé). 1969.
Niveau universitaire

——. <u>Wstęp do dydaktyki</u> (Introduction à la pédagogie).
Niveau universitaire
MATULKA, Z. <u>Programowane nauczanie gramatyki języka polskiego</u> (L'enseignement programmé de la grammaire de la langue maternelle).
Education des adultes

OKOŃ, W.; KUPISIEWICZ, Cz. Zarys dydaktyki ogólnej (Précis de pédagogie génér[ale])
Varsovie, Państwowe Zakłady Wydawnictw Szkolnych.
Niveau universitaire

PRZYJEMSKI, J. Kurs matematyki wyższej (Cours de mathématiques supérieures).
Niveau universitaire

TUKALSKI, A. Programowane nauczanie algebry (Enseignement programmé de l'algèb[re])
Niveau secondaire

WISZNIEWICZOWA, M. Programowane nauczanie geografii (Enseignement programmé de géographie).
Niveau primaire

3 - COMPUTER ASSISTED INSTRUCTION/ENSEIGNEMENT ASSISTE PAR ORDINATEUR

FIZYKA (PHYSIQUE)
Organisme: Ecole polytechnique silésienne de Gliwice - Centre expérimental des machines à enseigner de la Chaire d'électronique
Destinataires: Etudiants
Type de
  l'ordinateur: Machine de la série "Gamme"
Objet: Enseignement

UKŁADY ELEKTRONIKI (LES SYSTEMES D'ELECTRONIQUE)
Organisme: Ecole polytechnique silésienne de Gliwice - Centre expérimental des machines à enseigner de la Chaire d'électronique
Destinataires: Etudiants
Type de
  l'ordinateur: Machine électronique "Alfa"
Objet: Enseignement

ROMANIA/ROUMANIE

I - ORGANIZATIONS AND ACTIVITIES / STRUCTURES ET ACTIVITES

1 - CENTRES

INSTITUT DE RECHERCHES PEDAGOGIQUES
Sf. Apostoli 14, Bucarest 5
Nature de l'organisme: Gouvernemental

INSTITUT POLYTECHNIQUE
Str. 30 Decembrie 2, Timişoara
Nature de l'organisme: Universitaire

UNIVERSITE "BABEŞ-BOLYAI"
Str. M. Kogălniceanu 1, Cluj
Nature de l'organisme: Universitaire

2 - ACTIVITIES / MANIFESTATIONS

STAGE SUR LA FORMATION DES PROGRAMMEURS (Manifestation nationale)
Organisateur: Institut de recherches pédagogiques
Lieu et date: Bucarest, 22 mars - 3 avril 1969
Participants: Chercheurs. Enseignants scolaires et universitaires
Actes publiés par: Revista de pedagogie, 5, 1969

3 - PUBLISHERS / MAISONS D'EDITION

EDITURA DIDACTICĂ ŞI PEDAGOGICĂ
Str. Spiru Haret 12, Bucarest
Nature: Editions scolaires

4 - PERIODICALS / PERIODIQUES

REVISTA DE PEDAGOGIE
Editeur: Institut de recherches pédagogiques
Adresse: Sf. Apostoli 14, Bucarest 5
Périodicité: Mensuel
Centre d'intérêt: Réalisations pédagogiques

8 - DOCUMENTATION CENTRES / CENTRES DE DOCUMENTATION

CENTRE DE DOCUMENTATION PEDAGOGIQUE
Zalomit 12, Bucarest
Nature de l'organisme: Gouvernemental
Nature des services: Documentation. Bibliographies. Collection de
                       manuels et d'autre matériel programmé. Bibliothèque

II - PUBLICATIONS

1 - BOOKS / LIVRES

Creativitate, Modelare, Programare (Créativité, modèles, programmation). Travail collectif sous la direction de Al. Roşca. Editura Ştiinţifică, s.d.

Metode moderne de învăţămînt (Méthodes modernes d'enseignement). Bucarest, Universitatea populară, 1971.
Pédagogie cybernétique et technologie de l'enseignement programmé

RADULESCU, Şt.   Instruirea programată la limba română (L'enseignement programmé de la langue roumaine). Bucarest, Editura didactică şi pedagogică, 1971

Studii de pedagogie cibernetică şi instruire programată (Etude de la pédagogie cybernétique et de l'enseignement programmé). Travail collectif sous la direction de V. Bunescu. Bucarest, Editura didactică şi pedagogică, 1968, 208 p.
Compte rendu de recherches expérimentales organisées par l'Institut de recherches pédagogiques

2 - ARTICLES

MUNTEANU, G.   "Orientarea cercetaritor în domeniul instruirii programate în România" (L'orientation des recherches sur l'enseignement programmé en Roumanie), in <u>Revista de pedagogie</u>, No. 7-8, 1969.

NOVICICOV, E.   "Introducere in technologia instruirii programate" (Introduction aux techniques de l'enseignement programmé), in <u>Metode moderne de invatamint</u>. Bucarest, Universitatea populară, 1971.

——————.   "Introducere în tehnologia programării, I-VII". (Introduction aux techniques de l'enseignement programmé), in <u>Revista de fizică și chimie</u>, Série A, No. 7-12, 1970 et No. 1, 1971.

——————.   "Orientări și perspective ale pedagogiei cibernetice" (Orientations et perspectives de la pédagogie cybernétique), in <u>Revista de pedagogie</u>, No.2, 1971.

VAIDEANU, G.   "Reorganizarea tehnologiei didactice in funcție de obiectivele educaționale" (Adaptation des techniques pédagogiques en fonction des objectifs éducatifs), in <u>Revista de pedagogie</u>, No. 12, 1971.

III - RESEARCH AND APPLICATIONS / REALISATIONS

1 - RESEARCH / RECHERCHES

Thèmes: LANGUES ETRANGERES; MATHEMATIQUES; PHYSIQUE
Organisme: Institut de recherches pédagogiques, Secteur de l'enseignement programmé
Public intéressé: Elèves des lycées

Thème: LANGUE MATERNELLE
Organisme: Chaire de méthodologie de l'enseignement, Université "Babeș Bolyai", Cluj
Public intéressé: Elèves des écoles d'enseignement général

SINGAPORE/SINGAPOUR

I - ORGANIZATIONS AND ACTIVITIES / STRUCTURES ET ACTIVITES

1 - CENTRES

RESEARCH AND STATISTICS UNIT, MINISTRY OF EDUCATION
Kay Siang Road, Singapore 10
Nature of organization: Governmental

TEACHERS' TRAINING COLLEGE
Paterson Road, Singapore 9
Nature of organization: Pre-service and in-service teacher training institute

2 - ACTIVITIES/MANIFESTATIONS

WORKSHOP ON PROGRAMMED INSTRUCTION
Organized by: Ministry of Education
Place and date: Singapore, 11-15 August 1970
Participants: Teachers and teacher educators

FIVE WORKSHOPS ON PROGRAMMED INSTRUCTION
Organized by: Ministry of Education
Place and date: Singapore (during 1971)
Participants: Primary school principals and teachers

7 - TRAINING ORGANIZATIONS/ORGANISMES ASSURANT UNE FORMATION

TEACHERS' TRAINING COLLEGE
Paterson Road, Singapore 9
Nature of organization: Pre-service and in-service teacher training institute
Public concerned: College students and teachers

III - RESEARCH AND APPLICATIONS / REALISATIONS

1 - RESEARCH / RECHERCHES

Theme: AN INVESTIGATION INTO THE INTRODUCTION AND USE OF PROGRAMMED INSTRUCTION IN THE TEACHING OF MAP READING TO SECONDARY SCHOOL PUPILS
Organized by: University of Singapore and the Research and Statistics Unit,
                    Ministry of Education, Singapore
Public concerned: Swiss Cottage secondary school pupils

Theme: AN INVESTIGATION INTO TWO METHODS OF PROGRAMMED INSTRUCTION - THE VISUAL AND THE AUDIO-VISUAL MODES. THE ROLE OF REVIEW IN THE STUDY OF GEOGRAPHY
Organized by: University of Birmingham, Department of Education, United Kingdom
Public concerned: Secondary school pupils

SPAIN/ESPAGNE

I - ORGANIZATIONS AND ACTIVITIES / STRUCTURES ET ACTIVITES

1 - CENTRES

BEDAUX ESPAÑOLA, S.A.
Av. Generalísimo 30, Madrid 16
Nature de l'organisme: Privé

CENIDE (CENTRO DE INVESTIGACIONES PARA EL DESARROLLO DE LA EDUCACIÓN),
Departamento de Enseñanza Programada
Ciudad Universitaria, Madrid 3
Nature de l'organisme: Gouvernemental

ENSEÑANZA PROGRAMADA E INGENIERÍA DE SISTEMAS EDUCATIVOS (EPISE)
Muntaner 430, Barcelona 6
Nature de l'organisme: Privé

FACULTAD DE FILOSOFÍA Y LETRAS, Cátedra de Didáctica,
Sección de Pedagogía
Valencia
Nature de l'organisme: Université

INSTITUTO DE CIENCIAS DE LA EDUCACIÓN DE LA UNIVERSIDAD AUTÓNOMA
DE BARCELONA, División de Formación de Profesorado, División de
Investigación
San Antonio Ma Claret 171, Barcelona 13
Nature de l'organisme: Universitaire

2 - ACTIVITIES / MANIFESTATIONS

COURS D'ENSEIGNEMENT PROGRAMME
Organisateur: Escuela del Magisterio "Ausia March" de Valencia,
                Cátedra de Pedagogía
Lieu et date: Valence, octobre 1971 - juin 1972
Participants: Elèves - maîtres
Objet: Familiariser les futurs maîtres de l'enseignement
                général de base avec l'enseignement programmé, en vue,
                éventuellement, d'une application ultérieure dans les
                centres d'enseignement général de base

COURS D'ENSEIGNEMENT PROGRAMME
Organisateur: Facultad de Filosofía y Letras, Cátedra de Pedagogía
                General, Sociedad Española de Pedagogía
Lieu et date: Valence, janvier-avril 1969
Objet: Familiariser les maîtres de l'enseignement primaire
                avec l'enseignement programmé. Initier les professeurs
                du second degré et les étudiants à cette forme d'enseignement
Actes publiés par: Dra. Rosario de Pablo Vallejo, Cátedra de Didáctica,
                    Facultad de Filosofía y Letras, Valence

COURS D'ENSEIGNEMENT PROGRAMME
Organisateur: Instituto de Ciencias de la Educación, Universidad
                Autónoma de Barcelona
Lieu et date: Barcelone, novembre 1971 - avril 1972; trente heures de cours
Objet: Initiation à l'enseignement programmé. Aperçu historique et
                fondements théoriques de l'enseignement programmé. Mise au
                point par chaque participant de textes d'enseignement
                programmé. Essai et révision par les participants des
                textes d'enseignement programmé élaborés pendant le cours

COURS SUR L'ENSEIGNEMENT PROGRAMME DANS L'ENTREPRISE
Organisateur: Bedaux Española, S.A.
Lieu et date: Madrid, décembre 1971
Participants: Directeurs chargés de la formation
Objet: Faire connaître les possibilités de l'enseignement
                programmé pour la formation dans l'entreprise

REUNIONS NATIONALES SUR L'ENSEIGNEMENT PROGRAMME
Organisateur: CENIDE, Secretaría del Seminario Nacional Permanente de
                Enseñanza Programada y Automatizada
Lieu et dates: CENIDE, 13-17 juillet 1970; 8-9 février 1971; 25-26 juin
                1971; 20-23 janvier 1972

SEMINAIRE D'ENSEIGNEMENT PROGRAMME A L'INTENTION DES PROFESSEURS DE
L'UNIVERSITE LIBRE D'ENSEIGNEMENT A DISTANCE
Organisateur: CENIDE, Departamento de Enseñanza Programada
Lieu et date: CENIDE, 21-25 février 1972
Objet: Donner un aperçu général de l'enseignement programmé et en
                 faire connaître les possibilités

SEMINAIRE DE TECHNOLOGIE DIDACTIQUE
Organisateur: Facultad de Filosofía y Letras, Cátedra de Didáctica
Lieu et date: Valence, 1968
Participants: Etudiants
Objet: Faire connaître les techniques de programmation

3 - PUBLISHERS / MAISONS D'EDITION

EDICIONES ANAYA
Luis Braille 4, Salamanca
Nature: Editions générales

EDITORIAL EL MAGISTERIO ESPAÑOL
Calle Quevedo 1, Madrid 3
Nature: Editions scolaires

EDITORIAL PARANINFO
Magallanes 21, Madrid 15
Nature: Editions techniques

EDITORIAL TEIDE S.A.
Viladomat 291, Barcelona 15
Nature: Editions scolaires

4 - PERIODICALS / PERIODIQUES

EDUCADORES
Editeur: Federación Española de Religiosos de Enseñanza (FERE)
Adresse: Claudio Coello 32, Madrid 1
Périodicité: Bimensuel
Centre d'intérêt: Actualité pédagogique

7 - TRAINING ORGANIZATIONS / ORGANISMES ASSURANT UNE FORMATION

BEDAUX ESPAÑOLA SA
Av. Generalísimo 30, Madrid 16
Nature de l'organisme: Privé

ESCUELA SUPERIOR DE ADMINISTRACIÓN Y DIRECCIÓN DE EMPRESAS (ESADE)
Av. de la Victoria 60, Barcelona 17
Nature de l'organisme: Centre privé d'enseignement supérieur reconnu par
                        l'Etat
Public intéressé: Cadres. Etudiants

FACULTAD DE FILOSOFÍA Y LETRAS, Cátedra de Didáctica Experimental
Plaza de la Universidad, Barcelona
Nature de l'organisme: Université
Public intéressé: Etudiants

INSTITUTO DE CIENCIAS DE LA EDUCACIÓN, UNIVERSIDAD AUTÓNOMA DE BARCELONA
San Antonio Mª Claret 171, Barcelona 13
Nature de l'organisme: Universitaire
Public intéressé: Etudiants. Professeurs. Maîtres de l'enseignement général

II - PUBLICATIONS

1 - BOOKS / LIVRES

ESTARELLAS, J. Preparación y Evaluación de Objetivos para la enseñanza. Salamanca
    Ediciones Anaya, 1970

2 - ARTICLES

CANDAU, V.M.   "Las Máquinas de enseñar", in Eidos, No.28, juin 1968,
                    10 p.

FERNANDEZ HUERTA, J. "La enseñanza programada y máquinas de enseñar",
                    in Tiempo y Educación, vol.II, 1968, 16 p.

III - RESEARCH AND APPLICATIONS / REALISATIONS

2 - PUBLISHED PROGRAMMED COURSES / COURS PROGRAMMES PUBLIES

BEDAUX ESPAÑOLA, S.A. Contabilidad general de empresas. Bilbao 11,
        Iparraguirre 39, Centro Español de Gestión de Empresas.
        650 items
        Formation professionnelle

——————. Contabilidad y análisis de costes. Bilbao 11, Iparraguirre 39,
        Centro Español de Gestión de Empresas. 700 items
        Formation professionnelle

——————. El seguro privado. ICEA. 600 items
        Formation professionnelle

——————. Formación de telefonistas. Madrid, av. José Antonio 28,
        Compañía Telefónica Nacional de España. 1500 items
        Formation professionnelle

——————. Medida del trabajo. 580 items
        Formation professionnelle

——————. Normas de circulación - Señales - Mecánica del automóvil.
        Madrid, Cea Bermúdez 29, Jefatura Central de Tráfico
        1800 items

——————. Operaciones bancarias. Barcelona, av. José Antonio 615,
        Banca Catalana. 1400 items
        Formation professionnelle

——————. Organización bancaria - Derecho mercantil - Fundamentos de
        contabilidad - Contabilidad bancaria. Bilbao, Gran Via 1,
        Banco de Vizcaya. 1400 items
        Formation professionnelle

BUREAU INTERNATIONAL DU TRAVAIL.   Cómo interpretar un balance.   Genève, BIT, 1968
    Education des adultes. Enseignement technique

COMISIÓN MIXTA DE COORDINACIÓN ESTADÍSTICA.   Instrucción programada para preinstrucción de agentes censales. 1971
    Formation professionnelle

EPISE.   Curso de contabilidad general. Barcelona 6, Muntaner 430, EPISE. 1971. 12 thèmes
    Formation professionnelle

———; BANCO DE BILBAO.   Cálculo mercantil. 1972
    Formation professionnelle bancaire

———; ———.   Contabilidad general 1972
    Formation professionnelle bancaire

———; ———.   Derecho mercantil. 1971
    Formation professionnelle bancaire

———; ———.   Operaciones bancarias. 1972
    Formation professionnelle bancaire

———; GISPERT DIAZ.   Fundamentos de las computadoras de oficina. 1970
    Enseignement technique

HONEYWELL.   Formación de operadores keytape. 1971
    Enseignement technique

I.B.M.   Fundamentos de los ordenadores. I.B.M., 1968, 169 p.
    Enseignement technique

———.   Fundamentos de la programación. I.B.M., 1969
    Enseignement technique

———.   Generador automático de programas. I.B.M., 1968, 828 items
    Enseignement technique

———.   Lenguaje ensamblador. I.B.M., 1968, 187 p.
    Enseignement technique

———.   PL/I.   I.B.M., 1969, 1000 items
    Enseignement technique

———.   Sistema/3 R.P.G. II.   I.B.M., 1971
    Enseignement technique

LEARNING SYSTEMS ITALIANA S.P.A.   PERT como instrumento de dirección. Bilbao 11, Iparraguirre 39, Centro Español de Gestión de Empresas, 1969
    Education des adultes

VENTOSA, J.M.   Las 4 reglas. Barcelona 6, Muntaner 430, EPISE. Novembre 1969
    Niveau primaire. Education des adultes

———.   Seguridad en el manejo de puentes grúa. Barcelona 6, Muntaner 430, EPISE, 1969. 420 items
    Formation professionnelle. Education des adultes

SWEDEN/SUEDE

I - ORGANIZATIONS AND ACTIVITIES / STRUCTURES ET ACTIVITES

1 - CENTRES

ARMESTABENS UTBILDNINGSAVDELNING (ARMY SECTION FOR PROGRAMMED INSTRUCTION)
Östermalmsgatan 87, 11459 Stockholm 90
Nature of organization: Governmental

DEPARTMENT OF EDUCATION, UNIVERSITY OF GÖTEBORG
Mölndalsvägen 36, Göteborg
Nature of organization: University

DEPARTMENT OF EDUCATION, UNIVERSITY OF STOCKHOLM
Ynglingagatan 6, Stockholm 23
Nature of organization: University

DEPARTMENT OF EDUCATION, UNIVERSITY OF UPPSALA
St. Olofsgatan 12, 75221 Uppsala
Nature of organization: University

DEPARTMENT OF EDUCATIONAL AND PSYCHOLOGICAL RESEARCH, GÖTEBORG SCHOOL OF EDUCATION
Övre Husargatan 34, 41314 Göteborg
Nature of organization: Governmental

DEPARTMENT OF EDUCATIONAL AND PSYCHOLOGICAL RESEARCH, MALMÖ SCHOOL OF EDUCATION
Fack 20045, Malmö 23
Nature of organization: Governmental

DEPARTMENT OF EDUCATIONAL AND PSYCHOLOGICAL RESEARCH, STOCKHOLM SCHOOL OF EDUCATION
Fack 10026, Stockholm 34
Nature of organization: Governmental

DEPARTMENT OF EDUCATIONAL RESEARCH, LINKÖPING SCHOOL OF EDUCATION
Storgatan 28, 58223 Linköping
Nature of organization: Governmental

FÖRSVARETS BREVSKOLA (THE CORRESPONDENCE SCHOOL OF THE SWEDISH ARMED FORCES)
Fack, S-10045, Stockholm 90
Nature of organization: Military

HERMODS (CORRESPONDENCE SCHOOL, PUBLISHING HOUSE AND INSTITUTE FOR PERSONNEL TRAINING)
S-205 10 Malmö
Nature of organization: Independent, non-profit-making

LÄROMEDELSFÖRLAGEN
Fack, 10420 Stockholm 8
Nature of organization: Business

3 - PUBLISHERS / MAISONS D'EDITION

HERMODS (CORRESPONDENCE SCHOOL, PUBLISHING HOUSE AND INSTITUTE FOR PERSONNEL TRAINING)
S-205 10 Malmö
Nature of organization: Independent, non-profit-making

LÄROMEDELSFÖRLAGEN
Fack, 10420 Stockholm 8
Nature of organization: Commercial publisher

4 - PERIODICALS / PERIODIQUES

UTBILDNINGSTIDNINGEN
Publisher: Utbildningstidningen AB
Address: Fack 10422, Stockholm 22
Periodicity: 8-10 numbers per year

5 - PROFESSIONAL ORGANIZATIONS / ORGANISATIONS PROFESSIONNELLES

ASEA
Västerås

BULTFABRIKEN
Hallstahammar
Activities: Produced mechanical parts

MARINSTABEN (ROYAL SWEDISH NAVY)
Fack, Stockholm 80

STOCKHOLM PERSONALNÄMND, UTBILDNINGSAVDELNINGEN
Fack 10535, Stockholm 1
Public concerned: Adult education
Activities: Training organization (in-service)

6 - MANUFACTURERS OF TEACHING MACHINES / FABRICANTS DE MACHINES A ENSEIGNER

HÅKAN OLSSONS FÖRLAG
Box 1025, Lund
Type of machine: Pia-machine (audio-visual device)
Characteristics: Linear programme, storage of replies, audio-visual integrated, individual and collective use

7 - TRAINING ORGANIZATIONS / ORGANISMES ASSURANT UNE FORMATION

DEPARTMENT OF EDUCATIONAL AND PSYCHOLOGICAL RESEARCH, STOCKHOLM SCHOOL OF EDUCATION
Fack 100 26 Stockholm 34

FÖRSVARETS BREVSKOLA (SWEDISH ARMY)
Runs a series of courses on educational technology on a continual basis, with participants from universities, industry, and government authorities.
Within the normal courses in pedagogy there are short integrated courses in programmed instruction at some universities

8 - DOCUMENTATION CENTRES / CENTRES DE DOCUMENTATION

JÄRNBRUKSFÖRBUNDET
Hovslagargatan, Stockholm
Nature of organization: Business

DEPARTMENT OF EDUCATION, UNIVERSITY OF GÖTEBORG
Mölndalsvägen 36, Göteborg
Nature of organization: University

II - PUBLICATIONS

1 - BOOKS / LIVRES

BERNMALM, S. <u>Programmerad undervisning vid universitet och högskolor:
En granskning av förutsättningarna och ett försök.</u>
Göteborg, Pedagogiska Institutionen, Göteborg universitet,
1969, 93 p. + appendix

BJERSTEDT, Å. <u>Programmerad undervisning Språklaboratorier och grupp-
dynamisk kartläggning.</u> Lund, GLEERUPS, 1963 (Revised
1965-67-68), 224 p.

———. <u>Undervisningsprogrammering och utvärdering.</u> Stockholm
Sv. Bokförlaget, 1965, Rev.ed. 1970, 118 p.

GRUNDIN, H.U. <u>Svarskrav och facitsvar vid programmerad undervisning.
Bidrag till lösningen av ett praktiskt-pedagogiskt
problem.</u> Report from the Department of Ed. Res.,
Teachers College, Linköping, 1970, 200 p. (stencils)

JIVEN, L.M.; ÖREBERG, C. <u>The IMU Project : Preliminary plan for investi-
gating the effects of a system for individualised
mathematics teaching.</u> Malmö, Malmö School of Education,
Didakometry, No.22, 1968, 24 p.

WALLIN, E. <u>Undervisning - Konst eller teknik?</u> Stockholm, Almquist
and Wiksell, 1968, 173 p.

2 - ARTICLES

ANDERSSON, Å. "Matematik populärast i programmerat material", in
<u>Pedagogiska Meddelanden från Skolöverstyrelsen.</u> National Swedish Board
of Education, 1968

GRUNDIN, H.A. "Response Mode and Information about Correct Answers
in Programmed Instruction : a Discussion of Experimental Evidence and
Educational Decisions", in <u>Aspects of Educational Technology III.</u> Ed. Mann,
A.P., Brunstrom, C.K., London, 1969, p.65-71

3 - BIBLIOGRAPHIES

BERNMALM, S. <u>Programmerad undervisning vid universitet och
högskolor.</u> Göteborg, 1969, 93 p.

BJERSTEDT, Å. "Educational technology in Sweden". <u>Didakometry</u>
(Malmö School of Education), No.23, 1969, 22 p.

———. "Recent trends in educational technology: notes
from Munich, Nice and Amsterdam". <u>Didakometry</u>
(Malmö School of Education), No.21, 1968, 9 p.

———. "System analysis in instructional programming: The
initial phases of the programme construction process".
<u>Didakometry</u> (Malmö School of Education), No.30, 1971,
109 p.

———. "System modification and evaluation in instructional programming: the final phases of the programme construction process". Didakometry (The Malmö School of Education), No.33, 1971, 127 p.

———. "System synthesis in instructional programming: the intermediate phases of the programme construction process". Didakometry (Malmö School of Education), No.32, 1971, 80 p.

4 - AUDIO-VISUAL PRODUCTIONS / PRODUCTIONS AUDIO-VISUELLES

A.V. SIM (AUDIO-VISUELLT SJÄLVINSTRUERANDE MATERIEL)
Utbildningsförlaget, Stockholm

III - RESEARCH AND APPLICATIONS / REALISATIONS

1 - RESEARCH / RECHERCHES

Theme: COMPARISON OF THREE DIFFERENT MEDIA : FILM, PROGRAMMED INSTRUCTION AND TEACHER ASSISTED TEACHING
Organized by: Department of Education, University of Uppsala

Theme: GENERAL DESIGN OF PROGRAMMED MATERIALS (EFFECTS OF VARIATIONS AS TO RESPONSE REQUESTS, FREQUENCY, FEEDBACK INFORMATIONS, etc.)
Organized by: Department of Educational Research, School of Education, Linköping

Theme: GERMAN AS A FOREIGN LANGUAGE (ANALYSIS OF OBJECTIVES, METHODOLOGICAL COMPARISONS AND CONSTRUCTION OF INSTRUCTIONAL SYSTEMS)
Organized by: Department of Educational and Psychological Research, Malmö School of Education

Theme: LONG AND SHORT TIME EFFECTS FROM PARTIAL REINFORCEMENT
Organized by: Department of Education, University of Uppsala

Theme: MATHEMATICS LEARNING (CONSTRUCTION OF SELF-INSTRUCTIONAL MATERIALS IN MATHEMATICS AND COMPARISONS BETWEEN DIFFERENT ORGANIZATIONAL ARRANGEMENTS)
Organized by: Department of Educational and Psychological Research, Malmö School of Education

Theme: SELF-INSTRUCTIONAL COURSE IN INTRODUCTORY STATISTICS FOR STUDENTS OF EDUCATION, PSYCHOLOGY AND SOCIOLOGY
Organized by: Department of Education, University of Uppsala

Theme: SELF-INSTRUCTIONAL MATERIALS FOR PUPILS WITH SPECIAL LEARNING DIFFICULTIES
Organized by: Department of Educational and Psychological Research, Göteborg School of Education

Theme: SELF-INSTRUCTIONAL METHODS AND MATERIALS FOR TEACHING OF DEAF CHILDREN
Organized by: Department of Education, University of Uppsala

Theme: SWEDISH GRAMMAR (EXPERIMENTS WITH PROGRAMMED INSTRUCTION)
Organized by: Department of Educational and Psychological Research, Göteborg School of Education

2 - PUBLISHED PROGRAMMED COURSES / COURS PROGRAMMES PUBLIES

BYTTNER; NAESLUND; ROMARE. Swedish, Lång och kort vokal (2nd edition). Stockholm, Läromedelsförlagen, 1969, 160 items.
Primary level

DAHLQUIST. Mathematics, Det romerska talsystemet (2nd edition). Stockholm, Läromedelsförlagen, 1969, 40 items.
Primary and secondary levels

_____; HILDING. Mathematics, Procenträkningens grunder (3rd edition). Stockholm, Läromedelsförlagen, 1969, 179 items.
Primary level

EKSTRÖM; LINDELL. Swedish, Dubbelteckning av konsonant. Stockholm, Läromedelsförlagen, 1968, 127 items.
Primary level

HEMER; SANDER. Mathematics, Talföljder. Stockholm, Läromedelsförlagen, 1968, 162 items.
Secondary level

LARSSON; NILSSON; SJÖLIN. Chemistry, Grundkurs i kemi. Stockholm, Läromedelsförlagen, 255 items.
Vocational education

LUNDBERG; ÅNGSTRÖM. Swedish, Alfabetisk ordning 1-3. Stockholm, Läromedelsförlagen, 1968, 246 items.
Primary level

MELLGREN. English Adventure in the past (3rd edition). Stockholm, Läromedelsförlagen, 1968, 80 items.
Secondary level

STAFLIN. Physics, Grundläggande ellära. Stockholm, Läromedelsförlagen, 1968, 129 items.
Vocational education

THRONSTRÖM. Biology, Ögat och synen. Stockholm, Läromedelsförlagen, 1968, 707 items.
Secondary level

UNIVERSITETSPEDAGOGISKA UTREDNINGEN. Statistics, Elementär statistik. Stockholm, Universitetskanslersämbetet, 421 items, 259 p.
University level

UTBILDNINGSMETODIK AB. Den skoveltandade motorsogskedjan. Stockholm, Utbildningsmetodik AB & Skogsstyrelsen, 1971.
Forestry schools

_____. Växellära. Stockholm, Sr. Sparbanks-föreningen & Utbildningsmetodik AB, 1969.
Savings banks personnel

————————. Kommunikationssystem IBM on line (Savings banks terminal system). Stockholm, Spadab & Utbildningsmetodik, 1970 (Programmed instruction and computer-assisted instruction on line)
Savings banks personnel

WESTLING; WINKVIST. Physics, Atomen. Stockholm, Läromedelsförlagen, 1968.
Secondary level

SWITZERLAND/SUISSE

I - ORGANIZATIONS AND ACTIVITIES / STRUCTURES ET ACTIVITES

1 - CENTRES

CENTRE DE RECHERCHES PSYCHO-PEDAGOGIQUES DU CYCLE D'ORIENTATION
Chemin Briquet, 1211 Genève 19
Nature de l'organisme: Gouvernemental

ECOLE POLYTECHNIQUE FEDERALE, Chaire de didactique expérimentale
Pestalozzistrasse 24, 8032 Zürich
Nature de l'organisme: Universitaire

GLM (GESELLSCHAFT FUR LEHR- UND LERNMETHODEN)
Beckenhofstrasse 31, CH-8006 Zurich
Nature de l'organisme: Association sans but lucratif (Homologue du GRETI, mais pour la Suisse allemande)

GRETI (Groupement romand pour l'étude des techniques d'instruction)
Allinges 2, 1006 Lausanne
Nature de l'organisme: Association sans but lucratif

INSTITUT CENTRAL ORT
1247 Anières
Nature de l'organisme: Fondation indépendante. Institution internationale ayant organisé la première manifestation sur l'enseignement programmé en Europe

INSTITUT DE PSYCHOLOGIE DE L'UNIVERSITE (IPUN)
Avenue de Clos-Brochet 32, CH-2000 Neuchâtel
Nature de l'organisme: Universitaire

INSTITUT ROMAND DE RECHERCHES ET DE DOCUMENTATION PEDAGOGIQUES (IRDP)
Faubourg de l'Hôpital 43, CH-2000 Neuchâtel
Nature de l'organisme: **Association gouvernementale**

2 - ACTIVITIES / MANIFESTATIONS

COURS D'ENSEIGNEMENT PROGRAMME (Manifestation romande)

Organisateur:	Institut de psychologie de l'université de Neuchâtel (IPUN)
Lieu et date:	IPUN, une heure hebdomadaire
Participants:	Etudiants en psychologie du travail de 4e année
Objet:	Dériver une méthodologie de la programmation de l'enseignement à partir des fondements théoriques de l'enseignement programmé

JOURNEE D'ETUDE SUR L'ENSEIGNEMENT PROGRAMME ASSISTE PAR ORDINATEUR
(C.A.I.) (Manifestation romande)

Organisateur: GRETI
Lieu et date: Genève, 3 février 1968
Participants: Chercheurs. Enseignants scolaires et universitaires.
                Formateurs pour la formation professionnelle

JOURNEES POUR LA DETERMINATION DE L'OBJECTIF (Manifestation romande annuelle)

Organisateur: GRETI, Lausanne et réalisation par IPUN, Neuchâtel
Lieu et dates: Lausanne, 1, 12, 19 février 1969
Participants: Enseignants scolaires et universitaires.
                Formateurs pour la formation professionnelle
Objet: Système homme-machine, aspect critique de la performance,
                détermination du niveau opérationnel nécessaire,
                spécification des comportements nécessaires

SEMINAIRE DE FORMATION A LA C.A.I. (Manifestation romande)

Organisateurs: GRETI, CRPP et IBM
Lieux et dates: Lausanne, Genève et Neuchâtel, environ deux fois par an
Participants: Chercheurs. Enseignants scolaires et universitaires.
                Adultes. Professionnels

SEMINAIRE DE FORMATION POUR PROGRAMMEURS (Manifestation romande)
Organisateur: GRETI, Commission de formation
Lieux et dates: Leysin et Neuchâtel, environ tous les trois mois
Participants: Enseignants scolaires et universitaires
Objet: Initiation et perfectionnement

SEMINAIRES DE TECHNOLOGIE EDUCATIVE (Manifestation romande)

Organisateurs: GRETI et IPUN
Lieu et dates: Neuchâtel, une fois par an
Participants: Techniciens pédagogues pour la formation générale et
                professionnelle
Objet: Méthodologie de la planification totale de l'enseignement
                conçu comme application des systèmes hommes-machines

3 - PUBLISHERS / MAISONS D'EDITION

EDITIONS DELTA S.A.
Route de Chailly 40, CH-1814 La Tour-de-Pelz
Nature: Editeur scolaire et professionnel

EDITIONS SPES S.A.
St. Pierre 2, 1002 Lausanne
Nature: Editeur technique, scientifique, professionnel et scolaire

LIBRAIRIE PAYOT S.A.
1 rue du Bourg, 1003 Lausanne
Nature: Editeur scolaire

4 - PERIODICALS / PÉRIODIQUES

TECHNIQUES D'INSTRUCTION
Editeur: GRETI
Adresse: Chemin des Allinges 2, CH-1006 Lausanne
Périodicité: Trimestriel
Centres d'intérêt: Recherches. Réalisations. Actualités. Bibliographie.

5 - PROFESSIONAL ORGANIZATIONS / ORGANISATIONS PROFESSIONNELLES

FEDERATION SUISSE DES ASSOCIATIONS DE FABRICANTS D'HORLOGERIE (F.H.)
représentée par le C.I.D.
14 rue de la Gare, 2500 Bienne
Nature de l'organisation: Organisme patronal

SOCIETE DES PROFESSEURS ET DIRECTEURS DE COURS DE L'ASSOCIATION
STENOGRAPHIQUE AIME PARIS (SPDC)
5, rue de Beaumont, 1206 Genève
Nature de l'organisation: Association d'enseignants

SOCIETE PEDAGOGIQUE ROMANDE

chez M. Fernand Barbey, 1020 Renens
Activités: Information. Formation. Publications.
Nature de l'organisation: Association d'enseignants

6 - MANUFACTURERS OF TEACHING MACHINES / FABRICANTS DE MACHINES A ENSEIGNER

COMPAGNIE INDUSTRIELLE RADIO-ELECTRIQUE (C.I.R.)
Bundesgasse 16, 3000 Berne

PHILIPS S.A.
Edenstrasse 20 - CH-8027 Zurich

7 - TRAINING ORGANIZATIONS / ORGANISMES ASSURANT UNE FORMATION

CENTRE DE RECHERCHES PSYCHO-PEDAGOGIQUES DU C.O.
Chemin Briquet, 1211 Genève 19
Public intéressé: Enseignants scolaires

GESELLSCHAFT FUR LEHR- UND LERNMETHODEN (GLM)
Pestalozzianum, Beckenhofstrasse, Zurich
Nature de l'organisation: Société privée
Public intéressé: Enseignants, instructeurs

GROUPE ROMAND POUR L'ETUDE DES TECHNIQUES D'INSTRUCTION (GRETI)
Chemin des Allinges 2, CH-1006 Lausanne
Nature de l'organisation: Association sans but lucratif
Public intéressé: Formateurs pour la formation générale et professionnelle

INSTITUT DE PSYCHOLOGIE DE L'UNIVERSITE (IPUN)
32, Clos Brochet, CH-2000 Neuchâtel
Nature de l'organisation: Universitaire
Public intéressé: Formateurs pour la formation générale et professionnelle
                    et universitaires

Switzerland/Suisse

INSTITUT DE PSYCHOLOGIE DU TRAVAIL DE L'ECOLE POLYTECHNIQUE FEDERALE
Pestalozzistrasse 24, 8032 Zurich
Nature de l'organisation: Gouvernementale
Public intéressé: Enseignants et universitaires, instructeurs dans
l'industrie

SOCIETE PEDAGOGIQUE VAUDOISE
Allinges 2, CH-1006 Lausanne
Nature de l'organisation: Association d'enseignants
Public intéressé: Enseignants scolaires

8 - DOCUMENTATION CENTRES / CENTRES DE DOCUMENTATION

BIBLIOTHEQUE DE L'INSTITUT DE PSYCHOLOGIE DU TRAVAIL DE L'EPF
Pestalozzistrasse 24, 8032 Zurich
Nature de l'organisme: Gouvernemental

BUREAU INTERNATIONAL DU TRAVAIL (B.I.T.)
Rue de Lausanne 154, 1200 Genève
Nature de l'organisme: Intergouvernemental
Nature des services: Information. Consultation. Prêt

CENTRE GENEVOIS DE DOCUMENTATION PEDAGOGIQUE
Rue de Lyon 58, Genève 1203
Nature de l'organisme: Cantonal
Nature des services: Prêt

CENTRE NEUCHATELOIS DE DOCUMENTATION PEDAGOGIQUE DE RECHERCHE ET D'INFORMATION
Faubourg de l'Hôpital 65, 2000 Neuchâtel
Nature de l'organisme: Cantonal

GRETI, ADMINISTRATION
Allinges 2, CH-1006 Lausanne
Nature de l'organisme: Association sans but lucratif
Nature des services: Bibliographies

INSTITUT DE PSYCHOLOGIE DE L'UNIVERSITE (IPUN)
32, Clos Brochet, CH-2000 Neuchâtel
Nature de l'organisme: Universitaire

INSTITUT ROMAND DE RECHERCHES ET DE DOCUMENTATION PEDAGOGIQUES
Faubourg de l'Hôpital 43, CH-2000 Neuchâtel
Nature de l'organisme: Association gouvernementale

OFFICE DE DOCUMENTATION ET D'INFORMATIONS SCOLAIRES (ODIS)
Rawyl 47, 1950 Sion
Nature de l'organisme: Gouvernemental

SERVICE DE LA RECHERCHE PEDAGOGIQUE
Rue Sillem 11, 1207 Genève
Nature de l'organisme: Cantonal

UNESCO, BUREAU INTERNATIONAL D'EDUCATION
Rue des Pâquis 52, 1211 Genève 14
Nature de l'organisme: Intergouvernemental
Nature des services: Information. Consultation

II - PUBLICATIONS

1 - BOOKS / LIVRES

JOINSON, D.   Introduction à l'Enseignement Programmé. (Traducteur: Cardinet Jean). Neuchâtel, Institut de Psychologie, 1968, 33 p. Présentation du ramifié et du linéaire

SILVERMAN, R.   Comment utiliser l'Enseignement Programmé dans une classe. (Traducteur: Aboudaram Maurice). 1200 Genève, Rue Varembé 1, ORT Union, 1968, 67 p.
Fonction du professeur. Matières programmables. Appareils. Exemples

"WORLD HEALTH ORGANIZATION STUDY GROUP REPORT. Implications of Individual and Small Group Learning Systems in Medical Education. (W.H.O. Technical Publication No. 489). Geneva, World Health Organization. 1972"

2 - ARTICLES

Banque populaire suisse. "L'avenir des machines à enseigner", in Educateur, No. 25.- Montreux, Société pédagogique de la Suisse romande, 1971

BOBILIER, G.   "Informatique", in Educateur, No. 32, Montreux, Société pédagogique de la Suisse romande, 1971

CARDINET, Jean   "L'efficacité d'un cours programmé d'algèbre pour apprentis", in Techniques d'instruction, Vol. I, No. 3, 1969, 12 p.
Rapport d'expérience

GONTHIER, A.   "Un essai de contrôle de la méthode Ramain", in Orientation et formation professionnelles, No. 1/2, 1972, 9p.
Rapport d'analyse statistique

FISCHER, H.   "Verhaltenspsychologische Grundlagen des computerunterstützten Unterrichts", in IBM Bulletin, No. 70, mai 1970

————   "Principes de psychologie du comportement dans l'instruction par ordinateur", in IBM Bulletin, No. 70, mai 1970

FREI, Hans-Peter   "Computer-unterstützter Unterricht", in RZ Bulletin der ETH, No. 4, 1970, 12 p.

————   "Vom programmierten zum Computer-gesteuerten Lernen", in Archiv für das Schweizerische Unterrichtswesen. Frauenfeld. No. 56/57, 1970/71

————   "Betriebliche Schulung mit Hilfe eines Computers", in Planung und Produktion, No. 1, 1971

————   "Programmierter Unterricht und Verwendung des Computers im Unterricht in den USA", in Gymnasium Helveticum, No. 25, mars 1971

————   "Computer als Hilfsmittel der betrieblichen Instruktion", in Jahresbericht 1970 der Schweiz. Stiftung für Angewandte Psychologie

	"Der Computer als kybernetisches Unterrichtshilfsmittel", in *Gymnasium Helveticum*, No. 25, avril 1971
GONTHIER, A.	"L'enseignement programmé, essai de synthèse", in *La revue polytechnique*, No. 2, 1969, 2 p.
———.	"Divers traitements de l'information contenue dans l'objectif", in *Techniques d'instruction*, No. 2, 1972, 6 p. Proposition d'une phase complémentaire dans la programmation d'un cours
MARMY, E.	"Le traitement électronique de l'information par ordinateur", in *Techniques d'instruction*, No. 1, 1969, 5 p. Rapport d'expérience.
METRAUX, G.	"L'ordinateur au service de nouvelles stratégies pédagogiques", in *Techniques d'instruction*, No. 1, 1969, 2 p.
PAPALOIZOS, A.	"Les effets sociaux possibles de l'enseignement programmé", in *Techniques d'instruction*, No. 7, 1968, 9 p.
PLANQUE, B.	"Ordinateurs et satellites", in *Educateur*, No. 29, Montreux, Société pédagogique de la Suisse romande, 1971
TECOZ, H.F.	"Les techniques modernes de communication et l'école", in *Educateur*, No. 22, Montreux, Société pédagogique de la Suisse romande, 1970
TERRY, J.	"L'utilisation de l'ordinateur dans l'enseignement élémentaire", in *Educateur*, No. 2, Montreux, Société pédagogique de la Suisse romande, 1969

3 - BIBLIOGRAPHIES

GONTHIER, A.	*Bibliographie de l'enseignement programmé pour la formation professionnelle*, Neuchâtel, Institut de Psychologie, 1972, 60 p.
———.	*Catalogue des cours programmés pour la formation professionnelle*, Neuchâtel, Institut de Psychologie de l'Université, 1973, 50 p.
LAURENT, E.	*Les machines à enseigner et l'instruction au moyen des ordinateurs*. GRETI, 1968, 9 p.
METRAUX, G.	*Les machines à enseigner et l'instruction au moyen des ordinateurs*. GRETI, 1968, 10 p.

4 - AUDIO-VISUAL PRODUCTIONS / PRODUCTIONS AUDIO-VISUELLES

DER MATHEMATISCHE BEGRIFF DER INFORMATION. Bivision. 45 min. Couleur.
    Réalisateur: H. U. Baumann

DER KERN. Bivision, 10 min.
    Réalisateur: H.U. Baumann

LE PASSIF ET LE COMPLEMENT D'AGENT. 16 mm., 18 min., noir et blanc.
        Réalisateur: Laurent Wiblé

SI TU VEUX SAVOIR. 16 mm. 2 min., noir et blanc.
        Réalisateur: Jacqueline Veuve

III - RESEARCH AND APPLICATIONS / REALISATIONS

1 - RESEARCH / RECHERCHES

Thème: COMPARAISON DE L'ENSEIGNEMENT PROGRAMME A L'ENSEIGNEMENT CLASSIQUE POUR L'ALGEBRE ELEMENTAIRE
Organisme: Institut de psychologie de l'Université, Neuchâtel
Public intéressé: apprentis des branches techniques

Thème: CRITERES DE DECISION POUR ARRETER L'EXPERIMENTATION D'UN COURS PROGRAMME
Organisme: I.P.U.N.

Thème: DEVELOPPEMENT D'UNE LANGUE D'AUTEUR POUR LE CAI
Organisme: Institut de psychologie du travail de l'EPF

Thème: ELABORATION EXPERIMENTALE D'UN COURS DE PROPEDEUTIQUE GENERALE (STUDY SKILLS) PAR SYSTEMES COMBINES
Organisme: Département de l'instruction publique, Centre de recherches psychopédagogiques, Genève

Thème: MESURE DE L'EFFICACITE D'UN COURS SUR LE PARTICIPE PASSE
Organisme: Service de la recherche pédagogique du Département de l'instruction publique, Genève
Public intéressé: 600 élèves de 6ème primaire (Genève et Neuchâtel)

Thème: TECHNIQUES D'ELABORATION DIDACTIQUE (DETERMINATION DE LA TACHE DE FORMATION, DETERMINATION DE LA DIDACTIQUE, VALIDATION)
Organisme: I.P.U.N.

2 - PUBLISHED PROGRAMMED COURSES / COURS PROGRAMMES PUBLIES

CARDINET, J.; GONTHIER, A. <u>La formulation d'objectifs pédagogiques cognitifs.</u>
    Institut de psychologie de l'Université, 32 avenue de Clos-Brochet, CH-2000 Neuchâtel, 1970, 64 items
    Pédagogues praticiens et techniciens
    Cours édités: 200 en 1970
    En cours de validation

CAZIMIRSKI, J. <u>Création d'un marché</u> (Adaptation: I.P.U.N.). Genève, B.I.T., <u>1971, 440 items</u>
    Formation professionnelle

DE COULON, P.; GONTHIER, A. <u>Isochronisme du balancier-spiral.</u> Fédération horlogère, rue d'Argent 6, 2500 Bienne, 1968, 118 items.
    Livre et modèle à manipuler
    Formation professionnelle

GONTHIER, A. Mesurage au millième de millimètre par microcomparateur mécanique
I.P.U.N., 1968. 1055 items
Livre et diapositives ou photographies
Formation professionnelle

_____ ; AUROI, M.; TANNER, S. Les fibres artificielles. (Centre de
formation de la Fédération des coopératives Migros, 152 Limmatstrasse, CH-8005 Zürich, 1971, 56 items
Formation professionnelle

HALSHALL, Davey; DAVIDSON, Ward. Comment lire un bilan. (Adaptateur:
I.P.U.N.). Genève, B.I.T. 1970, 728 items
Formation professionnelle

INSTITUT FÜR ANGEWANDTE PSYCHOLOGIE, Zürich. Haushaltapparat: Dampfluft-
beleuchter. Centre de Formation de la Fédération des coopératives Migros, 152 Limmatstrasse, CH-8005 Zurich, 1969,
60 items
Formation professionnelle

_____, Zürich. Selbstbedienung mit Beratung
im Hemdenverkauf. Centre de Formation de la Fédération des
Coopératives Migros, 152 Limmatstrasse, CH-8005 Zürich, 1968,
162 items
Formation professionnelle

KUNZ, P.A.; LEPOUZE, J.; METIN, R. Comment garnir correctement les rayons
d'un magasin. CH-1814 La Tour-de-Peilz, Centre de Formation
AFICO, S.A., 1969, 80 items
Formation professionnelle

MAYENZET, P.; ARNOUX, M.; BIBERSTEIN, G.R.; CARDINET, J. L'algèbre par les
nombres positifs - Collection: GRETI-ICO-Cours programmé en
3 tomes. Editions DELTA S.A., CH-1814 La Tour-de-Peilz, 1972,
1600 items
Apprentis des branches techniques

METRAUX, G. Ton dictionnaire. Genève, Cycle d'orientation, 1968, 110 items.
Niveau secondaire

NICHOLS, L.A. (Adaptateur: Gonthier, A.) Alignement des organes des machines
accouplées. Editions DELTA S.A., CH-1814 La Tour-de-Peilz, 1972.
800 items (illustrations)
Formation professionnelle

SCHAEDELLI; R. Der Austausch von Paletten, Rahmen und Schutzbrettern. Beau-
lieustrasse 33, 3000 Berne. Service psychologique des C.F.F.,
1968, 111 items
Formation professionnelle

3 - COMPUTER ASSISTED INSTRUCTION / ENSEIGNEMENT ASSISTE PAR ORDINATEUR

CALCUL NUMERIQUE

Organismes: GRETI, CRPP et I.B.M.
Destinataires: Elèves de 12 à 15 ans
Type de l'ordinateur: I.B.M. 360

Type des terminaux: I.B.M. 1050
Langage utilisé: Coursewriter III
Objet: Contrôle des connaissances; enseignement

ELEMENTS DE PSYCHOPEDAGOGIE

Organismes: GRETI, CRPP et I.B.M.
Destinataires: Maîtres secondaires, débutants
Type de l'ordinateur: I.B.M. 360
Type des terminaux: I.B.M. 1050
Langage utilisé: Coursewriter III
Objet: Contrôle des connaissances; enseignement

ENSEIGNEMENT DU LATIN

Organisme: Ecole polytechnique fédérale, Zurich
Destinataires: Etudiants de l'Université de Zurich
Type de l'ordinateur: IBM 370/155
Type des terminaux: IBM 1050, 2741
Langage utilisé: Coursewriter III
Objet: Exercices

LES LOGARITHMES

Organisme: Ecole polytechnique fédérale, Zurich
Destinataires: Adultes moyens
Type de l'ordinateur: I.B.M. 1401
Type des terminaux: I.B.M. 1050/2741
Langage utilisé: Coursewriter I
Objet: Enseignement

SYRIAN ARAB REPUBLIC/REPUBLIQUE ARABE SYRIENNE

I - ORGANIZATIONS AND ACTIVITIES / STRUCTURES ET ACTIVITES

1 - CENTRES

FACULTE DE PEDAGOGIE, UNIVERSITE DE DAMAS
Damas
Nature de l'organisme: Universitaire

2 - ACTIVITIES / MANIFESTATIONS

ETUDE DES TECHNIQUES DE L'ENSEIGNEMENT PROGRAMME (Manifestation nationale)
Organisateur: Université de Damas
Lieu et date: Damas, 1969
Participants: Professeurs et étudiants d'université
Actes publiés par: Faculté de pédagogie, Université de Damas

7 - TRAINING ORGANIZATIONS / ORGANISMES ASSURANT UNE FORMATION

FACULTE DE PEDAGOGIE, UNIVERSITE DE DAMAS
Damas
Nature de l'organisme: Universitaire
Public intéressé: Enseignants (écoles et universités)

II - PUBLICATIONS

   1 - BOOKS / LIVRES

KALLA, Fakhridin. Fondements de la formation psychologique et de l'enseignement programmé. Damas, Faculté de pédagogie, 1969, 191 p. (En arabe.)
Cybernétique et enseignement programmé

——————. Programme de formation pour l'emploi des auxiliaires audio-visuels. Damas, Faculté de pédagogie, 1969, 61 p. (En arabe.)
Programme d'auto-instruction relatif à l'emploi des auxiliaires visuels

——————. Programme de grammaire arabe. Damas, Faculté de pédagogie, 1969, 156 p. (En arabe.)
Questions de grammaire arabe pour la cinquième classe du cours élémentaire

   2 - ARTICLES

KALLA, Fakhridin. "L'enseignement programmé de la grammaire arabe", in Al-Mu'allim al-'Arabi, Vol. 21, No. 2, 1968, 6 p. (En arabe).
Statistiques

——————. "L'enseignement programmé et les auxiliaires visuels", in Al-Mu'allim al-'Arabi, Vol. 21, No. 6, 1968, 6 p. (En arabe.)
Statistiques

——————. "Conditionnement d'un pigeon", in Al-Mu'allim al-'Arabi, Vol. 21, No. 7, 1968, 6 p. (En arabe)
Compte-rendu d'expérience: comment conditionner un pigeon pour qu'il tourne une clef avec son bec.

——————. "Programme de grammaire arabe (Article-Innah)", in Al-Mu'allim al-'Arabi, Vol. 21, No. 8, 1968, 6 p. (En arabe.)
Compte-rendu d'expériences

——————. "Programme de grammaire arabe (cinq substantifs)", in Al-Mu'allim al-'Arabi, Vol. 21, No. 9, 1968, 5 p. (En arabe.)
Compte-rendu d'expériences

THAILAND/THAILANDE

I - ORGANIZATIONS AND ACTIVITIES / STRUCTURES ET ACTIVITES

   1 - CENTRES

THE EDUCATIONAL MATERIALS CENTRE OF THE DEPARTMENT OF EDUCATIONAL TECHNIQUES
Ministry of Education
Rajadamnern Avenue, Bangkok
Nature of organization: Governmental

2 - ACTIVITIES/MANIFESTATIONS

A TRAINING SEMINAR (National annual conference)
Organized by: The Educational Materials Centre of the Department of Educational Techniques, with the co-operation of the Rural Education Development Project. A joint venture, sponsored by U.S.A.I.D. and the Thai Government.
Place and date: Auditorium of the Educational Materials Centre, Bangkok, October 1969.
Participants: Research workers. Supervisors.
Purpose: To train a group of Thai supervisors and specialists of different disciplines and level of education in the techniques.

3 - PUBLISHERS/MAISONS D'EDITION

DEPARTMENT OF EDUCATIONAL TECHNIQUES
Ministry of Education, Rajadamnern Avenue, Bangkok
Nature of organization: Governmental

8 - DOCUMENTATION CENTRES/CENTRES DE DOCUMENTATION

DEPARTMENT OF EDUCATIONAL TECHNIQUES
Ministry of Education, Rajadamnern Avenue, Bangkok
Nature of organization: Governmental

II - PUBLICATIONS

1 - BOOKS/LIVRES

KUMUT, Prueng. A Programmed Text in Education. Bangkok, May 1969, 60 p.
Preparing instruction objectives of any subjects to be taught. Material supplementing courses on general method of teaching or educational measurement.

TUNISIA/TUNISIE

I - ORGANIZATIONS AND ACTIVITIES / STRUCTURES ET ACTIVITES

1 - CENTRES

INSTITUT DES SCIENCES DE L'EDUCATION
17, rue Fénelon, Tunis
Nature de l'organisme: Universitaire

2 - ACTIVITIES / MANIFESTATIONS

CYCLE DE FORMATION: L'ENSEIGNEMENT PROGRAMME
Organisateur: Institute des sciences de l'éducation, Tunis
Lieu et dates: Lycée mixte de Grombalia, 21-28 avril 1971, 6-13 mai 1971, 20 mai 1971
Participants: Professeurs de l'enseignement secondaire

CYCLE DE FORMATION: LA REALISATION DES COURS D'ENSEIGNEMENT PROGRAMME
Organisateur: Institut des sciences de l'éducation, Tunis
Lieu et date: Tunis, 13 avril - 27 mai 1970
Participants: Chercheurs. Enseignants scolaires et universitaires

CYCLE D'INITIATION A L'ENSEIGNEMENT PROGRAMME
Organisateur: Institut des sciences de l'éducation, Tunis
Lieu et date: Collège nord-africain de machinisme agricole et
                  de génie rural, 15 mai - 4 juin 1970
Participants: Professeurs de l'enseignement secondaire

CYCLE D'INITIATION A L'ENSEIGNEMENT PROGRAMME ET EXPOSITION
Organisateur: Institut des sciences de l'éducation, Tunis
Lieu et dates: Lycée de garçons de Sousse, 16-17 avril 1971,
                  22-23 avril 1971
Participants: Professeurs de l'enseignement secondaire

CYCLE D'INITIATION ET DE FORMATION
Organisateur: Institut des sciences de l'éducation, Tunis
Lieu et date: Institut des sciences de l'éducation, 24-28 mai 1971
Participants: Office professionnel de l'emploi, Radès (techniciens)

CYCLE D'INITIATION ET DE FORMATION: LA REALISATION DES COURS
D'ENSEIGNEMENT PROGRAMME
Organisateur: Institut des sciences de l'éducation, Tunis
Lieu et date: Institut des sciences de l'éducation, 22-24 décembre 1971
Participants: Educateurs spécialisés du Centre de réadaptation
                  "La Volonté", Tunis

L'ENSEIGNEMENT PROGRAMME (conférence-débat)
Organisateur: Maison de l'éducateur, 45, avenue Bab Djedid, Tunis
Lieu et date: Tunis, 21 avril 1969
Participants: Enseignants scolaires et universitaires
Compte rendu: Journal l'Action, 24 avril 1969

JOURNEES D'ETUDE: THEORIE ET PRATIQUE DE L'ENSEIGNEMENT PROGRAMME
Organisateur: Institut des sciences de l'éducation, Tunis
Lieu et date: Tunis, avril 1970
Participants: Chercheurs. Enseignants scolaires et universitaires

7 - TRAINING ORGANIZATIONS / ORGANISMES ASSURANT UNE FORMATION

INSTITUT DES SCIENCES DE L'EDUCATION
17, rue Fénelon, Tunis
Nature de l'organisme: Universitaire
Public intéressé: Enseignants scolaires et universitaires

UNIVERSITE DE TUNIS
94, boulevard du 9 avril 1938, Tunis
Nature de l'organisme: Universitaire
Public intéressé: Universitaires

8 - DOCUMENTATION CENTRES / CENTRES DE DOCUMENTATION

INSTITUT DES SCIENCES DE L'EDUCATION
17, rue Fénelon, Tunis
Nature de l'organisme: Universitaire
Nature des services: Information. Formation. Elaboration de
                         cours d'enseignement programmé

III - RESEARCH AND APPLICATIONS / REALISATIONS

  1 - RESEARCH / RECHERCHES

  Thème: DEVELOPPEMENT DE L'ENSEIGNEMENT PROGRAMME:
  1. Constitution d'une documentation
  2. Publication d'un manuel pratique: L'ABC de l'enseignement programmé par Soyez JOANNES
  3. Tenue de seminaires (initiation et formation)
  4. Essais en calcul-niveau: enseignement primaire
  5. Programmation de la grammaire arabe (niveau: fin du cycle primaire)
  6. Publication d'un article de Abdelaziz CHETTAOUI: "L'enseignement programmé" in Bulletin Pédagogique, No.1 (en arabe).
  Organisme: Institut des sciences de l'éducation, 17, rue Fénelon, Tunis
  Public intéressé: Enseignants et enseignés

UNION OF SOVIET SOCIALIST REPUBLICS/
UNION DES REPUBLIQUES SOCIALISTES SOVIETIQUES

I - ORGANIZATIONS AND ACTIVITIES / STRUCTURES ET ACTIVITES

  1 - CENTRES

  INSTITUT OBŠEJ I PEDAGOGIČESKOJ PSIKOLOGII (Institut de psychologie et de psychopédagogie de l'Académie des sciences pédagogiques de l'URSS)
  Laboratoire d'enseignement programmé
  Marx Prospekt 20, Moscou K 9
  Nature de l'organisme: Centre de recherche gouvernemental

  MOSKOVSKIJ PEDAGOGIČESKIJ INSTITUT "LENIN" (Institut pédagogique "Lénine" de Moscou)
  M. Ul. Pirogovskaja 1, Moscou
  Nature de l'organisme: Gouvernemental

  MOSKOVSKIJ PEDAGOGIČESKIJ INSTITUT "LENIN"
  Laboratorija programmirovannogo obučenija (Laboratoire de l'enseignement programmé)
  M. Ul. Pirogovskaja 1, Moscou
  Nature de l'organisme: Gouvernemental

  2 - ACTIVITIES / MANIFESTATIONS

  CONFERENCE SUR L'INSTRUCTION PROGRAMMEE ET LES APPLICATIONS DES MOYENS TECHNIQUES EN EDUCATION (Conférence nationale, tous les deux ou trois ans)
  Organisateur: Pedagogičeskoe obščestvo RSFSR (Société des pédagogues de la RSFSR)
  Lieu et date: Moscou, 24-28 juin 1969
  Participants: Chercheurs. Universitaires. Adultes. Professionnels. Enseignants scolaires.

Union of Soviet Socialist Republics/
Union des républiques socialistes soviétiques

Actes publiés par: Vserossijskaja Konferencija po tehničeskim sredstvam i programmirovannomu obučeniju (Conférence russe sur les moyens techniques et l'enseignement programmé). Symposiums N.1-20. Rédaction scientifique: L. Landa et N.M. Sahmaeva, Moscou, M. Pedag. Ofščestvo. 1969.

MANIFESTATION REGIONALE
Organisateur: Pedagogičeskij Institut "Lenin" (Institut Pédagogique Lénine de Moscou), Ministère de l'Instruction publique RSFSR.
Lieu et date: Moscou, 26-28 mars 1968
Participants: Chercheurs. Enseignants scolaires. Universitaires. Adultes. Professionnels.
Objet: Echange d'expériences en matière de recherches
Actes publiés par: Tezisy dokladov mežvuzovskoj konferencii programmirovannogo obučenija v skole. M. 1968 (Résumé des communications, Conférence inter-universitaire sur les problèmes de l'enseignement programmé et des élèves, Moscou 1968).

3 - PUBLISHERS / MAISONS D'EDITION

PEDAGOGIKA
M. Pagodinskaja Ul. 8, Moscou

PROSVEŠČENIE
M. 3 Proezd Marinoj Rošči, 41, Moscou

ZNANIE
M. Novaja Ploščad', 3/4 Moscou

4 - PERIODICALS / PERIODIQUES

SOVETSKAJA PEDAGOGIKA (Pédagogie soviétique)
Editeur: Académie des sciences pédagogiques de l'U.R.S.S.
Adresse: M. Ul. Makarenko, 5/16
Périodicité: Mensuel
Centres d'intérêt: Recherche. Réalisations. Actualités

7 - TRAINING ORGANIZATIONS / ORGANISMES ASSURANT UNE FORMATION

INSTITUT OBŠEJ I PEDAGOGIČESKOJ PSIKOLOGII A.P.N. - S.S.S.R.
(Institut de psychologie et de psychopédagogie de l'Académie des Sciences pédagogiques de l'URSS)
Marx Prospekt 20, Moscou K9
Nature de l'organisme: Gouvernemental
Public intéressé: Enseignants scolaires

MOSKOVSKIJ PEDAGOGIČESKIJ INSTITUT "LENIN" (Institut pédagogique Lénine)
M. Ul. Pirogovskaja 1, Moscou
Nature de l'organisme: Gouvernemental
Public intéressé: Enseignants scolaires

8 - DOCUMENTATION CENTRES / CENTRES DE DOCUMENTATION

INFORMACIONNYJ CENTRE VYSŠEJ ŠKOLY (Centre d'information sur l'instruction supérieure)

M. Izmajlovskoe Šosse 4, Moscou
Responsable: Ministère de l'enseignement supérieur de l'URSS
Nature de l'organisme: Gouvernemental
Nature des services: Recherche et diffusion d'information sur
les méthodes nouvelles d'enseignement

II - PUBLICATIONS

1 - BOOKS / LIVRES

_____. "Actes de la Conférence russe sur les moyens techniques et l'enseignement programmé", Pedagogičeskoe Obščestvo RSFSR, Moscou, 1969

ARCHANGELSKIJ, S.I. Kiberneticeskie analogii v obučenii (Les analogies cybernétiques dans l'enseignement), Moscou, Znanie, 1968

BIZJUKOV, B.V.; GRANIK, G.G.; PETROV, Y.A.; LANDA, L.N.; SENŠEV, L.V.; JUDINA, O.N.; ORLOVA, A.M. Voprosy algoritmizacii i programmirovanie obučenija (Algorithmisation et programmation dans l'enseignement), Vol. I (sous la direction de L.N. Landa). Moscou, Prosveščenie, 1969, 231 p.
Problèmes théoriques de l'algorithmisation de l'enseignement avec ou sans machines à enseigner.

IL'INA, T.A. Problèmes de la méthodologie de la programmation. Moscou, Znanie, 1969, 127 p.

_____. Pedagogika (Pédagogie). Moscou, Prosveščenie, 1969, 574 p.
Chapitre 19: L'enseignement programmé.

_____. Voprosy eksperimentalnoj proverki metodiki programmirovannogo obučenija (Vérification expérimentale des méthodes de l'enseignement programmé). Moscou, Institut Pédagogique Lénine de Moscou. 1970, 170 p.
Résultat de recherches sur l'évaluation de l'enseignement programmé

OGORODNIKOV, I.T. Pedagogika (Pédagogie), Moscou, Prosveščenie, 1968.
Manuel à l'intention des institutions pédagogiques

2 - ARTICLES

IL'INA, T.A. "Ponjatie" pedagogicheskaja technologiia v sovremennoi Zarubežnoi pedagogike", in Sovietskaja Pedagogika, 1971, No. 8, 10 p.

KONDRATENKO, G.N.; ROZENBERG, N.M. "Obučajuščaja programma s adaptaciej po složnosti" (Programme à enseigner avec adaptation de la complexité), in Sovietskaja Pedagogika, 1969, Vol. 33, No. 9, 10 p. Rapport d'expérience.

MEL'NIKOVA, V.A. "Eksperimental'noje issledovanie effektivnosti sistemy programmirovannyh materialov dlja IX klassa" (Recherche expérimentale de l'efficacité de la programmation de la géométrie pour la classe de 9e), in Sovietskaja Pedagogika, 1968, Vol. 32, No. 7, 10 p. Rapport d'expérience.

SEMENOVA, G.F. "Kompleksnoe ispol'zovanie tehničeskih sredstv obučenija i ělementov programmirovanija v maldkomplektnoj nacal'noj škole" (Utilisation complexe des moyens techniques de l'enseignement et éléments de l'enseignement programmé dans les petites écoles primaires), in Sovetskaja Pedagogika, Vol. 31, No. 7, 7 p. Rapport d'expérience.

3 - BIBLIOGRAPHIES

Bibliografičeskij ukazatel' literatury po programmirovannomu obučeniu (Répertoire bibliographique de la littérature sur l'enseignement programmé). Moscou, Informacionnyj centr vysšej skoly (Centre d'information sur l'enseignement supérieur), 1968, 394 p. Collectif

ERŠOV, B.V. Ukazatel' literatury po naučnoj organizacii truda v učebnom processe (Répertoire de la littérature sur l'organisation scientifique du travail pédagogique). Moscou, Informacionnyj centre vysšej školy, 1968, 35 p.

III - RESEARCH AND APPLICATIONS / REALISATIONS

1 - RESEARCH / RECHERCHES

Thème: CYBERNETIQUE ET EDUCATION. ALGORITHMISATION ET HEURISTIQUE DANS L'ENSEIGNEMENT, LA FORMATION DES ELEVES (METHODES GENERALES DU RAISONNEMENT), ET LE DIAGNOSTIC DES CAUSES PSYCHOLOGIQUES DES ERREURS FAITES PAR LES ELEVES
Organisme: Institut de psychologie et de psychopédagogie de l'Académie des sciences pédagogiques de l'URSS, Laboratoire d'enseignement programmé
Public intéressé: Elèves des écoles secondaires

Thème: EVALUATION DE L'EFFICACITE DES METHODES DE L'E.P.
Organisme: Moskovskij Pedagogičeskij Institut "Lenin" (Institut pédagogique Lénine de Moscou), Laboratoire d'enseignement programmé
Public intéressé: Elèves des écoles secondaires

Thème: DETERMINATION DES PRINCIPES ET CREATION DE NOUVELLES MACHINES A ENSEIGNER SUR LA BASE DE LA MEMOIRE CYCLIQUE
Organisme: Institut de psychologie et de psychopédagogie de l'Académie des Sciences pédagogiques de l'URSS, Laboratoire d'enseignement programmé
Public intéressé: Elèves de tous les degrés et de tous les types d'écoles

Thème: DETERMINATION DES PRINCIPES ET ELABORATION D'UN MANUEL PROGRAMME DE LANGUE RUSSE POUR LES ECOLES PRIMAIRES ET SECONDAIRES
Organisme: Institut de psychologie et de psychopédagogie de l'Académie des Sciences pédagogiques de l'URSS, Laboratoire d'enseignement programmé
Public intéressé: Elèves des écoles secondaires

2 - PUBLISHED PROGRAMMED COURSES / COURS PROGRAMMES PUBLIES

GRANIK, G.G. (éd.) Syntaxe et ponctuation dans la langue russe. Moscou, Laboratoire d'enseignement programmé, Institut de psychologie et de psychopédagogie de l'Académie des Sciences pédagogiques de l'URSS, 1970.
Cours expérimentaux à l'usage des classes III-IV

————. BOŠOVIČ, Ed. Le russe programmé. Partie I. Moscou, Laboratoire d'enseignement programmé, Institut de psychologie et de psychopédagogie de l'Académie des Sciences pédagogiques de l'URSS, 1970.
Niveau secondaire

————.; YUDINA, O.N. Le russe programmé. Partie II. Moscou, Laboratoire d'enseignement programmé, Institut de psychologie et de psychopédagogie de l'Académie des Sciences pédagogiques de l'URSS, 1970.
Niveau secondaire

IL'INA, T.A.; HAR'KOVSKIJ, Z.S. Programmed English. Moscou, Institut Pédagogique Lénine de Moscou, 1967-1968, 14 fascicules.
Niveau secondaire

UNITED KINGDOM/ROYAUME UNI

I - ORGANIZATIONS AND ACTIVITIES / STRUCTURES ET ACTIVITES

1 - CENTRES

ARMY EDUCATION SERVICES
Old War Office Building,
Whitehall, London SW1A 2EU
Nature of organization: Governmental

ASSOCIATION FOR PROGRAMMED LEARNING AND EDUCATIONAL TECHNOLOGY (APLET)
33 Queen Anne Street, London W1M 0AL
Nature of organization: Independent

BATH UNIVERSITY OF TECHNOLOGY, SCHOOL OF EDUCATION
Northgate House,
Upper Borough Walls, Bath, Somerset
Nature of organization: University

BRITISH ASSOCIATION FOR COMMERCIAL AND INDUSTRIAL EDUCATION (BACIE)
16 Park Crescent, London W1N 4AP
Nature of organization: Registered as an educational charity organization

CENTRE FOR INDIVIDUAL LEARNING MATERIAL IN MEDICINE, DEPARTMENT OF AUDIO-VISUAL COMMUNICATION, BRITISH MEDICAL ASSOCIATION AND BRITISH LIFE ASSURANCE TRUST FOR HEALTH EDUCATION
B.M.A. House, London WC1H 9JP

EDUCATIONAL TECHNOLOGY CENTRE, UNIVERSITY OF SUSSEX
Falmer, Sussex
Nature of organization: University

GLASGOW UNIVERSITY DEPARTMENT OF EDUCATION
4 University Gardens, Glasgow G12 8QJ
Nature of organization: University

INSTITUTE OF CYBERNETICS, BRUNEL UNIVERSITY
Uxbridge, Middlesex
Nature of organization: University

NAVY EDUCATION SERVICES
Archway South,
Spring Gardens,
London SW1A 2BE
Nature of organization: Governmental

OPEN UNIVERSITY INSTITUTE OF EDUCATIONAL TECHNOLOGY
Bletchley, Bucks
Nature of organization: University

PROGRAMMED INSTRUCTION CENTRE, ENFIELD COLLEGE OF TECHNOLOGY,
Enfield, Middlesex
Nature of organization: College of technology

PROGRAMMED INSTRUCTION CENTRE FOR INDUSTRY (PICI)
University of Sheffield, Sheffield
Nature of organization: Governmental (Industrial Training Board)

PROGRAMMED LEARNING CENTRES NETWORK
c/o APLET
33 Queen Anne Street, London W1M OAL
Nature of organization: Independent

ROYAL AIR FORCE EDUCATIONAL BRANCH
Ministry of Defence (ED Ed S1 (RAF))
Adastral House
Theobalds Road,
London WC1X 8RV
Nature of organization: Governmental

(THE) ROYAL LIBERTY SCHOOL, COMPUTER DEPARTMENT
Hare Hall,
Upper Brentwood Road,
Romford RM2 6HJ

SCHOOL OF EDUCATION, UNIVERSITY OF BIRMINGHAM
P.O. Box 363, Birmingham 15
Nature of organization: University

SYSTEM RESEARCH LTD.,
2 Richmond Hill, Richmond, Surrey

2 - ACTIVITIES/MANIFESTATIONS

INTERNATIONAL CONFERENCE ON PROGRAMMED LEARNING AND EDUCATION TECHNOLOGY
(International annual conference)
Organized by: APLET

Places and dates: Bath University, 1972
Brighton College of Education, 1973
Participants: Research workers. School, university and vocational teachers. Adult educators.
Proceedings: <u>Aspects of Educational Technology</u>, London, Pitman & Co., Ltd.

OCCASIONAL SEMINARS AND CONFERENCES
Organized by: BACIE
Participants: Adult educators representing industry, commerce, education and organizations interested in educational technology.
Purpose: Promotion of the development of education and instruction in commerce and industry.

PROGRAMME WRITING WORKSHOPS (Regional conference)
Organized by: PIC, Enfield College of Technology
Place and dates: Enfield College, Enfield, February, May, October
Participants: School and vocational teachers
Purpose: Practical experience of programme writing

PROGRAMMES IN ACTION (Regional annual conference)
Organized by: Scotland Programmed Learning Group in conjunction with APLET
Date: September
Participants: Research workers. School, university and vocational teachers. Adult educators.
Purpose: Exchange information on practical uses for Programmed Learning.
Proceedings: Programmed Learning, Research Unit, University of Glasgow, University Gardens.

REGIONAL ONE DAY APLET CONFERENCE (Regional conference)
Organized by: APLET in conjunction with Enfield College of Technology, Loughborough College of Education, Bradford Technical College and others.
Place and date: Programme from APLET, 33 Queen Anne Street, London W1M OAL
Participants: Research workers. School, university and vocational teachers.

3 — PUBLISHERS/MAISONS D'EDITION

AUTOBATES LEARNING SYSTEMS LTD.
Whitestone House, Lutterworth Road, Nuneaton, Warwickshire
Nature of organization: Commercial publisher

KOGAN-PAGE
16 Grays Inn Road, London W.C.1
Nature of organization: Commercial publisher

LONGMAN GROUP LTD.,
Longman House, Burnt Mill, Harlow, Essex.
Nature of organization: Commercial publisher

METHUEN EDUCATIONAL LTD.,
11 New Fetter Lane, London EC4P 4EE
Nature of organization: Commercial publisher

OPEN UNIVERSITY PRESS LIMITED,
Bletchley, Bucks.
Nature of organization: University press

PERGAMON PRESS LTD.,
Headington Hill Hall, Oxford
Nature of organization: Commercial publisher

SIR ISAAC PITMAN AND SONS LTD.,
39 Parker Street, Kingsway, London W.C.2
Nature of organization: Commercial publisher

PROGRAMMED INSTRUCTION CENTRE FOR INDUSTRY (PICI)
University of Sheffield
Nature of organization: Associated with a university

STILLITRON
72 New Bond Street, London W1Y OQT
Nature of organization: Language and programme publisher

UNIVERSITY OF LONDON PRESS
8 Warwick Lane, London E.C.4
Nature of organization: University press

JOHN WILEY AND SONS LTD.,
Baffin Lane, Chichester, Sussex
Nature of organization: Commercial publisher

4 - PERIODICALS/PERIODIQUES

INSTRUCTIONAL SCIENCE
Publisher: Elsevier
Address: 61 Pall Mall, London SW1Y 5HZ

(THE) JOURNAL OF EDUCATIONAL TECHNOLOGY
Publisher: Councils and Education Press Ltd. (NCET)
Address: 10 Queen Ann Street, London W.1
Field of
  interest: Survey. Application

JOURNAL OF MAN-MACHINES STUDIES
Publisher: Academic Press (London Ltd.)
Address: Berkeley Square House, Berkeley Square, London, W.1

PROGRAMME
Publisher: Programmed Instruction Centre for Industry
Address: 32 Northumberland Road, Sheffield S10 2TX
Periodicity: Fortnightly
Field of
  interest: Application (industrial). News

PROGRAMMED LEARNING AND EDUCATIONAL TECHNOLOGY
Publisher: Sweet & Maxwell
Address: 11 New Fetter Lane, London E.C.4P 4EE
Periodicity: Bi-monthly
Field of
  interest: Research. Reviews and descriptions of innovation in education

RECALL (REVIEW OF EDUCATIONAL CYBERNETICS AND APPLIED LINGUISTICS)
Publisher: Longmac Ltd.,
Address: Victoria Hall, East Greenwich, London SE10 ORF
Periodicity: 3 times a year
Field of
  interest: Research

5 - PROFESSIONAL ORGANIZATIONS/ORGANISATIONS PROFESSIONNELLES

APLET
33 Queen Anne Street, London W1M OAL
Activities: Dissemination of information about programmed instruction

BRITISH ASSOCIATION FOR COMMERCIAL AND INDUSTRIAL EDUCATION
16 Park Crescent, London W1N 4AP
Public
  concerned: Members of the association representing industry, commerce, education and government
Activities: Promotion of the development of education and instruction in commerce and industry

CONSTRUCTION INDUSTRY TRAINING BOARD
Radnor House, London Road, Norbury, London S.W.16
Nature of
  organization: Industrial training board
Activities: Has its own programme writing department

INBUCON LEARNING SYSTEMS
Ancaster Lodge, Queens Road, Richmond, Surrey
Public
  concerned: Adult industrial training
Activities: Training consultants, writers of programmed materials

NATIONAL COUNCIL FOR EDUCATIONAL TECHNOLOGY
160 Great Portland Street, London W1N 5TB
Activities: To develop and promote the application of educational technology at all levels of education and training throughout the United Kingdom. The Council is an independent body financed in the main by Government Departments, but also accepting support for its projects from other sources.

NETWORK OF PROGRAMMED LEARNING CENTRES
St. Albans College, St. Albans, Herts
Public
  concerned: Full-time practitioners in educational technology
Activities: To support the work of the teachers and instructors responsible for the use of Programmed Instruction, and similar techniques within organizations in school districts

SYSTEM RESEARCH LTD.,
2 Richmond Hill, Richmond, Surrey
Public
  concerned: Adult. Industrial training
Activities: Simulation. Computer simulated model for learning in a CAI system. Adaptively controlled compensatory tacking. CAI System for rule application learning. CAI System for probability. CAI System for statistics. CAI System for taxonomies. CAI System for biological systems. CAI System for learning to learn

6 - MANUFACTURERS OF TEACHING MACHINES/FABRICANTS DE MACHINES A ENSEIGNER

E.J. ARNOLD
Butterley Street, Leeds LS10 1AX
Characteristics: Linear programme. Storage of replies. Integrated audio-visual device. Using paper roll. Individual use

AUTOBATES LEARNING SYSTEMS LTD.,
Whitestone House, Lutterworth Road, Nuneaton, Warwickshire
Characteristics: a) Linear programme. Storage of Replies. Integrated audio-visual device. Using paper roll. Individual use.
b) Linear or branching programme. Flash frames. Storage of replies. Using paper roll. Individual use

E.S.L. BRISTOL LTD.,
St. Lawrence House, 29-31 Broad Street, Bristol BS1 E HF
Type of machine: Bristol tutor, Auto tutor
Characteristics: Branching programme. Individual use

INTERNATIONAL TUTOR MACHINES
Ashford Road, Ashford, Middlesex
Type of machine: a) Grandytutor, b) Grundymaster, c) ITM group tutor
Characteristics: a) Branching programme. Individual use
b) Linear programme. Storage of replies. Individual use
c) Branching programme. Collective use

PACKMAN RESEARCH LTD.,
Twyford RG 10, 9BB, Berkshire
Type of machine: Tutorpack Linear
Characteristics: Loose sheet linear programme. Answer slips for storage of answers.

PLESSEY LTD.,
Abbey Works, Tichfield, Fareham, Hampshire
Type of machine: Supervisor (linked tap and filmstrip-automatic stop + rewi
Characteristics: Linear programme. Audio-visual integrated. Individual-collective use

STILLITRON
72 New Bond Street, London W.1
Type of machine: Stillitron (multiple-choice, response board)
Characteristics: Individual use, giving immediate confirmation of correctness or error with green and red lights. Portable.

SYSTEM RESEARCH LTD., (GOVERNANCE LTD., IN COLLABORATION WITH ELECTROSONICS)
2 Richmond Hill, Richmond, Surrey
Type of machine: Boss, Master, Caste I

7 - TRAINING ORGANIZATIONS/ORGANISMES ASSURANT UNE FORMATION

CENTRE FOR EDUCATIONAL TECHNOLOGY
Sussex University, Falmer, Sussex
Public concerned: School, university and adult teachers. Vocational teachers. Adult educators.

CENTRE FOR INDIVIDUAL LEARNING MATERIAL IN MEDICINE, DEPARTMENT OF AUDIO VISUAL COMMUNICATION, BRITISH MEDICAL ASSOCIATION AND BRITISH LIFE ASSURANCE TRUST FOR HEALTH EDUCATION
B.M.A. House, London, WC1H 9JP

CITY AND GUILDS OF LONDON INSTITUTE
76 Portland Place, London W1N 4AA
Nature of
  organization: Examining Board
Public concerned: School and vocational teachers. Adult educators. Training officers and directors.

E.S.L. BRISTOL
St. Lawrence House, 29-31 Broad Street, Bristol
Nature of
　organization:　　Business
Public concerned:　School and vocational teachers.

OPEN UNIVERSITY INSTITUTE OF EDUCATIONAL TECHNOLOGY
Bletchley, Bucks.
Public concerned:　University teachers

PROGRAMMED INSTRUCTION CENTRE
College of Technology, Enfield
Nature of
　organization:　　College of technology
Public concerned:　School and vocational teachers. Adult educators.

PROGRAMMED INSTRUCTION CENTRE FOR INDUSTRY (PICI)
University of Sheffield
Nature of
　organization:　　Governmental
Public concerned:　Vocational teachers

PROGRAMMED LEARNING CENTRE, UNIVERSITY OF BIRMINGHAM
50 Wellington Road, Edgbaston, Birmingham 15
Nature of
　organization:　　University
Public concerned:　School and university teachers

8 - DOCUMENTATION CENTRES/CENTRES DE DOCUMENTATION

APLET
33 Queen Anne Street, London W1M 0AL
Type of services:　　Individual advice list of all programmes in
　　　　　　　　　　　print. Yearbook of Educational Technology

BRITISH ASSOCIATION FOR COMMERCIAL AND INDUSTRIAL EDUCATION (BACIE)
16 Park Crescent, London W1N 4AP
Type of services:　　Register of programmed instruction teaching aids
　　　　　　　　　　　index. Collects books and documents on all aspects
　　　　　　　　　　　of programmed instruction and vocational training
　　　　　　　　　　　in general.

DEPARTMENT OF AUDIO VISUAL COMMUNICATION. BRITISH MEDICAL ASSOCIATION AND
BRITISH LIFE ASSURANCE TRUST FOR HEALTH EDUCATION
B.M.A. House, London WC1H 9JP
Nature of organization:　Professional
Type of services:　　Publication of bi-monthly bulletin Information,
　　　　　　　　　　　catalogues on learning materials and bibliographies.
　　　　　　　　　　　Individual advice on techniques, applications, equipment
　　　　　　　　　　　and available programmes. Certification of films and
　　　　　　　　　　　audio tapes which meet specific educational criteria.

OPEN UNIVERSITY LIBRARY
Bletchley, Bucks.
Type of services:　　Educational technology collection. All normal
　　　　　　　　　　　library services.

PROGRAMMED INSTRUCTION CENTRE
Enfield College of Technology, Enfield, Middlesex
Nature or organization: College of technology
Type of services: Individual advice surveys on the use of programmes.
                          Surveys of research.

PROGRAMMED INSTRUCTION CENTRE FOR INDUSTRY
University of Sheffield
Type of services: Advice on the application of programmed instruction
                          to industry and commerce. Bibliographies

II - PUBLICATIONS

1 - BOOKS / LIVRES

Aspects of Educational Technology (II). Ed. by W.R. Dunn and C. Holroyd. London, Methuen, 1969, 670 p.
Proceedings of 1968 APLET conference

Aspects of Educational Technology (III). Ed. by A.P. Mann et al. London, Isaac Pitman, 1969.
Proceedings of 1969 APLET conference

Aspects of Educational Technology (IV). Ed. by F.J. Leedham et al. London, Isaac Pitman, 1970, 420 p.
Proceedings of 1970 APLET conference

Aspects of Educational Technology (V). Ed. by Packham et al. London, Isaac Pitman, 1971, 488 p.
Proceedings of 1971 APLET conference

Aspects of Educational Technology (VI). Ed. by K. Austwick et al. London, Isaac Pitman, 1972.
Proceedings of 1972 APLET conference

BUNG, Klaus. Programmed learning and the language laboratory. 2 vols. 1967 and 1968. Longmac, London

GILBERT, Thomas F. Mathetics. An explicit theory for the design of teaching programmes. Longmac, London

LEITH, G.O.M. Second thoughts on programmed learning. London, National Council for Educational Technology, 1969, 16 p.
Survey of impact of programmed instruction critic pointing out valuable features, future trends

LYNE, R.W. Programmed instruction in industry. Training system in industry. A series of case-studies. Oxford, Pergamon, volume 2, 1969

ROMISZOWSKI, A.J. The selection and use of teaching aids. A system approach to course design. London, Kogan-Page Publishers Ltd., 1968, 166 p.
The application of programmed instruction principles to the design of efficient teaching and training aids and exercices

————. Yearbook of educational and instructional technology. London, Kogan-Page Publishers Ltd., 1972/73, 412 p.

TANSEY, P.J.; UNWIN, D. Simulation and Gaming. London, Methuen, 1969.
A general survey

TAYLOR, George (ed.) The teacher as manager: A symposium. National Council for Educational Technology Publications

UNWIN, D. Media and methods. London, MacGraw Hill, 1969, 219 p. Survey of media and methods in educational technology with special reference to higher education

2 - ARTICLES

"Applications of theoretical principles to a miniature teaching system. A diagnostic branching system for remedial training in the manipulation of vulgar fractions", in P.I.C.I., 1968-1969, 14 p.

CAVANAGH, P.; JONES, C. "Programmed learning in the universities, local educational authorities, colleges of further education", in Programmed Learning and Educational Technology, January, April 1968.

_____; _____. "Programmes in action" in Yearbook of educational and instructional technology, 1969, 35 p. Survey.

DODD, B.T.; HUDSON, E.A.; BECK, J.E. "Introduction to the programmed instruction centre for industry", in P.I.C.I., 1968-1969, 3 p.

_____; _____; _____. "Training for decimilisation", in P.I.C.I., 1968-1969, 27 p.

ENGEL, C.E. "Preparation of Audio Tapes for Self-Instruction", in Medical and Biological Illustration, No.21, 1971, p. 14-18.

_____; COOPER, W.J. "Television Replay Systems", in Medical Teacher, No.2, 1972, p. 5-9.

"Experiments with machine-like teaching at the undergraduate and management level", in P.I.C.I., 1968-1969, 4 p.

"The evaluation of programmed instruction: does it teach?", in P.I.C.I., 1968-1969, 12 p.

"The evaluation of programmed instruction: how much does it cost?", in P.I.C.I., 1968-1969, 22 p.

GILBERT, L.A. "Educational technology in the United Kingdom", in Educational Technology, Vol.9, No.II, 1969, 5 p.

"Mathetics, a procedural guide", in P.I.C.I., 1968-1969, 18 p.

PASK, Gordon. "The meaning of Cybernetics in the Behavioural Sciences", in Progress of Cybernetics, Vol. 1 (J. Rose, ed.) p. 15-45, Gordon and Breach, 1970. Reprinted in Cybernetics No.3, 1970, p. 140-159 and in No.4, 1970, p.240-250. Reprinted in Artoga Communications p. 146-148, 1971.

_____. "Teaching machines" in Modern Trends in Education (Dr. B. Rose, ed.). Macmillan, Sept. 1971. p.216-259.

_____; SCOTT, B.C.E. "Learning and Teaching Strategies in a Transformation Skill", in British Journal of Mathematical and Statistical Psychology, Vol.24, November 1971, p. 205-229.

_____. "Fundamental Aspects of Educational Technology Illustrated by the Principles of Conversational Systems", in Proceedings IFIP World Conference on Computer Education, Vol. 1, Invited papers. Ed. by Sheepmaker, R. p. 1-29 to 1-52, Amsterdam, IFIP, 1970.

_____. "Computer Assisted Learning and Teaching" in Proceedings of the Leeds Seminar on Computer Based Learning (Annett J. Duke, ed.). NCET, 1970, p.50-63.

_____. "Interaction between individuals, its stability and style", in Mathematical Biosciences vol. II (Richard Bellman ed.), American Elsevier Publication, June 1971, p.59-84

_____. "A cybernetic experimental method and its underlying philosophy", in International Journal Man-Machine Studies. London, January 1972, p.279-337

ROMISZOWSKI, A.J. "Trends in programmed instruction in industry", in Aspects of Educational Technology, Vol. 2, 1968. Survey.

_____; BIRAN, L.A. "Survey of research and development in programmed instruction in Member Countries".(A Council of Europe publication.)

TOBIN, M. "A series of case histories of the use of programmed learning", London, National Committee for Audio-Visual Aids in Education, 1969.

WAKEFORD, R.E. "Some observations on multiple choice questions used in conjunction with self-instructional materials", in Medical and Biological Illustration, No. 21, 1971, p. 25-26.

_____. "Preparing Audio-tape recordings for individual study: notes on the relative acceptability of different speakers", in Medical and Biological Illustration, No. 22, 1972, p. 13-14.

3 - BIBLIOGRAPHIES

BIRAN, L.A.; WAKEFORD, R.E. Programmes in the health sciences. National Centre for Programmed Learning, 1970.

ERAUT, Michael; SQUIRES, Geoffrey. An Annotated Select Bibliography of Educational Technology, National Council for Educational Technology, 1970.

PERRY, P.J.C. (ed.) Registers of Programmed Instruction, London, British Association for Commercial and Industrial Education, 1968, 189 p.

P.I.C.I. Programmes for Industry. Subject Lists. Sheffield University, 1968-1969. Topics: Decimalization 27 p.; Metrication 19 p.; Sales training 49 p.; Work study 17 p.; Managers 16 p.; Textiles 33 p.; Programmed Learning and Educational Technology 60 p.; Safety training 18 p.; Network analysis 16 p.; Chemical process operators 23 p.; Computers 60 p.

ROMISZOWSKI, A.J. (ed.) 'APLET' Yearbook of Educational and Instructional Technology 1972/73, London, Kogan-Page Publishers Ltd.

TAMSEY, P.J., UNWIN, D. Simulation and gaming in education and training: a bibliography. New University of Ulster, Coleraine, Northern Ireland, 1969.

United Kingdom/Royaume-Uni

III - RESEARCH AND APPLICATIONS/REALISATIONS

1 - RESEARCH/RECHERCHES

Theme: ANALYSIS OF TASKS FOR TRAINING
Organized by: Department of Psychology, University of Hull
Public concerned: Adults, technical training

Theme: APPLICATION OF SELF-INSTRUCTION
Organized by: University of Glasgow
Public concerned: Medical and educational students

Theme: COLLEGES OF EDUCATION LEARNING PROGRAMMES PROJECT
A small team has assessed the needs of colleges of education for multi-media learning materials for use by students, preparatory to the planning of a large scale project.
Organized by: National Council for Educational Technology

Theme: CONTINUING MATHEMATICS PROJECT
Organized by: National Council for Educational Technology
Public concerned: Non-specialist mathematicians in the 16-20 age group

Theme: CO-OPERATION IN THE PRODUCTION AND USE OF VISUAL INSTRUCTION MATERIALS BETWEEN FIVE UNIVERSITIES
Organized by: Universities of Bath, Birmingham, Glasgow, London and Sussex, under auspices of the Nuffield Foundation (Nuffield Inter-University Biology Teaching Project)
Public concerned: University students

Theme: DEVELOPMENT AND USE OF PROGRAMMED MATERIALS IN UNIVERSITIES
Organized by: University of Sussex

Theme: DEVELOPMENT IN THE USE OF SIMULATION AND GAMING AS TEACHING TECHNIQUES WITHIN PROGRAMMED COURSES
Organized by: The Education Centre, New University of Ulster
Public concerned: School children

Theme: DEVELOPMENT OF TESTING AND PRODUCTION PROCEDURES FOR INDIVIDUALIZED INSTRUCTION. A SYSTEM APPROACH IS USED IN THE DEVELOPMENT OF COURSES FOR TEACHERS
Organized by: Jordanhill College of Education, Glasgow
Public concerned: School children

Theme: DEVELOPMENT AND TESTING OF MULTI-MEDIA TEACHING METHODS
Organized by: College of Education, Loughborough, Leics.
Public concerned: School children

Theme: DEVELOPMENT AND EVALUATION OF THE USE OF ALGORITHMIC JOB-AID FOR FAULT-FINDING TASKS
Organized by: Training Command, Royal Air Force, Brompton, Huntington
Public concerned: Airmen

Theme: DEVELOPMENT AND EVALUATION OF THE USE OF AUDIO-VISUAL PROGRAMMES IN MEDICAL TRAINING
Organized by: Department of Audio-Visual Communication, British Medical Association and British Life Assurance Trust for Health Education

Theme: DEVELOPMENT OF A COMPUTER-BASED FEEDBACK CLASSROOM
Organized by: Department of Electrical Engineering Science, University of Essex, Wirenhoe Park, Colchester, Essex.
Public concerned: University students

Theme: DEVELOPMENT AND TESTING OF METHODS OF TASK ANALYSIS
Organized by: Department of Psychology, University of Hull
Public concerned: Industrial employees

Theme: ESTABLISHMENT OF THE FEASIBILITY OF USING PROGRAMMED INSTRUCTION AMONG OTHER TECHNIQUES, TO INCREASE THE EFFICIENCY/EFFECTIVENESS OF EDUCATION
Organized by: Various educational institutions on contracts under the Nuffield Resources for Learning Project
Public concerned: School children

Theme: FAMILIARIZATION COURSE IN EDUCATIONAL TECHNOLOGY
Preparation of packages of 'core' materials for use by organizers of courses in educational technology.
Organized by: National Council for Educational Technology

Theme: FEASIBILITY STUDY OF THE SYSTEMS APPROACH TO DESIGN, AND EVALUATION OF CONTINUING EDUCATION IN MEDICINE
Organized by: Department of Audio-Visual Communication, British Medical Assoc. and British Life Assurance Trust for Health Education and Department of General Practice, University of Manchester.

Theme: FEASIBILITY STUDY OF THE SYSTEMS APPROACH TO DESIGN AND EVALUATION OF POSTGRADUATE EDUCATION IN MEDICINE
Organized by: Department of Audio-Visual Communication, British Medical Assoc. British Life Assurance Trust for Health Education and St. Mary's Hospital, Medical School, London

Theme: INCREASE EFFECTIVENESS OF TEACHING SECONDARY SCHOOL MATHEMATICS THROUGH PROGRAMMED INSTRUCTION
Organized by: France Hill Comprehensive School, Camberley, Surrey, and other schools
Public concerned: School children. School teachers and programmers of E.S.L. Bristol

Theme: MEDIA CATALOGUING RULES
A joint project with the Library Association for the establishment of a specialist group to formulate rules for the cataloguing of non-print materials
Organized by: National Council for Educational Technology

Theme: PREPARATION OF PROGRAMME UNITS IN PRE-UNIVERSITY CHEMISTRY AND UNIVERSITY BIOLOGY
Organized by: College of Science and Technology, Centre for Science Education, Bridges Place, London.
Public concerned: School students (16-20 years)

United Kingdom/Royaume-Uni

Theme: **PRIMARY EXTENSION PROGRAMME**
Development of audio-visual materials to help with the education of young disadvantaged children
Organized by: National Council for Educational Technology

Theme: **PROGRAMMED LANGUAGE INSTRUCTION. DEVELOPMENT OF ALGORITHMS AND EXPLICIT PROCEDURES IN EDUCATION AND TRAINING**
Organized by: Department of Linguistics, University of Cambridge
Public concerned: Adolescents. Adults

Theme: **RESOURCE CENTRES IN COLLEGES OF EDUCATION**
An investigation of the current provision, aims and use of Resource Centres, which lead to a report at the end of 1971 giving guidelines for the future of this important new development.
Organized by: National Council for Educational Technology

Theme: **SURVEY OF THE REACTION OF PRIMARY SCHOOL COMMUNITIES TO A TECHNOLOGICAL LEARNING ENVIRONMENT**
A survey in connexion with the Primary Extension Programme of experience in organizing the use of equipment and materials by pupils, and the reactions of teaching staff in schools making major use of audio-visual techniques.
Organized by: National Council for Educational Technology

Theme: **SYSTEMATIC ANALYSIS OF FORESTRY SKILL TRAINING**
Co-operative project with the Agricultural Horticultural and Forestry Industry Training Board concerned with on-the-job training of forestry workers at skilled operative level.
Organized by: National Council for Educational Technology

Theme: **TRANSLATION FROM THE DANISH OF A COMPLETE SET OF BEHAVIOURAL LEARNING OBJECTIVES FOR AN UNDERGRADUATE MEDICAL COURSE IN PHYSIOLOGY AT AARHUS UNIVERSITY**
Organized by: Department of Audio-Visual Communication, British Medical Assoc., and British Life Assurance Trust for Health Education

Theme: **VARIETY OF PROJECTS COVERING MOST ISSUES IN PROGRAMMED INSTRUCTION**
Organized by: R.A.F. School of Education and Army School of Instructional Technology
Public concerned: Military personnel

2 - PUBLISHED PROGRAMMED COURSES/COURS PROGRAMMES PUBLIES

BLARHE, J. _Arithmetic, understanding number base._ A first book of notation, Longmans, Green & Co., Ltd., 1969, 72 items.

_____. _Arithmetic + place value._ A second book of notation, Longmans.

CAMBRIDGE CONSULTANTS LTD. _Programmed Introduction to Critical Path Methods._ Oxford, Pergamon.

CONSTRUCTION INDUSTRY TRAINING BOARD. _Arrow Diagram Planning._ London, Pitman Publishing.

———————. Mathematics. Retraining for metrication. C.I.T.B. 1969, 10 p. 7 programmes (8, 27, 18, 74, 50, 65, 65 pages each).

———————. Precedence Diagram Planning. London, Pitman Publishing.

CRAFT ENGINEERING APPRENTISER. Basic Workshop Techniques. International Tutor Machines, 1966-1968, 60 programme modules, average of 150 frames each.

DAVIES, J.; OWEN, J.W. Laboratory Procedures: Pipette, Volumetric Flask, and Burette. Pitman Publishing, 1969.

————; ————. Laboratory Procedures: Weighing. London, Pitman Publishing, 1969, 82 frames.

DODD, B.; HUDSON, E.A.; BECK, J.E. Decimalisation. University of Sheffield, P.I.C.I., 14 p.

EARNSHAW, J.D.; BLACKFORD, W. Algol. London, Pitman Publishing, 1970, 521 frames.

ERAUT, M.R. Fundamentals of Arithmetic: A Programme for Self-Instruction. McGraw-Hill, 1970.

———————. Fundamentals of Elementary Algebra: A Programme for Self-Instruction. McGraw-Hill, 1970.

———————. Fundamentals of Intermediate Algebra: A Programme for Self-Instruction. McGraw-Hill, 1970.

GEORGE, F.H. The Brain as a Computer. 2nd edition. Oxford, Pergamon.

———————. Computer Arithmetic. Oxford, Pergamon

———————. Introduction to Computer Programming. Oxford, Pergamon

———————. An Introduction to Digital Computing. Oxford, Pergamon

———————. A Survey of Digital Computing. Oxford, Pergamon

GUNSTONE, F.D. Programmes in organic chemistry. London, The English University Press, 77 + 129 + 203 items, 32 + 44 + 68 p.

HODGE, H.P.R.; COULL, D.; WEIR, R.D. The prescription and administration of drugs in hospital. Glasgow, Jordanhill College of Education, 1968, 98 p.

KIND, R.W.; LEEDHAM, J. Contraception, Programmed Sex, Information Series. Longmans, 1968, 42 frames.

LEARNING SYSTEMS LTD. Break Even Charts. Oxford, Pergamon

———————. Discounted cash flow. Oxford, Pergamon

———————. Industrial Training Act: How it Affects You. Oxford, Pergamon.

———————. Manager and Programmed Learning. Oxford, Pergamon.

———————. Filing and Indexing. London, Pitman Publishing, 1971, 144 frames.

LEWIS, B.N.; WOOLFENDEN, P.J. Algorithms and logical trees. Cambridge, Algorithms Press, 1969, 55 p.

OLIVER, W.D. Science for beginners, (III), London, Stillit Books. Book I; How liquids behave, Book 2; Water, Book 3; Solids.

P.I.C.I. Chemical Process Operator. Sheffield, 23 p.

_____ . Computer. Sheffield, 60 p.

_____ . Network Analysis. Sheffield, 16 p.

_____ . Numerical Techniques (for managers). Sheffield, 11 p.

_____ . Programmed Learning and Educational Technology. Sheffield, 60 p.

_____ . Safety Training. Sheffield, 18 p.

_____ . Sales Training. Sheffield, 54 p.

_____ . Statistics, Sheffield, 14 p.

_____ . Textiles. Sheffield, 33 p.

_____ . Understanding accounting. Sheffield, 19 p.

_____ . Work study. Sheffield, 16 p.

STONES, E. Psychology of learning. Learning and Teaching: A Programmed Introduction. J. Wiley & Sons Ltd., 1968, 458 items, 114 p.

STRUCTURAL COMMUNICATIONS CENTRE LTD. Structural Communications Topics: (1) Chemical Structure; (2) The Biology and Energetics of Nutrition. London University Press, 1969, 96 p.

WILSON, Susan. Introduction to Logic. Open University Press, 1971.

WINGATE, T.H. Systematic Electronic Fault Diagnosis. London, Pitman Publishing, 1968.

The following programmes have been prepared and published by The Audio-Visual Communications Department of the British Medical Association for use in teaching hospitals

BARNETT, Professor C.H. Congenital abnormalities.

MARSHALL, Dr. P.B. Drugs acting on the peripheral nervous system.

SMAJE, Dr. L. Haemostasis and blood groups.

WORLLEDGE, Dr. Sheila. Blood transfusion laboratory exercises.

_____ . Blood transfusion (lectures): Blood group antigens; Blood group antibodies; Antigen-Antibody reactions.

3 - COMPUTER-ASSISTED INSTRUCTION / ENSEIGNEMENT ASSISTE PAR ORDINATEUR

ADAPTIVE TRAINING FOR MANUAL AND PERCEPTIVE SKILLS
Organization: Department of Electrical Engineering Science, University of Essex
Public concerned: Pilots. Technicians
Purpose: Evaluation

BIOLOGY, COMPUTER MANAGED COURSE
Organization: International Computer Ltd.
Public concerned: 12-15 year old school children
Type of computer: I.C.L.
Purpose: Evaluation, teaching

COMPUTER BASED TEACHING SYSTEMS FOR MATHEMATICS, STATISTICS, CHEMISTRY, MEDICINE (DIAGNOSTIC SKILLS), TEACHER TRAINING.
Organization: Department of Education, University of Leeds
Public concerned: University students and schools (pupils 9-13 years)
Purpose: Evaluation, teaching

DEVELOPMENT OF COMPUTER-BASED FEEDBACK CLASSROOM AND OF TERMINALS FOR C.A.I.
Organization: University of Essex
Public concerned: Schools
Purpose: Evaluation, teaching, technical training

DEVELOPMENT OF COMPUTER MANAGED INSTRUCTION AND USE OF COMPUTER IN STUDY OF MATHEMATICS, COMPUTING, PURE AND APPLIED SCIENCE AND THE HUMANITIES
Organization: Royal Liberty School, Computer Department
Public concerned: Secondary education and school children
Type of language: ALGOL, Basic
Purpose: Evaluation, teaching

REMEDIAL MATHEMATICS (MANAGEMENT OF TESTING, GUIDANCE BY COMPUTER)
Organization: Programmed Instruction Centre, Enfield College of Technology
Type of computer: Honeywell 200
Type of terminals: Off-line car punchers
Type of language: Fortran (for programming)
Purpose: Evaluation, teaching

RESEARCH ON COMPUTER MANAGED INSTRUCTION (TEST MARKING, RECORD KEEPING ETC.)
Organization: International Computer Ltd.
Public concerned: Schools
Type of computer: I.C.L.
Purpose: Evaluation

SIMULATION
Organization: System Research Ltd.
Public concerned: Adults. Industrial training
Purpose: Teaching. Research into psychological issues (learning strategies, cognitive representation ...)

UNITED STATES OF AMERICA/ETATS-UNIS D'AMERIQUE

I - ORGANIZATIONS AND ACTIVITIES / STRUCTURES ET ACTIVITES

1 - CENTRES

A - UNIVERSITY AND RESEARCH CENTRES / UNIVERSITES ET CENTRES DE RECHERCHES

AMERICAN INSTITUTE FOR RESEARCH
710 Chatham Center, Pittsburgh, Pennsylvania 15219

AREA OF INSTRUCTIONAL TECHNOLOGY, SYRACUSE UNIVERSITY
123 College Place, Syracuse, New York 13210

AUTOMATED LEARNING CENTER, NEW MEXICO UNIVERSITY
Portales, New Mexico 88130

CENTER FOR EDUCATIONAL TECHNOLOGY, CATHOLIC UNIVERSITY OF AMERICA
Washington, D.C. 20017

CENTER FOR EDUCATIONAL TECHNOLOGY, FLORIDA STATE UNIVERSITY
Tallahassee, Florida 32306

CENTER FOR PROGRAMMED LEARNING, UNIVERSITY OF MICHIGAN
Bureau of Industrial Relations, Annarbor, Michigan 48104

CENTER FOR THE STUDY OF PROGRAMMED LEARNING, UNIVERSITY OF MINNESOTA
Minnepolis, Minnesota 55455

COMPUTER ASSISTED INSTRUCTION CENTER, HARVARD UNIVERSITY
Cambridge, Massachusetts 02138

COMPUTER ASSISTED INSTRUCTION LABORATORY, PENNSYLVANIA STATE UNIVERSITY
University Park, Pennsylvania 16802

EDUCATIONAL TECHNOLOGY CENTER, UNIVERSITY OF MARYLAND
College Park, Maryland 20742

INSTITUTE FOR COMMUNICATION RESEARCH, UNIVERSITY OF STANFORD
Palo Alto, California 94305

INSTITUTE FOR EDUCATIONAL DEVELOPMENT
999 North Sepulveda Boulevard, El Segundo, California 90245

INSTITUTE FOR EDUCATIONAL TECHNOLOGY, COLUMBIA UNIVERSITY
525 West 120th Street, New York, N.Y. 10027

INSTITUTE OF HUMAN LEARNING, UNIVERSITY OF CALIFORNIA
Berkeley, California 94720

INSTRUCTIONAL MEDIA RESEARCH UNIT, PURDUE UNIVERSITY
Lafayette, Indiana 47907

INSTRUCTIONAL RESOURCES CENTER, UNIVERSITY OF ILLINOIS AT CHICAGO CIRCLE
Chicago, Illinois 60608

LAWRENCE HALL OF SCIENCE, UNIVERSITY OF CALIFORNIA
Berkeley, California 94720

LEARNING RESEARCH AND DEVELOPMENT CENTER, UNIVERSITY OF PITTSBURGH
160 North Craig St., Pittsburgh, Pennsylvania 15213

OFFICE OF INSTITUTIONAL RESEARCH
Washington, D.C. 20002

OFFICE FOR INSTRUCTIONAL DEVELOPMENT, HARVARD SCHOOL OF PUBLIC HEALTH
55 Shattuck Street, Boston (Mass. 02115)

ROCHESTER CLEARINGHOUSE ON SELF-INSTRUCTIONAL MATERIALS FOR HEALTH CARE
FACILITIES, UNIVERSITY OF ROCHESTER
River Campus Station, Rochester, New York 14627

B - REGIONAL EDUCATIONAL LABORATORIES/LABORATOIRES PEDAGOGIQUES REGIONAUX

APPALACHIA EDUCATIONAL LABORATORY
Atlas Building, P.O. Box 1348, Charleston, West Virginia 25301

CENTER FOR URBAN EDUCATION
105 Madison Avenue, New York 10016

CENTRAL MIDWESTERN REGIONAL EDUCATIONAL LABORATORY (CEMREL)
10646 St. Charles Rock Road, St. Ann, Missouri 63074

FAR WEST LABORATORY FOR EDUCATIONAL RESEARCH AND DEVELOPMENT
Claremont Hotel, 1 Garden Circle, Berkeley, California 94705

MID-CONTINENT REGIONAL EDUCATIONAL LABORATORY
104 East Independence Avenue, Kansas City, Missouri 64106

NATIONAL CENTER FOR EDUCATIONAL TECHNOLOGY
U.S. Office of Education
Washington D.C. 20202

NATIONAL LABORATORY FOR HIGHER EDUCATION
Mutual Plaza, Durham, North Carolina 27701

NORTHWEST REGIONAL EDUCATIONAL LABORATORY
400 Lindsay Building, 710 Southwest Second Avenue, Portland, Oregon 97204

RESEARCH FOR BETTER SCHOOLS, INC.,
1700 Market Street, Philadelphia, Pennsylvania 19103

SOUTHEASTERN EDUCATION LABORATORY
Georgetown Square Office Park, Suite 207,
1750 Old Springhouse Lane, N.E., Atlanta, Georgia 30341

SOUTHWEST EDUCATIONAL DEVELOPMENT LABORATORY
800 Brazos Street, Austin, Texas 78701

SOUTHWEST REGIONAL LABORATORY FOR EDUCATIONAL RESEARCH AND DEVELOPMENT
4665 Lampson Avenue,
Los Alamitos, California 90720

SOUTHWESTERN COOPERATIVE EDUCATIONAL LABORATORY
404 S. Mateo Boulevard, Albuquerque, New Mexico 87108

C - RESEARCH AND DEVELOPMENT CENTERS / CENTRES DE RECHERCHE ET DE DEVELOPPEMENT

CENTER FOR THE ADVANCED STUDY ON EDUCATIONAL ADMINISTRATION, UNIVERSITY OF OREGON
Eugene, Oregon 97401
Activities: Control of instructional policy. Organizational implications of instructional change. Strategies of organizational change. Procedures of System Planning Instructional Materials Development.

CENTER FOR OCCUPATIONAL EDUCATION, NORTH CAROLINA STATE UNIVERSITY
1 Maiden Lane, Raleigh, North California

CENTER FOR RESEARCH AND DEVELOPMENT IN HIGHER EDUCATION, UNIVERSITY OF CALIFORNIA
Berkeley, California 94704
Activities: Developing relevant programmes for new studies. Appropriate structures. Participants and processes for development. Educational impact and student development.

CENTER FOR RESEARCH AND LEADERSHIP DEVELOPMENT IN VOCATIONAL AND TECHNICAL EDUCATION, OHIO STATE UNIVERSITY
1900 Kenny Road, Columbus, Ohio 43210

CENTER FOR THE STUDY OF EVALUATION, UNIVERSITY OF CALFORNIA
905 Hilgard Avenue, Los Angeles, California 90024

EDUCATION DEVELOPMENT CENTER
55 Chapel Street, Newton, Massachusetts 02160

LEARNING RESEARCH AND DEVELOPMENT CENTER, UNIVERSITY OF PITTSBURGH
Pittsburgh, Pennsylvania 15213
Activities: Learning research. Instructional design and evaluation

RESEARCH AND DEVELOPMENT CENTER FOR TEACHER EDUCATION, UNIVERSITY OF TEXAS
303 Sutton Hall, Austin, Texas 78712
Activities: Personalized teacher education. Personalized school

STANFORD CENTER FOR RESEARCH AND DEVELOPMENT IN TEACHING
Stanford, California 94305
Activities: Heuristic teaching. Teaching students from low-income areas. Environment for teaching

WISCONSIN RESEARCH AND DEVELOPMENT CENTER FOR COGNITIVE LEARNING, UNIVERSITY OF WISCONSIN
1404 Regent Street, Madison, Wisconsin 53705
Activities: Conditions and processes of learning. Processes and programmes of instruction. Facilitative environments

D - EDUCATIONAL POLICY RESEARCH CENTRES / CENTRES DE RECHERCHES SUR LA POLITIQUE DE L'EDUCATION

EDUCATIONAL POLICY RESEARCH CENTER, STANFORD UNIVERSITY
Menlo Park, California 94025
Nature of organization: Research Institute

EDUCATIONAL POLICY RESEARCH CENTER, SYRACUSE UNIVERSITY
1206 Harrison Street, Syracuse, N.Y. 13210
Nature of organization: Research Corporation

E - RESEARCH COORDINATING UNITS FOR VOCATIONAL EDUCATION / UNITES DE COORDINATION DES RECHERCHES SUR L'ENSEIGNEMENT PROFESSIONNEL [1]

OCCUPATIONAL RESEARCH AND DEVELOPMENT UNIT, AUBURN UNIVERSITY
115 Petrie Hall, Alabama 36830

ALASKA RESEARCH COORDINATING UNIT, STATE OF ALASKA
Alaska Office Building Pouch F., Juneau, Alaska 99801

OCCUPATIONAL RESEARCH COORDINATING UNIT
1626 West Washington, Phoenix, Arizona 85007

ARKANSAS RESEARCH COORDINATING UNIT FOR OCCUPATIONAL EDUCATION
Department of Vocational Education
Fayetteville, Arkansas 72701
Nature: University

RESEARCH COORDINATING UNIT FOR VOCATIONAL EDUCATION
721 Capitol Hall, Sacramento, California 95814

RESEARCH AND PLANNING UNIT, DIVISION OF VOCATIONAL EDUCATION, CONNECTICUT STATE DEPARTMENT OF EDUCATION
Hartford, Connecticut 06115

DELAWARE OCCUPATIONAL RESEARCH COORDINATING UNIT, DEPARTMENT OF PUBLIC INSTRUCTION
P. O. Box 697, Dover, Delaware 19901

FLORIDA RESEARCH COORDINATING UNIT FOR VOCATIONAL EDUCATION
Room 258, Knott Building, Tallahassee, Florida 32304

GEORGIA OCCUPATIONAL RESEARCH COORDINATING UNIT, LEADERSHIP SERVICES UNIT, VOCATIONAL EDUCATION DIVISION, STATE DEPARTMENT OF EDUCATION
Atlanta, Georgia 30334

HAWAII VOCATIONAL-TECHNICAL RESEARCH COORDINATING UNIT, OFFICE OF THE STATE DIRECTOR FOR VOCATIONAL EDUCATION
2327 Dole Street, Honolulu, Hawaii 96822

STATE OCCUPATIONAL RESEARCH COORDINATING UNIT, STATE DEPARTMENT OF VOCATIONAL EDUCATION
518 Front Street, Boise, Idaho 83702

ILLINOIS RESEARCH COORDINATING UNIT, DIVISION OF VOCATIONAL AND TECHNICAL EDUCATION
1035 Outer Park Drive, Springfield, Illinois 62706

INDIANA RESEARCH AND DEVELOPMENT COORDINATING UNIT FOR VOCATIONAL AND TECHNICAL EDUCATION
600 Old Trails Building, 309 West Washington Street,
Indianapolis, Indiana 46204

SUPPORT SERVICES SECTION, CAREER EDUCATION DIVISION, IOWA DEPARTMENT OF PUBLIC INSTRUCTION
Grimes   State Office Building, Des Moines, Iowa 50319

---

[1] In alphabetical order by State - plus Puerto Rico / Selon l'ordre alphabétique des Etats, plus Puerto Rico

KANSAS VOCATIONAL EDUCATION RESEARCH COORDINATING UNIT
Ralada Executive Building, Room 22, Topeka, Kansas 66607

KENTUCKY RESEARCH COORDINATING UNIT FOR VOCATIONAL-TECHNICAL EDUCATION,
UNIVERSITY OF KENTUCKY
152 Taylor Building, Lexington, Kentucky 40506

LOUISIANA RESEARCH COORDINATING UNIT, STATE DEPARTMENT OF EDUCATION,
DIVISION OF VOCATIONAL EDUCATION
Capitol Building Baton Rouge, Louisiana 70874

MASSACHUSETTS RESEARCH COORDINATING UNIT, STATE DEPARTMENT OF EDUCATION,
DIVISION OF OCCUPATIONAL EDUCATION
182 Tremont St., Boston, Massachusetts 02111

RESEARCH COORDINATION UNIT, RESEARCH, EVALUATION AND ASSESSMENT SERVICES,
MICHIGAN DEPARTMENT OF EDUCATION
Lansing, Michigan 48902

RESEARCH COORDINATING UNIT FOR VOCATIONAL EDUCATION, UNIVERSITY OF MINNESOTA
145 Peik Hall, Minneapolis, Minnesota 55455

MISSISSIPI RESEARCH AND CURRICULUM COORDINATING UNIT FOR VOCATIONAL-TECHNICAL
EDUCATION
P. O. Drawer DX, State College, Mississipi 39762

MISSOURI RESEARCH COORDINATING UNIT, STATE DEPARTMENT OF EDUCATION
Jefferson City, Missouri 65101

MONTANA RESEARCH PLANNING DEVELOPMENT AND EVALUATION COMPONENT, DEPARTMENT
OF PUBLIC INSTRUCTION
Helena, Montana 59601

NEBRASKA RESEARCH COORDINATING UNIT
Box 33, Henzlik Hall, Lincoln, Nebraska 89507

NEVADA RESEARCH COORDINATING UNIT, COLLEGE OF EDUCATION, UNIVERSITY OF NEVADA
Reno, Nevada 89507

NEW HAMPSHIRE RESEARCH COORDINATING UNIT, STATE DEPARTMENT OF EDUCATION
Stickney Avenue, Concord, New Hampshire 03301

NEW JERSEY STATE DEPARTMENT OF EDUCATION, DIVISION OF VOCATIONAL EDUCATION,
BUREAU OF OCCUPATIONAL RESEARCH DEVELOPMENT
225 W. State Street, Trenton, New Jersey 08625

NEW MEXICO OCCUPATIONAL RESEARCH AND DEVELOPMENT COORDINATING UNIT,
STATE DEPARTMENT OF EDUCATION
Capitol Building, Santa Fe, New Mexico 87501

BUREAU OF OCCUPATIONAL EDUCATION RESEARCH, NEW YORK STATE DEPARTMENT OF
EDUCATION
Room 468, Albany, N.Y. 12224

NORTH CAROLINA OCCUPATIONAL RESEARCH UNIT, DIVISION OF RESEARCH,
STATE DEPARTMENT OF PUBLIC INSTRUCTION
Raleigh, North Carolina 27602

NORTH DAKOTA RESEARCH COORDINATING UNIT FOR VOCATIONAL EDUCATION
Box 8009, University Station, Grand Forks, North Dakota 58201

United States of America/Etats-Unis d'Amérique

EDUCATIONAL PROGRAMS AND STUDIES INFORMATION SERVICE (EPSIS), STATE
EDUCATION DEPARTMENT
Room 330, Albany, New York 12224

OHIO RESEARCH COORDINATING UNIT
65 South Front Street, Columbus, Ohio 43215

OKLAHOMA RESEARCH COORDINATING UNIT, STATE DEPARTMENT OF VOCATIONAL EDUCATION
1515 West 6th Avenue, Stillwater, Oklahoma 74074

OREGON RESEARCH COORDINATING UNIT, OREGON STATE UNIVERSITY
317 Education Hall, Corvallis, Oregon 97331

RESEARCH COORDINATING UNIT FOR VOCATIONAL EDUCATION, DEPARTMENT OF PUBLIC
INSTRUCTION
Box 911, Harrisburg, Pennsylvania 17126

RESEARCH COORDINATING UNIT FOR RHODE ISLAND COLLEGE
600 Mount Pleasant Avenue, Providence, Rhode Island 02908

SOUTH CAROLINA RESEARCH COORDINATING UNIT FOR VOCATIONAL EDUCATION
101 Godfrey Hall, Clemson, South Carolina 29631

RESEARCH COORDINATING UNIT FOR VOCATIONAL EDUCATION, UNIVERSITY OF TENNESSEE,
COLLEGE OF EDUCATION
909 Mountcastle Street, Knoxville, Tennessee 37916

DIVISION OF OCCUPATIONAL RESEARCH AND DEVELOPMENT, DEPARTMENT OF OCCUPATIONAL
EDUCATION AND TECHNOLOGY, TEXAS EDUCATION AGENCY
201 East Eleventh Street, Austin, Texas 78701

UTAH RESEARCH COORDINATING UNIT
University Club Building, Salt Lake City, Utah 84111

WASHINGTON STATE RESEARCH COORDINATING UNIT
216 Old Capitol Building, Olympia, Washington 98504

WEST VIRGINIA RESEARCH COORDINATING UNIT FOR VOCATIONAL EDUCATION,
MARSHALL UNIVERSITY
Huntington, West Virginia 25701

DEPARTMENT RESEARCH CENTER (R.C.U.), WISCONSIN BOARD OF VOCATIONAL,
TECHNICAL AND ADULT EDUCATION
137 East Wilson Street, Madison, Wisconsin 53702

WYOMING RESEARCH COORDINATING UNIT, OCCUPATIONAL EDUCATION PROGRAM SERVICES,
STATE DEPARTMENT OF EDUCATION
Cheyenne, Wyoming 82001

RESEARCH DISSEMINATION AND CURRICULUM DEVELOPMENT UNIT, STATE AREA OF
VOCATIONAL AND TECHNICAL EDUCATION, STATE DEPARTMENT OF EDUCATION
Box 759, Hato Rey, Puerto Rico 00919

F - INSTRUCTIONAL MATERIALS CENTRES FOR HANDICAPPED CHILDREN AND YOUTH /
CENTRES DE MATERIEL D'INSTRUCTION POUR LES ENFANTS ET LES JEUNES HANDICAPES

UNIVERSITY OF ALABAMA AT MONTGOMERY
Montgomery, Alabama 36104

UNIVERSITY OF SOUTHERN CALIFORNIA, SCHOOL OF EDUCATION
17 Chester Place, Los Angeles, California 90007

COLORADO STATE COLLEGE
Greeley, Colorado 80631

DEPARTMENT OF EXCEPTIONAL CHILDREN, SUPERINTENDENT OF PUBLIC INSTRUCTION
1020 South Spring Street, Springfield, Illinois 62706

UNIVERSITY OF KANSAS, SCHOOL OF EDUCATION
Lawrence, Kansas 66044

UNIVERSITY OF KENTUCKY
641 South Limestone Street, Lexington, Kentucky 40506

INSTRUCTIONAL MATERIALS REFERENCE CENTER
American Printing House for the Blind, 1839 Frankfort Avenue
Louisville, Kentucky 40206

BOSTON UNIVERSITY SCHOOL OF EDUCATION
765 Commonwealth Avenue, Boston, Massachusetts 02215

MICHIGAN STATE UNIVERSITY
Room 216, Eirckson Hall East, Lansing, Michigan 48823

NEW YORK STATE DEPARTMENT OF EDUCATION, BUREAU FOR PHYSICALLY HANDICAPPED
CHILDREN
Albany, N.Y. 12201

UNIVERSITY OF OREGON
Clinical Services Building, Eugene, Oregon 97403

UNIVERSITY OF TEXAS
2613 Wichita, Austin, Texas 78712

GEORGE WASHINGTON UNIVERSITY, DEPARTMENT OF SPECIAL EDUCATION
2201 - G Street, N.W. Washington, D.C. 20006

UNIVERSITY OF WISCONSIN
2570 University Avenue, Madison, Wisconsin 53706

3 - PUBLISHERS / MAISONS D'EDITION[1]/

ADDISON-WESLEY PUBLISHING CO. Inc.
Reading, Mass. 01867

ALLYN & BACON, Inc.
470 Atlantic Ave., Boston, Mass. 02210

AMERICAN BOOK CO., Division of Litton Educational Pul., Inc.
450 W. 33 Street, New York 10001

ANCO TECHNICAL SERVICES, Inc.
80 Boylston Street, Boston, Massachusetts 02116

---

[1]/ Reprinted by permission of R.R. Bowker Company. (Extracts from Literary Market Place, 1971-72.) /Reproduit avec l'autorisation de R.R. Bowker Company. (Extrait de Literary Market Place, 1971-72).

APPLETON-CENTURY-CROFTS
440 Park Ave. South, New York 10016

AUTOMATED EDUCATION CENTER
22929 Industrial Dr. E. Street Clair shores, Michigan 48080

BEACON PRESS
25 Beacon Street, Boston, Massachusetts 02108

BEHAVIORAL RESEARCH LABORATORIES
Ladera Professional Ctr., Box 577, Palo Alto, California 94302

BROLET PRESS
18 John St., 15 Maiden Lane, New York 10038

BURGESS PUBLISHING Co.
426 Sixth Street, Minneapolis, Minnesota 55415

CTB/McGRAW-HILL, Div. of McGraw-Hill Book Co.
Del Monte Research Park, Monterey, California 93940

THE CENTER FOR CURRICULUM DEVELOPMENT, Inc.
401 Walnut Street, Philadelphia, Pa. 19106

CONSOLIDATED EDUCATIONAL PUBLISHING, Inc.
Glen Cove & Voice Roads, Carle Place, N.Y. 11514

CORONET LEARNING PROGRAMS
65 E South Water Street, Chicago, Illinois 60601

DEVEREUX FOUNDATION
Devon, Pa. 19333

E-Z SORT SYSTEMS Ltd.
351 Bryant Street, San Francisco, California 94107

EDUCATIONAL DEVELOPMENT LABORATORIES, Inc., Div. of McGraw-Hill Book Co.
284 Pulaski Road, Huntington, N.Y. 11744

EDUCATIONAL METHODS, Inc.
500 N. Dearborn Street, Chicago, Illinois 60610

EDUCATIONAL RESEARCH ASSOCIATES
1019 SW Tenth Avenue, Portland, Oregon 97205

EDUCREATIVE SYSTEMS, Inc.
435 E. 79 St., New York 10021

ENCYCLOPAEDIA BRITANNICA EDUCATIONAL CORP.
425 N. Michigan Avenues, Chicago, Ill. 60611

ENTELEK, Inc.
42 Pleasant Street, Newburyport, Mass. 01950

FEARON PUBLISHERS, Lear Siegler Inc., Educational Division
6 Davis Drive, Belmont, California 94002

FIELD ENTERPRISES EDUCATIONAL CORPORATION
510 Merchandise Mart Plaza, Chicago, Illinois 60654

FORDHAM PUBLISHING CO.
2377 Hoffman St., Bronx, N.Y. 10458

GENERAL ELECTRONIC LABORATORIES
1085 Commonwealth Avehue, Boston, Massachusetts 02215

GENERAL PROGRAMMED TEACHING, Div. of Commerce Clearing House, Inc.
Quail Hill, San Rafael, California 94903

GINN & Co.
Statler Office Building, Back Pay P.O. 191, Boston, Massachusetts 02117

GRAFLEX DIVISION, The Singer Co.
3750 Monroe Avenue, Rochester, N.Y. 14603

GROLIER EDUCATIONAL CORPORATION, Teaching Materials Division
845 Third Avenue, New York 10022

HARCOURT BRACE JOVANOVICH, Inc.
757 Third Avenue, New York 10017

HARPER & ROW, PUBLISHERS, Inc.
10 E. 53d Street, New York 10022

C. RICHARD HATCH ASSOCIATES, Inc.
989 Fifth Avenue, New York 10019

HOLT, RINEHART & WINSTON, Inc.
383 Madison Avenue, New York 10017

HOUGHTON MIFFLIN Co.
110 Tremont Street, Boston, Massachusetts 02107

JEPPESEN & Co., Subs. of Times-Mirror Co.
8025 E. 40 Avenue, Denver, Colorado 80207

LEARNING RESEARCH ASSOCIATES
1501 Broadway, New York 10036

LEARNING SYSTEMS Co., Div. of Richard D. Irwin, Inc.
1818 Ridge Road, Homewood, Illinois 60430

J.B. LIPPINCOTT Co.
E. Washington Sq., Philadelphia, Pa. 19105

LITTLE, BROWN & Co.
34 Beacon St., Boston, Massachusetts 02106

McGRAW-HILL BOOK Co.
330 W. 42nd St., New York 10036

MACMILLAN Co.
866 Third Avenue, New York 10022

MATERIAL FOR TODAY'S LEARNING Inc.
679 Harrison Street, San Francisco, California 94107

MEDIA MASTERS Inc.
400 W. Sixth Street, Tustin, California 92680

MEDIA PLUS Inc.
60 Riverside Drive, New York 10024

C.V. MOSBY CO., (THE)
11830 Westline Industrial Drive, St. Louis, Mo. 63141

NEW DIMENSIONS IN EDUCATION, Inc.
131 Jericho Tpke, Jericho, N.Y. 11753

PRENTICE-HALL, Inc.
Englewood Cliffs, N.J. 07632

PRESCHOOL PRESS Inc.
159 W. 53 Street, New York 10019

G.P. PUTNAM'S SONS
200 Madison Avenue, New York 10016

W.B. SAUNDERS Co.
W. Washington Sq., Philadelphia, Pa. 19105

SCHOLASTIC MAGAZINES, Inc.
50 W. 44 Street, New York 10036

SCHOLASTIC SYSTEMS, Inc. Div. of General Educational Services Corp.
90 Main Street, Hackensack, N.J. 07601

SCIENCE RESEARCH ASSOCIATES
259 E. Erie St., Chicago, Illinois 60611

SULLIVAN ASSOCIATES
3000 Sand Hill Road, Menlo Park, California 94025

VOCATIONAL MEDIA
400 W. Sixth St., Tustin, California 92680

WFF'N PROFF PUBLISHERS
Box 71, New Haven, Connecticut 06501

JOHN WILEY & SONS, Inc.
605 Third Avenue, New York 10016

WILLIAMS & WILKINS CO., (THE)
428 Preston St., Baltimore, Md. 21202

4 - PERIODICALS/PERIODIQUES

A.V. COMMUNICATION REVIEW
Publisher: Association for Educational Communications and Technology
Address: 1201 Sixteenth Street, N.W. Washington, D.C. 20036
Periodicity: Quarterly
Field of interest: Research

AUDIOVISUAL INSTRUCTION (Journal of the Association for Educational Communications and Technology)
Publisher: Association for Educational Communications and Technology
Address: 1201 Sixteenth Street, N.W. Washington, D.C. 20036
Periodicity: Monthly (except August; June-July issues combined)
Field of interest: Research

CURRENT CONTENTS EDUCATION
Publisher: Institute for Scientific Information
Address: 325, Chestnut Street, Philadelphia, Pa. 19106
Periodicity: Weekly
Field of interest: Current or pre-publication tables of contents of educational journals

DATAMATION
Publisher: Gardner F. Landon, F.D. Thompson Publication Inc., Executive Circulation and Advertising Offices 35 Mason Street, Greenwich, Connecticut
Periodicity: Monthly
Field of interest: Application. Topical events

EDUCATIONAL TECHNOLOGY
Publisher: Educational Technology Publications Inc.,
Address: 140 Sylvan Avenue, Englewood Cliffs, New Jersey 07632
Periodicity: Monthly
Field of interest: Application. Topical events. Research

EMC DIRECTORY OF SUMMER SESSION COURSES ON EDUCATIONAL MEDIA
Publisher: Educational Media Council
Address: 1346 Connecticut Avenue, N.W. Washington D.C. 20036
Periodicity: Annual

N.S.P.I. JOURNALS
Publisher: National Society for Programmed Instruction, School of Education, Catholic University
Address: Washington, D.C. 20017
Periodicity. Monthly newsletter. Research quarterly. Improving human performance
Field of interest: Research. Topical events

5 - PROFESSIONAL ORGANIZATIONS / ORGANISATIONS PROFESSIONNELLES

ASSOCIATION FOR EDUCATIONAL COMMUNICATIONS AND TECHNOLOGY
1201 16th Street, N.W., Washington D.C. 20036
Nature of organization: National Education Association
Public concerned: Teachers' Associations
Activities: The improvement of educational and public welfare through the use of educational communications, technology and media, and audio-visual materials and methods

EDUCATIONAL MEDIA COUNCIL
1346 Connecticut Avenue, N.W. Washington, D.C. 20036
Public concerned: All those interested in educational media
Activities: Federation of 14 national professional associations of educators, producers of educational materials, and specialists in the development and use of educational media, conduction, research, dissemination of conference activities

NATIONAL AUDIO-VISUAL ASSOCIATION
3150 Spring Street, Fairfax, Virginia 22030
Activities: Dealers, manufacturers, producers and suppliers of audio-visual products and materials such as movie projector film, tape recorders, etc.

NATIONAL SOCIETY FOR PROGRAMMED INSTRUCTION, THE CATHOLIC UNIVERSITY OF AMERICA
123 William Street, New York, N.Y. 10038
Activities: To advance education and training through collection, development and diffusion of information concerned with programmed instruction. Has 14 chapters throughout the U.S. Issues monthly journal from headquarters in San Antonio, Texas 78212

8 - DOCUMENTATION CENTRES / CENTRES DE DOCUMENTATION

CENTRAL E.R.I.C. CLEARING HOUSE ON EDUCATION MEDIA AND TECHNOLOGY
National Center for Educational Communications
400 Maryland Avenue, S.W., Washington D.C. 20202
Nature of organization: Governmental
Type of services: Organizing and disseminating information on instructional films, television, programmed instruction, computer-assisted instruction and other audio-visual means of teaching, including individualized instruction, alternative education, simulation games and communication. (There are 18 others throughout the country, performing the same functions.)

INSTRUCTIONAL MEDIA LABORATORY
University of Wisconsin
Nature of organization: University
Type of services: Publishes indexes to all available programmed and computer instruction programmes

II - PUBLICATIONS

1 - BOOKS / LIVRES

ALLEN, D. Calvin, Ed. _Programmed Instruction: Bold New Venture_, Bloomington, Indiana University Press, 1969, 250 p.

CHU, Godwin C.; SCHRAMM, Wilbur. _Learning from television: what the research says_, ERIC Document Reproduction Service, ED.014900, Bethesda, Maryland, 213 p.

————; ————. _Educational Product Report_. Educational Products Information. Exchange Institute, Publication Office, N. Fair Street, Guildford, Connecticut, October 1968, vol. 2, No. 1, 55 p.

MEYER MARKLE, Susan. _Good frames and bad - A grammar of frame-writing_. New York, John Wiley & Sons (1964) 1969 (2nd ed.), 308 p.

NATIONAL AUDIO-VISUAL ASSOCIATION, Inc. _The Audio-visual equipment directory_. The National Audio-Visual Association, Fairfax, Virginia 22030. Copyright 1972 by the National Audio-visual Association, Inc.

OFIESH, Gabriel D. Dial access information retrieval systems: Guidelines handbook for educators. Final report, Project No. BR 7, 1042, Bureau of Research, Office of Education, Department of Health, Education and Welfare, Washington D.C., 1968. ERIC Document Reproduction Service, ED.025682, Bethesda, Maryland, 152 p.

WANGER, Judy, (comp.) Directory of educational information resources. New York: CCM Information Corp., 1971, 181 p.

3 - BIBLIOGRAPHIES

GLASER, Robert; MARINE, Mary Louise. A basic Reference Shelf on Programmed Instruction. E.R.I.C. Clearinghouse on Educational Media and Technology, Institute for Communication Research, Stanford University, June 1968. 8 p.

NATIONAL INFORMATION CENTER FOR EDUCATIONAL MEDIA. A catalog of Major Programs of Programmed Instruction. New York, N.Y., R.R. Bowker Co., 1969, Index to 16 mm educational films, 2nd edition, 4 p.

————. Programmed Instruction in Adult Education, Current Information Sources, E.R.I.C. Clearinghouse on Adult Education, Syracuse University, Syracuse, N.Y. February 1968

WOODBURY, Marda A Guide to Educational Resources, Far West Laboratory for Educational Research and Development, Berkeley, California, 1971

NCTE/ERIC A current bibliography on Programmed Instruction in English for remedial students in junior colleges. 1970

————. A current bibliography on Programmed Instruction of English as a second language. 1971

————. Selected bibliography on Programmed Instruction in the English language arts. 1969, Addenda 1971.

VENEZUELA

I - ORGANIZATIONS AND ACTIVITIES / STRUCTURES ET ACTIVITES

1 - CENTRES

DEPARTAMENTO DE NUEVOS MÉTODOS, DIRECCIÓN DE PROGRAMACIÓN Y SERVICIOS TÉCNICOS, INSTITUTO NACIONAL DE COOPERACIÓN EDUCATIVA (INCE)
A.P. 40340 - Av. Nueva Granada, Caracas 104
Nature de l'organisme: Gouvernemental

4 - PERIODICALS / PERIODIQUES

BOLETÍN TÉCNICO
Editeur: Departamento de Nuevos Métodos, INCE
Périodicité: Trois numéros par an
Centres d'intérêt: Articles divers sur la formation professionnelle

7 - TRAINING ORGANIZATIONS / ORGANISMES ASSURANT UNE FORMATION

INSTITUTO NACIONAL DE COOPERACIÓN EDUCATIVA (INCE)
Nature de l'organisme: Gouvernemental
Public intéressé: Adultes et jeunes

8 - DOCUMENTATION CENTRES / CENTRES DE DOCUMENTATION

DEPARTAMENTO DE NUEVOS MÉTODOS, INCE
Nature de l'organisme: Gouvernemental
Nature des services: Registre des programmes, livres, articles en
                     espagnol. Préparation de matériel d'enseignement programm

- PUBLICATIONS

1 - BOOKS / LIVRES

INSTITUTO NACIONAL DE COOPERACIÓN EDUCATIVA, Departamento de Nuevos Métodos
     Monografía sobre la instrucción programada. Caracas, INCE,
     1969, 50 p.

MAGER, Robert. Objetivos para la enseñanza efectiva. Caracas, Paradero
     a Salesianos, 1968

2 - ARTICLES

BANEGAS, A.   "Principios de la instrucción programada", in Boletín
              Técnico, INCE, No. 6, 1969, 10 p.
              Etude

———.   "Algunas apreciaciones sobre el estado actual de la instrucción
              programada en los Estados Unidos", in Boletín Técnico, INCE,
              No. 7, 1969, 4 p.
              Etude

GIBBS, A.   "La instrucción programada en el proceso electoral", in
              Boletín Técnico, INCE, No. 7, 1969, 6 p.

———.   "La instrucción programada en Venezuela", in Boletín Técnico,
              INCE, No. 11, 1970, 6 p.

RODRIGUEZ, M. "Sugerencias para la especificación de objetivos", in Boletín
              Técnico, INCE, No. 6, 1969, 5 p.
              Rapport d'expérience

SCHESTAKOW, M. "El concepto soviético de las máquinas de enseñar", (traduit
              par Alberto Gibbs), in Boletín Técnico, INCE, No. 4, 1968, 15 p.
              Etude

Venezuela

III - RESEARCH AND APPLICATIONS / REALISATIONS

2 - PUBLISHED PROGRAMMED COURSES / COURS PROGRAMMES PUBLIES

ÁLVAREZ, M.R. Contabilidad básica. Caracas, Instituto Nacional de Cooperación Educativa, 1969.
Formation professionnelle

GIBBS, A. Curso de votación y escrutinio. Caracas, Consejo Supremo Electoral, 1968, 62 p.
Education des adultes

————. Elaboración de listas de electores. Caracas, Consejo Supremo Electoral, 1968, 21 items
Education des adultes

————; BANEGAS, A. Control de participantes. Caracas, Instituto Nacional de Cooperación Educativa, 1969, 70 items.
Fonctionnaires de l'INCE

————; et al. Registro electoral. Caracas, Consejo Supremo Electoral 1968, 63 items.
Education des adultes

INSTITUTO NACIONAL DE COOPERACIÓN EDUCATIVA, Departamento de Nuevos Métodos.
Operaciones con decimales. INCE, 1972
Education des adultes et apprentissage

————. Operaciones con enteros. INCE, 1969, 437 items.
Education des adultes et apprentissage

————. Operaciones con fracciones. INCE, 1971.
Education des adultes et apprentissage

————. Orientación INCE. INCE, 1971.
Fonctionnaires de l'INCE

Z
5814
A85
I 57
1973